Concise Medical Textbooks

Cardiology

'Medical teachers know that half of what they teach
is untrue — the trouble is that they don't know which half.'

Attributed to Dr C. S. Burwell
(formerly Dean, Harvard Medical School)

Concise Medical Textbooks

Fourth Edition

Cardiology

Desmond G. Julian MA, MD, FRCP, FRCP(E), FRACP

British Heart Foundation Professor of Cardiology,
University of Newcastle upon Tyne

Baillière Tindall · London

Published by Baillière Tindall,
a division of Cassell Ltd,
Greycoat House, 10 Greycoat Place,
London SW1P 1SB

© 1983 Baillière Tindall
a division of Cassell Ltd

First published 1970
Second edition 1973
  Reprinted 1975
Third edition 1978
  Reprinted 1979, 1980
Fourth edition 1983
ISBN 0 7020 0953 9

Turkish Edition (University of Istanbul) 1974

Printed and bound in Great Britain by
Robert Hartnoll Ltd. Bodmin, Cornwall

British Library Cataloguing in Publication Data
Julian, Desmond G.
    Cardiology — 4th ed. — (Concise medical textbooks)
    1. Cardiology
    I. Title
    616.1'2   RC 681

    ISBN 0-7020-0953-9

Contents

Preface

The primary purpose of this small book is to describe and explain cardiac disease in a way that is comprehensible to the student embarking on clinical medicine. It is also intended as a short handbook for the physician and the advanced nurse.

Cardiology, and particularly cardiac surgery, has progressed very rapidly in the last few years and much that was experimental at the time when the third edition was published has now become established. This applies particularly to non-invasive methods of investigation and to the vasodilator and calcium antagonist drugs.

In a book as short as this, over-simplification and dogmatism are inevitable. Those wishing to go more deeply into the subject are advised to consult the references provided at the end of each section as well as one of the several larger textbooks available.

I am again indebted to Dr J. I. Hall for providing many of the illustrations for this edition and to Mr D. P. Hammersley who contributed some new ones and to Dr S. Hunter for the echocardiograms.

In preparing this edition, I have been greatly helped by the medical, nursing, technical and secretarial staff of Freeman Hospital, to whom I express my gratitude.

August 1982   D. G. Julian

1

The Incidence and Prevalence of Heart Disease

Diseases of the cardiovascular system are the main causes of death in the richer countries of the world and are of increasing importance in underdeveloped areas. In most Western countries, cardiovascular disease is responsible for approximately 50% of deaths, of which about half are due to ischaemic (coronary) heart disease. After increasing in nearly all countries, deaths due to coronary disease have diminished during the last decade in the United States, Australia and some European countries but continue to rise in others. Hypertension is the other main cardiovascular cause of death, and predominates in some countries, especially Japan. Rheumatic heart disease is responsible for perhaps 2% of all deaths but is the most important cardiac cause of disability and death in many parts of Asia, Africa and South America. Pulmonary heart disease is commonest in communities which have a heavy consumption of cigarettes and which are exposed to severe atmospheric pollution.

Because congenital and rheumatic heart diseases and hypertension are compatible with a long life span the relative prevalence of these conditions in the community differs from their incidence as causes of death.

The importance of the different types of heart disease varies considerably with age. Under the age of 15, heart disease is most commonly congenital, whereas between the ages of 20 and 35 rheumatic heart disease is the major problem. Over this age cardiac disease is most likely to be due to coronary disease or hypertension (or a combination of the two). Pulmonary heart disease is largely confined to men over 45.

The epidemiology of each of these types of heart disease is discussed in the relevant chapter.

2

Myocardial Function: Heart Failure

Normal myocardial function

The primary function of the heart is to provide the tissues and organs of the body with a flow of oxygenated blood sufficient for their metabolic needs. In order to do this, it must pump a cardiac output (in the adult) of about 5 litres per minute at rest, and be able to increase this to 15 litres per minute or more on exercise. It must also adjust to great variations in peripheral resistance and venous return without substantially altering arterial, venous or intracardiac pressures. This ability both to maintain an adequate flow and to keep intracardiac and vascular pressures within a limited range is lost when cardiac failure develops.

The ways in which the ventricles as a whole respond to changing demands can be, to a considerable extent, explained by the structure and function of the sarcomere, the fundamental unit of cardiac contraction.

The structure and function of the sarcomere

Each muscle cell contains, amongst other structures, a nucleus, numerous mitochondria, and a number of parallel fibrils. Each fibril is made up of functional sub-units or sarcomeres. The sarcomere is composed of parallel actin and myosin filaments, arranged with the thin actin filaments attached to its limiting membrane (or Z line) and interdigitating with the thicker myosin filaments which are placed centrally (Fig. 1). When contraction occurs, the actin filaments slide towards each other over the myosin filaments and thus bring the Z lines closer together. Bridges, at which the forces responsible for sliding (or contraction) are generated, connect the two types of filament. The myosin filaments, which are a constant 1.5 μm in length, have a central area 0.2 μm wide which is free of bridges; the actin filaments are always 1.4 μm in length. It has been postulated that the greater the number of bridges (or sites for interaction) there are between myosin and actin filaments, the more forceful the resulting contraction. It is apparent that the maximum interaction between the

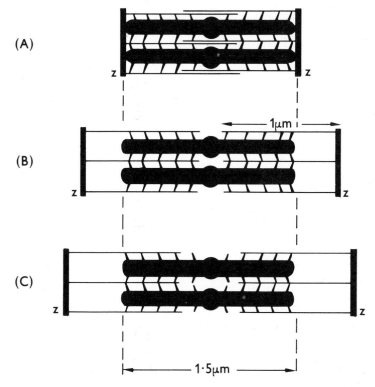

Fig. 1.   Relationship of actin (thin horizontal lines) and myosin (thick horizontal bars) in the sarcomere. In (A) the actin filaments are overriding each other. In (B) the overall sarcomere length is 2.2 μm and all bridges (vertical lines) are available for binding. In (C) the sarcomere is overextended; some sites are not engaged. Contraction is maximal when the greatest number of sites are available for interaction as in (B).

actin and myosin filaments occurs when the overall sarcomere length lies between 2.0 and 2.2 μm. If it exceeds this, some sites become disengaged; if it is less than this, actin filaments override each other and interfere with binding.

The law of the heart, as enunciated by Starling, states that the more myocardial fibres are stretched (or the greater the diastolic volume of the heart) within physiological limits, the greater the energy of the ensuing contraction. Beyond these limits, the energy of contraction falls off. As the diastolic volume of the heart is directly related to sarcomere length, it is reasonable to explain Starling's law in terms of the ultrastructure of the myocardial cell. As the sarcomere is progressively stretched to its optimal length, and the diastolic fibre lengthens proportionately, the force of contraction progressively increases. If the sarcomere (or heart muscle) is stretched excessively, less force is generated.

This relatively simple concept must be amplified to take into account another protein, troponin, which is attached to the actin filaments. Troponin has an inhibitory effect on the interaction between actin and myosin which must be counteracted before contraction can occur. Troponin has a great affinity for calcium; when this ion is present in sufficient concentration, the inhibitory effect is overcome and the actin–myosin bridges can form. The number of bridges activated and, therefore, the contractility of the muscle, is proportional to the quantity of available calcium.

The mechanics of the myocardium

Two important characteristics of heart muscle are the force with which it contracts, and the velocity with which it shortens, for these determine the volume of blood expelled during systole. Three major factors are responsible for the force and velocity of cardiac contraction: (1) the extent to which the muscle is stretched prior to contraction ('preload'), (2) the load that the ventricle faces during contraction ('afterload'), and (3) the contractile state of the myocardium.

Preload

If other factors are held constant, the force with which the heart contracts depends on the extent to which it has been stretched prior to contraction. This is a restatement of Starling's law. In effect, the preload is the volume of the ventricle at the end of diastole, i.e. the *end-diastolic volume*. The end-diastolic volume is largely determined by the venous return, which is, in turn, dependent upon a number of influences including the blood volume and venous tone. Another important factor affecting venous return is the distensibility (compliance) of the ventricle. Atrial contraction contributes appreciably to ventricular end-diastolic volume as it occurs immediately before ventricular systole. This atrial component of ventricular filling assumes importance when the ventricle is hypertrophied because passive filling is then impeded by the indistensibility (lack of compliance) of the ventricle.

Afterload

The ventricle has to develop sufficient tension during systole to expel blood into the aorta in the face of the resistance (or, more correctly, impedance) imposed by the aorta and peripheral arterial vessels. A further factor which becomes of importance in the dilated ventricle is the end-diastolic volume (see p. 11).

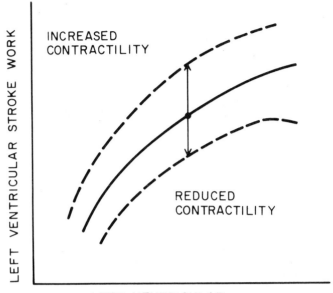

Fig. 2. The relationship between end-diastolic fibre length and the left ventricular stroke work. For any given end-diastolic fibre length, increased contractility, such as is produced by sympathetic action, produces more stroke work. Reduced contractility, as occurs in cardiac failure, produces less work. Similarly, if the arrows were drawn horizontally instead of vertically, it would be seen that for any given amount of work, increased contractility enables this to be performed at a smaller end-diastolic fibre length. In cardiac failure, a given amount of stroke work can only be achieved with a greater end-diastolic fibre length.

The contractile state of the myocardium

If the end-diastolic volume and the aortic impedance are held constant, the force and velocity of contraction of the myocardium depend upon its contractile state. For a given end-diastolic volume, therefore, changes in contractility can alter the performance of the ventricle (see Fig. 2). Myocardial contractility is largely dependent upon the activity of the cardiac sympathetic nerves, but it can also be increased by circulating catecholamines, tachycardia, cardiac glycosides and isoprenaline. Myocardial contractility is depressed by hypoxia, quinidine and procainamide.

Mechanisms which lead to an increased ventricular performance, such as an enlarged end-diastolic volume or sympathetic stimulation, also involve an increase in myocardial oxygen consumption. The greater ventricular performance does not necessarily, therefore, mean an increase in cardiac efficiency. Indeed, the increase in myocardial oxygen consumption is disproportionately great in relation to the increase in work performed.

The effect of exercise

Cardiovascular changes take place as soon as exercise is anticipated — as a result of vagal inhibition and a generalized sympathetic discharge. Both heart rate and myocardial contractility increase. The resistance vessels in the muscles dilate whilst those supplying the kidneys, abdominal viscera and skin constrict. The overall effect is to increase cardiac output and, specifically, the blood supply to the muscles.

With the onset of exercise, further dilatation of muscular arterioles and capillaries occurs and venous return is augmented by the pumping action of the muscles.

The systolic blood pressure rises, the increase roughly corresponding to the severity of the exercise. Diastolic pressure changes little.

The energy supply of the myocardial cell

Energy is produced in the heart by the process of oxidative phosphorylation. This results from the conversion of the energy produced by the oxidation of substrates such as glucose, lactate and fatty acids into the energy of adenosine triphosphate (ATP) and creatine phosphate (CP). These substances provide the energy source for muscular contraction.

Excitation–contraction coupling

The electrical excitation of the cell leads to a series of events which results in contraction of the heart muscle. This process, which is not as yet fully understood, involves transverse channels ('T' tubules) formed by invagination of the sarcolemma ensheathing the cell, and the sarcoplasmic reticulum, a network of membrane-lined channels which run longitudinally in contact with the individual sarcomeres (Fig. 3). It has been postulated that the electrical stimulus traverses the transverse channels and then proceeds along the longitudinal channels releasing calcium. The calcium is then transferred into the fibril and causes contraction by activating ATPase. Repolarization is associated with a reversal of the process and the active pumping of calcium back into the sarcoplasmic tubules.

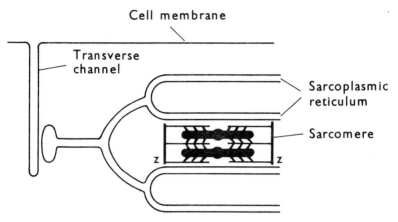

Fig. 3. Note the relationship between the longitudinal tubules of the sarcoplasmic reticulum and the sarcomere, and between the lateral sac of the sarcoplasmic reticulum and the transverse channel ('T' tubule).

The pressure and volume changes in the heart and great vessels during the cardiac cycle (Figs. 4 and 5)

With the onset of left ventricular systole, the mitral valve closes and the pressure in the ventricle rises rapidly. Until the aortic valve opens, the volume of the ventricle remains unchanged, this being the period of isovolumetric contraction. As soon as the aortic valve opens, blood is rapidly ejected from the ventricle into the aorta. This phase is followed by one of relatively slow ejection. Shortly after ejection ceases, the aortic valve closes. As the ventricle relaxes, the pressure within it falls rapidly, but until it has fallen to the level present in the left atrium, the volume in the ventricle remains unchanged, this being the period of isovolumetric relaxation. When the pressure in the ventricle falls below that in the atrium, the mitral valve opens and a period of rapid ventricular filling ensues. This is followed by a slow phase, or diastasis, during which the pressure rises slowly. This continues until atrial contraction propels more blood through the mitral valve and causes a small increase in left ventricular volume and pressure prior to the onset of the next ventricular systole.

In the left atrium, there are three waves in the cardiac cycle, the crests being designated 'a', 'c' and 'v', and the troughs 'x', 'y' and 'z'. The 'a' wave is due to atrial contraction, which is followed by a 'z' trough associated with atrial relaxation. After this, there is a 'c' wave as a result of upward movement of the mitral valve cusps, with a subsequent 'x' descent as the mitral valve ring descends as the ventricle contracts. During the latter portion of ventricular systole,

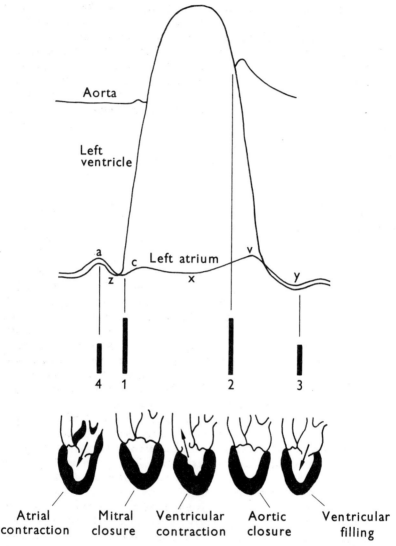

Fig. 4. Pressure pulses in the left atrium, left ventricle and aorta (see text).

with the mitral valve closed, there is a build up of pressure in the atrium with increasing pulmonary venous return. This rising pressure is terminated when the mitral valve opens. At this point, the peak of the 'v' wave is produced. The 'y' descent follows as blood flows into the ventricle during ventricular diastole. (From the opening of the mitral valve to its closure at the onset of ventricular systole, the pressures in the atrium and the ventricle are almost identical.) Events on the right side of the heart mirror those on this left but they take place slightly later so that tricuspid valve closure occurs shortly after mitral valve closure, and closure of the pulmonary valve follows that of the aortic valve. The timing of pulmonary valve closure varies with respiration. The increased negative pressure in the thorax during inspiration results in an augmented venous return to the right side of the heart. As a consequence of this transient increase in blood flow, ejection of blood in the right side of the heart is delayed and pulmonary valve closure occurs relatively later during inspiration than it does during expiration.

Heart failure

Failure in anything implies expectations unfulfilled, and one's definition of heart failure depends upon what one expects of the heart. No single definition suffices because the clinical and physiological criteria necessarily differ.

The clinician regards his patient as having heart failure when there are symptoms or physical signs attributable to inadequate cardiac performance. The physiologist regards the heart as failing when the contractility of the ventricles or the cardiac output fall outside the statistically defined normal range. There is no clear distinction between normality and abnormality; values in the 'abnormal' range may be found in normal hearts in the face of extreme demand, and 'normal' values may be encountered in diseased hearts when the demands are slight. None the less, if one is aware of the shortcomings, some definitions of heart failure may be accepted.

To Sir Thomas Lewis, heart failure was 'an inability of the heart to discharge its contents adequately'; to Paul Wood it was 'a state in which the heart fails to maintain an adequate circulation for the needs of the body despite a satisfactory venous filling pressure' (thereby excluding from consideration inadequate cardiac output due to insufficient venous return).

Cardiac failure, as it is understood in clinical practice, denotes the presence of one of the complexes of symptoms and signs associated with the 'congestion' of tissues and organs which result from fluid retention and venous engorgement. Congestive cardiac failure is a term understood by some to mean congestion of both pulmonary and systemic veins, by others to mean congestion of either of these two systems and by yet others to apply only to systemic venous congestion. In the author's view, it is a term better avoided; one should refer to pulmonary venous congestion or systemic venous congestion as appropriate.

Pulmonary venous congestion results from disordered function of the left ventricle or left atrium.

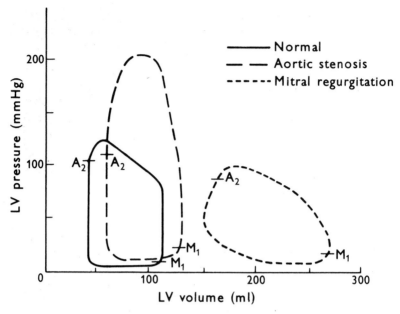

Fig. 5.   Relationships between left ventricular pressure and left ventricular volume in the normal heart, in aortic stenosis and in mitral regurgitation. In the normal heart, following the closure of the mitral valve (M_1), there is a rapid rise in pressure without any change in volume until the aortic valve opens. Pressure then rises more slowly as the left ventricle ejects blood; in later systole, there is a fall-off in pressure, though ejection continues until the aortic valve closes (A_2). The phase of isovolumetric relaxation then occurs followed by diastolic filling with little change in pressure. The salient feature of aortic stenosis is the pressure load; mitral regurgitation is associated with a volume load leading to an increase in ventricular volume at the end of both systole and diastole.

Systemic venous congestion is similarly due to disorders of the right ventricle and atrium, but is often the end-result of left-sided heart failure. The clinical features derive, in the main, from engorgement of the systemic veins and capillaries.

The heart has also failed when it cannot maintain an adequate blood pressure in spite of a peripheral vascular resistance that is normal or high, but, by convention, this type of cardiac failure is referred to as acute circulatory failure or cardiogenic shock rather than heart failure.

The causes of heart failure

The heart fails either because it is subjected to an overwhelming load, or because the heart muscle is disordered, or as a result of a combination of the two.

An increased work load (Fig. 5) can be of two different types — a volume load (preload) and a pressure load (afterload). A volume load is imposed by disorders which demand that the ventricle expels more blood per minute than is normal. Examples include thyrotoxicosis and anaemia, in which the total cardiac output is increased; and mitral regurgitation and aortic regurgitation, in which the left ventricle has to expel not only the normal forward flow into the aorta but also the large volume of regurgitated blood as well.

Pressure loads are imposed by disorders which increase resistance to outflow from the ventricles (typified by systemic hypertension due to increased impedance of the peripheral arterioles and by aortic stenosis in which there is narrowing of the outflow orifice of the left ventricle).

Disorders of myocardial function result not only from diminished contractility but also from loss of contractile tissue, as occurs in myocardial infarction. An additional factor in this condition is a paradoxical movement of infarcted muscle which further increases the work of the remaining myocardium.

In rheumatic heart disease, the different mechanisms of heart failure are often combined, with myocarditis, valve narrowing and valvar regurgitation all participating in its production.

Cardiac and circulatory responses in heart failure

The heart at first responds in much the same way as it does to normal increases in demand, such as those imposed by exercise. As the disorder progresses, more cardiac and circulatory adjustments take place which, for a time, maintain an adequate circulation. At a later stage, these compensatory mechanisms are either overwhelmed or lead themselves to a worsening of the clinical situation. Indeed, the clinical manifestations of heart failure are largely those of 'compensatory' mechanisms which eventually embarrass the circulation.

These mechanisms are, to some extent, compensatory but some of them, such as severe vasoconstriction, which would be appropriate in counteracting a fall in cardiac output from blood loss, may be inappropriate when the primary fault is in the heart itself.

Dilatation of the heart — increase in end-diastolic volume

In response to a volume load, the heart dilates, i.e. the ventricular volume is increased. Up to a point, dilatation is a normal and efficient response but it is abnormal when it cannot be wholly ascribed to the volume load. Pathological dilatation of this kind occurs when there is myocardial disease, when, because of decreased contractility, the ventricle must be stretched to a greater extent for a given stroke volume. Even in those cases in which dilatation may at first be regarded as a physiological response, it eventually becomes disadvantageous because, as the ventricle increases in size, greater tension is required in the myocardium to expel a given volume of blood. This is in accordance with the law of Laplace which indicates that the tension in the myocardium (T) is proportional to the intraventricular pressure (P) multiplied by the radius (R) of the ventricular chamber (T∞PR). The greater tension results in increased oxygen requirements and eventually leads to hypertrophy.

Hypertrophy of the heart

When the ventricle has to face a chronic increase of pressure load, such as that imposed by arterial hypertension, aortic stenosis or pulmonary hypertension, the myocardium hypertrophies, i.e. it increases in weight as a result of an enlargement of individual muscle fibres. The process affects only those chambers upon which there are increased demands. The mechanism responsible for the development of cardiac hypertrophy is uncertain but it seems likely that it is a response to increased stretching or tension in muscle fibres which results from a raised diastolic volume or pressure. Hypertrophy may be regarded as a normal compensatory mechanism which permits the heart to cope with the increased demands, but becomes self-defeating when it is excessive. The thickening of the fibres increases the distance which oxygen has to diffuse from the capillaries; eventually this leads to impaired oxygenation of the centre of the fibre. It is probable that this hypoxia is an important factor in the fibrosis which frequently develops in hypertrophied muscle.

Impaired myocardial contractility

In many types of heart disease, the major defect lies in the myocardium itself. This is the case in ischaemic heart disease, myocarditis and cardiomyopathy, and myocardial involvement is often considerable in rheumatic heart disease. Even when the primary disturbance is that of a volume or pressure overload, intrinsic myocardial function may be eventually affected adversely by dilatation and hypertrophy. Why the impaired myocardial contractility develops is uncertain, but it has been attributed by some to overstretching of the sarcomeres (see p. 2). There is, as yet, no evidence to support the suggestion that there is a defect of production or storage of creatine phosphate or adenosine triphosphate (ATP) in ·cardiac failure. However, there may be a slowing up in the conversion of chemical energy into muscular work as a result of depression in the activity of ATPase, the enzyme responsible for the release of energy from ATP. There may also be a defect in excitation–contraction coupling in heart failure because it has been noted that the cardiac glycosides which improve myocardial function in heart failure appear to enhance the release of calcium by the sarcoplasmic reticulum (see p. 9). A further factor which may reduce myocardial contractility is a depletion of noradrenaline (norepinephrine) stores in the myocardium.

Increased sympathetic activity

Counteracting these effects is an increase in sympathetic nervous activity, manifested by sinus tachycardia and by venous and arterial vasoconstriction. These responses may be disadvantageous by increasing preload, afterload and myocardial oxygen consumption.

The cardiac output in heart failure

By definition cardiac failure is present when the cardiac output is insufficient for the needs of the body, but some patients with an output in the normal range manifest the clinical features of cardiac failure, whereas other patients with low outputs are free of symptoms and signs. However, in cardiac failure, even if the cardiac output is normal at rest it usually responds inadequately to exercise. In conditions, such as beri-beri and thyrotoxicosis, in which the cardiac output is abnormally high, it is still insufficient for the exceptional metabolic demands.

The regional circulations in cardiac failure

There is a redistribution of blood flow to different organs and tissues in cardiac failure, as there is on exercise. This redistribution is mediated through vasoconstriction in certain areas, notably the renal arterioles. The renal blood flow falls disproportionately, and may be reduced to one-quarter of normal. There is little reduction in the coronary or cerebral blood flow, but there is vasoconstriction of the skin and splanchnic vessels.

Salt and water retention

An almost invariable feature of cardiac failure is the retention of sodium and water. This leads to a substantial increase in extracellular and plasma volume and plays a large part in the production of the clinical features of cardiac failure. The mechanism of the sodium and water retention is still far from clear, but there is no doubt that the retention of water is secondary to that of sodium.

Two factors which have been implicated in impaired renal excretion of sodium are diminished glomerular filtration and increased tubular reabsorption.

Diminished glomerular filtration. Glomerular filtration is reduced in cardiac failure, although to a lesser extent than is renal blood flow. Diminished glomerular filtration may play some part in sodium retention, but it is probably not an important factor except when the failure is severe.

Increased tubular reabsorption. There is abundant experimental evidence that tubular reabsorption of sodium is increased in cardiac failure. There is no doubt that, in certain patients, there is increased aldosterone secretion, and that this hormone, by its action on the distal tubule, promotes the reabsorption of sodium whilst increasing the excretion of potassium and hydrogen. However, evidence of hyperaldosteronism is confined to advanced failure; aldosterone antagonists are relatively ineffective in the treatment of sodium retention in early failure. The enhanced tubular reabsorption of sodium found in cardiac failure seems to be mediated through some mechanism as yet undiscovered.

As mentioned, water retention in heart failure is usually secondary to sodium retention. In some patients with advanced cardiac failure, however, there is a disproportionate retention of water. In these patients, the kidneys can no longer excrete solute-free water and the serum sodium concentration falls as a result of dilution ('dilutional hyponatraemia').

Raised venous pressure in cardiac failure

When the left ventricle fails the pulmonary venous pressure rises, and when the right ventricle fails the pressure rises in the systemic veins. This can be largely explained by the inability of the failing ventricle to discharge the blood presented to it effectively. The increased blood volume resulting from sodium and water retention contributes to the venous return and is thus a factor in producing the raised venous pressure as is venoconstriction.

The effect of left ventricular failure on the lungs

As explained above, when the left ventricle fails, the diastolic pressure in the left ventricle rises and with it the left atrial pressure. Since the pulmonary veins and capillaries are in continuity with the left atrium, the pressures in these vessels rise concomitantly. In mild left ventricular failure, the pressures in the left atrium and pulmonary veins are within normal limits at rest but rise on exercise. As failure advances, the left atrial pressure progressively increases from its normal level of 5 to 10 mmHg to one of 25 to 30 mmHg. The hydrostatic pressure in the capillaries is then close to that needed to overcome the osmotic pressure exerted by the plasma proteins and may lead to an exudation of fluid from the capillaries into the alveolar walls and alveoli. If the pressure in the atrium rises rapidly, there may be a sudden exudation of fluid into the alveoli. If this process takes place slowly, exudation may proceed gradually with a slow build up of tissue tension occurring in the alveolar wall. This restricts further exudation of fluid and limits the risk to the alveoli. In response to this process, some fibrosis may take place in the alveolar wall. The pulmonary congestion caused by the high pulmonary venous pressure and by the changes in the alveolar walls makes the lung more rigid (less compliant). As a result of this, more work must be done by the respiratory muscles to move a given volume of air. The stretch receptors in the lung are stimulated and lead to hyperventilation.

Left heart failure

Aetiology

The features of left heart failure develop when there is a major obstruction to outflow from the left atrium (e.g. mitral stenosis) or when the left ventricle can no longer cope with the demands upon it. The common causes of left ventricular failure are systemic hypertension, aortic valve disease, mitral regurgitation, myocardial infarction and cardiomyopathy.

Clinical features

The clinical features of left-sided cardiac failure are largely the consequence of pulmonary congestion. The symptoms are, therefore, those of dyspnoea on exertion, orthopnoea, paroxysmal dyspnoea and acute pulmonary oedema. Pulmonary congestion may lead to the physical signs of tachypnoea, crepitations in the lungs and, sometimes, hydrothorax. More direct evidence that the left ventricle is failing is supplied by the presence of pulsus alternans and by a third heart sound.

The chest radiograph shows pulmonary venous congestion and, in the more severe cases, oedema.

The electrocardiogram may be of value although it does not provide direct evidence of left heart failure. For example, it is unusual for hypertension or aortic valve disease to lead to the symptoms of left heart failure without producing ECG evidence of left ventricular hypertrophy first. Again, it is unusual for coronary artery disease to lead to left heart failure if the ECG is normal. This is not, however, true of mitral regurgitation.

The diagnosis of left heart failure is usually not difficult when there is progressive dyspnoea coupled with clinical evidence of advanced left-sided heart disease. However, this evidence may not always be unequivocal and there may be difficulty in distinguishing the symptoms of heart failure from those of pulmonary disease. The dyspnoea of left heart failure is more likely to be provoked by lying down flat. Patients with dyspnoea due to pulmonary disease usually have a history of asthmatic attacks or of chronic cough and sputum.

Paroxysmal nocturnal dyspnoea and acute pulmonary oedema may be difficult to differentiate from acute respiratory attacks. The latter are commonly associated with bronchospasm and purulent sputum. In contrast, the patient with acute pulmonary oedema is usually free of pulmonary infection, has fine crepitations rather than rhonchi and is liable to cough up pink frothy sputum. Furthermore, examination usually reveals the signs of left-sided heart disease. Correct diagnosis is of great importance because the therapy of the two conditions is different. For example, morphine may be lethal in respiratory failure, but invaluable in acute pulmonary oedema. Similarly, high concentrations of oxygen are useful in acute pulmonary oedema but may be dangerous in respiratory failure. The chest radiograph is also helpful in showing signs of oedema or infection. In cases of doubt, estimation of the arterial CO_2 tension is of value because this is usually low in acute pulmonary oedema and high in respiratory failure.

Right heart failure

Aetiology
Failure of the right side of the heart occurs when the right ventricle can no longer cope with the demands upon it, or when there is tricuspid stenosis. Right ventricular failure often follows left ventricular failure, with its consequent effects upon the pulmonary circulation. It also results from pulmonary disease, particularly chronic bronchitis and emphysema, pulmonary valve disease and tricuspid regurgitation.

Clinical features
The characteristic features of right heart failure are those of raised systemic venous pressure and its effects. In the normal individual, the venous pressure in the internal jugular veins does not exceed 2 cm vertically above the sternal angle when the patient is reclining at 45 degrees. In right heart failure this figure is exceeded. Even if normal at rest, it rises on exercise.

Almost as important as the rise in venous pressure is enlargement of the liver which, if chronic, may result in cirrhosis. The third important feature of right heart failure is oedema, which is of the dependent type and usually most evident in the pretibial and ankle regions. Less frequently, ascites occurs.

Other clinical features of cardiac failure

There are a number of common but less specific features of cardiac failure. Fatigue is a frequent symptom which is difficult to evaluate.

The nutrition of patients with cardiac failure is often good in the early stages, but cachexia sets in as disability increases. In the very advanced case, cerebral symptoms may develop with dulling of consciousness, confusion or changes in personality. Patients with cardiac failure are prone to develop venous thrombosis and pulmonary emboli are common. Mild jaundice, due to hepatic congestion or cirrhosis, is quite frequent in right-sided heart failure. Proteinuria due to renal congestion is often present.

Precipitating factors in cardiac failure

Cardiac failure is often precipitated or exacerbated by factors superimposed on the underlying heart disease. Amongst these are arrhythmias, infections, pulmonary embolism, pregnancy, anaemia, excessive sodium intake and over-exertion. The recognition of precipitating factors is of great importance in the management of heart failure, because the correction of these complicating conditions will often result in the abolition of symptoms.

The management of cardiac failure

Ideally, the treatment of cardiac failure is the correction of the cause, but for a variety of reasons this may not be possible, at least initially. In some conditions, such as ischaemic heart disease and the cardiomyopathies, no currently available methods of treatment affect the underlying lesions. In other disorders, the radical treatment necessary for cure, such as major surgery, cannot be safely undertaken until cardiac failure has been corrected.

The principles of treating cardiac failure may be enumerated as follows:

1. The correction or amelioration of the underlying disease.
2. The control of complicating factors.
3. The reduction of demands on the heart by the restriction of physical activity and weight loss.
4. The improvement of myocardial function by the administration of inotropic drugs such as the digitalis glycosides.
5. The correction of sodium and water retention.
6. Vasodilator therapy.

The correction or amelioration of the underlying cause

When heart disease is due to such causes as thyrotoxicosis or hypertension, corrective treatment can be started immediately. In congenital and rheumatic heart disease, surgical management is usually required, but this may have to be deferred until the maximum benefit has been achieved from medical treatment.

The correction of complicating factors

The control of arrhythmias, the correction of anaemia and the treatment of infections play important roles in the management of cardiac failure.

Restriction of activity

Rest reduces the demands on the heart and leads to a fall in venous pressure and a reduction in pulmonary congestion. It allows a relative increase in renal blood flow and often leads to a diuresis. However, bed rest also encourages the development of venous thrombosis and pulmonary embolism.

The degree of physical restriction necessary depends upon the severity of the cardiac failure. When there is severe pulmonary congestion or peripheral oedema, a period of complete rest may be required. At this time, the patient is usually most comfortable propped up by two or more pillows in bed or in an armchair. Complete bed rest is seldom necessary for more than a few days, after which a gradual increase in activity may be encouraged, depending upon the response. In patients with lesser degrees of cardiac failure, there may be no need to enforce bed rest, but excessive activity, particularly walking up hills and stairs, should be temporarily avoided. The degree of physical restriction necessary can be largely determined by the relief of symptoms and the disappearance of the signs of failure.

When the patient has improved, moderate exercise should be encouraged if this does not produce symptoms.

Therapy with inotropic drugs

Drugs which increase myocardial contractility (inotropic agents) are undoubtedly effective in improving cardiac performance, increasing cardiac output and relieving the clinical features of cardiac failure. Such effects are more evident when the drugs are given acutely; their long-term effectiveness is disputed but most cardiologists believe in their value, particularly in patients with dilated hearts. Although new inotropic drugs, such as prenalterol and pirbuterol, are becoming available, the digitalis glycosides are the drugs usually used for this purpose.

Digitalis and related compounds play a uniquely important part in the management of heart disease. Not only can they be used over a long period of time to improve myocardial contractility but they have an additional role in controlling the ventricular rate in atrial arrhythmias.

Digitalis compounds are composed of a steroid compound, a lactone ring and a sugar residue. The steroid and lactone ring together are known as an aglycone and it is this fraction which is responsible for the cardiotonic effect. Different sugar residues are attached which alter potency and duration of action.

The chief effect of digitalis is to increase myocardial contractility — that is, it has a positive inotropic effect both in the normal and in the failing heart. In the normal heart the increase in contractility is accompanied by an increase in oxygen utilization, but in the failing dilated heart, digitalis causes a reduction in end-diastolic volume and therefore a fall in myocardial tension (see p. 12). In this way, oxygen utilization may remain the same or be reduced and the efficiency of the myocardium increased.

It seems most probable that the positive inotropic action of digitalis is mediated through an effect upon intracellular ionic transport. It has been postulated that digitalis blocks the sodium-potassium activated ATPase in the cell membrane and in doing so leads to an accumulation of intracellular sodium. Because of the sodium-calcium carrier system, this results in an increase in the amount of calcium available to activate contraction.

Digitalis slows the heart rate in three ways: (i) by ameliorating cardiac failure and thus reversing the associated tachycardia; (ii) by vagal stimulation; (iii) by slowing atrioventricular conduction through prolongation of the refractory period of the atrioventricular node.

Digitalis reduces the refractory period of atrial and ventricular muscle and therefore enhances the risk of ectopic rhythms.

Digitalis produces sagging of the ST segment in the ECG in those leads in which there is a dominant R wave, especially lead II.

In normal individuals, digitalis glycosides produce arterial and venous constriction. However, in patients with cardiac failure they produce arterial and venous dilatation. This is probably explained by the fact that there is widespread vasoconstriction in cardiac failure which is reversed when the failure is controlled.

Digitalis has an unimportant direct diuretic effect on the kidney. The striking diuresis that may follow digitalis therapy is largely due to the increase in renal plasma flow and glomerular filtration rate that accompanies increased cardiac output.

Cardiac glycosides produce anorexia, nausea, vomiting and diarrhoea both by a direct action on the gastrointestinal tract and by stimulating central emetic centres.

There are a large number of different preparations available, but digoxin in one or other of its forms is suitable for nearly all cases. The most commonly used tablet contains 0.25 mg; tablets containing 125 and 62.5 μg are useful in children and the elderly. Suggested dosage schemes are shown in Table 1.

Most preparations are well absorbed from the intestinal tract, although with differing degrees of completeness. Digitoxin is almost 100% absorbed in contrast with about 80% in the case of digoxin. Because oral therapy is safest, this route should be used if possible.

Table 1. Some cardiac glycoside preparations

INTRAVENOUS

Preparation	Onset of action (min)	Peak effect (min)	Dis-appear-ance (days)	Dose (mg)
Ouabain	5	30–120	3	0.25–0.5
Digoxin	15	120	7	0.5–1.0

ORAL

Preparation	Onset of action (hr)	Peak effect (hr)	Dis-appear-ance (weeks)	Initial dose (mg)	Daily mainte-nance dose (× 1–4) (mg)
Digoxin	1–3	6–12	1	0.5–1.0	0.25
Digitoxin	2–4	6–12	3	0.2–0.4	0.1

Note: Smaller doses are required for children, the elderly and patients with renal failure.

The intravenous route should be employed only in cases of urgency and should always be avoided if a digitalis preparation has been administered within the previous week.

Intravenous digoxin produces an effect within 15 minutes and has peak activity in about 2 hours. When given by mouth, the effects start in about half an hour and are maximal at about 6 hours.

Digoxin is excreted in an unchanged form by the kidneys. This is normally complete in 4 to 5 days, but is delayed in the presence of renal failure.

The earliest toxic effects of digitalis therapy are usually malaise, anorexia, nausea and, later, vomiting. In some patients, there is excessive salivation or diarrhoea.

More serious than these symptoms are the many different types of conduction and rhythm disturbance that may occur. The most frequent are ventricular ectopic rhythms, often taking the form of coupling (bigeminy). This may be well tolerated, but is an indication for reducing digitalis dosage. Ventricular tachycardia and ventricular fibrillation may also be induced.

Supraventricular rhythm disturbances may be provoked, of which the most important is atrial tachycardia with block (p. 54). Atrioventricular dissociation (p. 69) and junctional rhythms (p. 53) may also occur.

Prolongation of the PR interval is common, as is partial heart block of the Wenckebach type (p. 65). In more severe cases, complete heart block can develop.

Potassium depletion promotes the development of digitalis-induced disturbances of rhythm and conduction, and should be assumed to be present when these occur, in spite of a normal serum potassium. In all cases, digitalis should be discontinued immediately and potassium depletion corrected either by oral therapy such as 2 g of potassium chloride 6-hourly, or intravenously with 20 to 40 mmol potassium chloride in 500 ml or 5% dextrose in water over a period of 4 hours. In treating ventricular tachycardia due to digitalis intoxication, beta-adrenoceptor blocking drugs or phenytoin may be used. It is important never to use dc shock therapy in the treatment of digitalis-induced arrhythmias.

The digitalis glycosides are used chiefly for two purposes: the management of cardiac failure; and slowing the ventricular response to supraventricular arrhythmias.

Digitalis is indicated in nearly all types of cardiac failure except when there are contraindications, such as severe potassium depletion, pre-existing digitalis toxicity and partial heart block. However, it is comparatively ineffective in heart failure associated with acute myocarditis, thyrotoxicosis, beri-beri and anaemia. It is unlikely to be helpful in cases of constrictive pericarditis or in mitral stenosis without atrial fibrillation, except when there is right- as well as left-sided failure. It is potentially dangerous in hypertrophic obstructive subaortic stenosis (p. 173). Its role in the treatment of arrhythmias is discussed in Chapter 4.

It is relatively easy to assess the therapeutic effectiveness of digitalis therapy in patients with tachycardia when this is a direct result of cardiac failure or is due to an arrhythmia. When there is atrial fibrillation, a satisfactory result is usually obtained when the heart rate has been slowed to 70 per minute at rest. If such a rate is difficult to achieve, it suggests some complicating factor, such as infection, pulmonary infarction or thyrotoxicosis. Bradycardia should be avoided. It may be difficult to assess the effectiveness of digitalis therapy in the patient in regular sinus rhythm. However, improvement in symptoms and the disappearance of the signs of cardiac failure suggest that an adequate dose is being given.

The management of sodium and water retention

Low salt diets effectively counteract cardiac failure. However, with the availability of potent diuretic drugs, no extreme limitation of sodium intake is usually necessary. Nevertheless, some restriction is desirable and inability to control cardiac failure is quite often due to the patient not reducing sodium intake sufficiently. All patients should be advised not to add salt at meals and to avoid obviously salty foods.

Occasionally, a strict salt restriction must be applied. It is seldom necessary to practise water restriction, but in cases of dilutional hyponatraemia, limitation to one litre per day may be helpful. These may be identified by a lack of response to conventional treatment for cardiac failure in association with a low serum sodium concentration.

Diuretics are valuable in the treatment of those cases of cardiac failure that do not respond to restriction of activity and limitation of salt intake supplemented, if necessary, by digitalis therapy. All the commonly used diuretics act by promoting sodium excretion, with enhanced water excretion as a secondary effect. There are now a large number of diuretics available, but it is necessary for the physician to be familiar with only three or four varieties.

The loop diuretics: frusemide (Lasix, Dryptal, Frusid), bumetanide (Burinex) and ethacrynic acid (Edecrin). These drugs prevent reabsorption at multiple sites including the proximal and distal tubules and the ascending limb of the loop of Henle. They produce a profound diuresis with the excretion of large quantities of sodium and chloride. When given by mouth, action commences in about one hour and is complete in 6 to 8 hours. If given intravenously, the onset of action is almost immediate.

Because these drugs are expensive and very potent, their use should be reserved for situations of urgency and for those patients who are resistant to less powerful diuretics.

Frusemide may be given in a dosage of 20–40 mg intravenously, but this occasionally produces hypotension. The oral dose is usually 40–80 mg, but 120 mg or more may be necessary. Bumetanide (1 or 5 mg) is another potent diuretic with a similar action.

Ethacrynic acid is helpful in some patients with severe heart failure who have failed to respond to other drugs. An oral dose of 50 mg may be adequate, but 100 mg once or twice a day may be necessary. Supplements of potassium chloride should be given to all patients receiving these drugs for heart failure.

Thiazide diuretics and chlorthalidone (Table 2).   The many drugs in this group are essentially similar except in their potency and duration of action. Most of the thiazide diuretics act for 12 to 24 hours whereas polythiazide and chlorthalidone exert their effect for 48 hours or more. They may have several sites of action, but the main mechanism is the inhibition of sodium reabsorption in the distal convoluted tubule.

These diuretics are less potent than the loop diuretics, but are rather more likely to produce hypokalaemia. If the serum potassium is low, or if the drugs are being given more than once a week, supplements of slow release potassium chloride should be used.

These drugs sometimes cause hyperglycaemia and hyperuricaemia, and may precipitate diabetes and clinical gout. Other occasional

Table 2. Diuretics

Drug	Tablet size (mg)
Thiazide diuretics:	
Chlorothiazide (Saluric, Diuril)	500
Hydrochlorothiazide (Hydrosaluric, Direma, Esidrex)	25, 50
Hydroflumethiazide (Hydrenox)	50
Chlorthalidone (Hygroton)	50
Bendrofluazide (Aprinox, Centyl, Berkozide, Neonaclex)	2.5, 5
Methylclothiazide (Enduron)	5
Polythiazide (Nephril)	1
Cyclopenthiazide (Navidrex)	0.5
Aldosterone antagonists and similar drugs:	
Triamterene (Dytac)	50
Triamterene (50 mg) with Hydrochloro-thiazide (25 mg) (Dyazide)	
Spironolactone (Aldactone)	25, 100
Spironolactone with Hydroflumethiazide (Aldactide) (25 or 50 mg of each)	
Amiloride (Midamor)	5
Amiloride (5 mg) with Hydrochlorothiazide (50 mg) (Moduretic)	
Loop diuretics:	
Frusemide (Lasix, Dryptal, Frusid)	20, 40
Ethacrynic acid (Edecrin)	50
Bumetanide (Burinex)	1, 5

undesirable effects include agranulocytosis, thrombocytopenia, nausea, abdominal discomfort, impotence and skin rashes.

Aldosterone antagonists. In some cases of cardiac failure, particularly when there is advanced right-sided heart failure, there is excessive aldosterone secretion. This results in sodium retention and potassium excretion, which can be mitigated by the aldosterone antagonist spironolactone.

It is relatively ineffective when given alone and is best prescribed in combination with a thiazide diuretic. There is a risk of hyperkalaemia; in most cases potassium supplements should be omitted. Some 3 days is necessary before its full effect is produced. Because of its expense, its use should be restricted to cases with refractory heart failure, and it should be discontinued when a good diuresis has been achieved. Gynaecomastia is a common side-effect. The usual dose of spironolactone is 100 mg daily, but occasionally up to 400 mg per day is required.

Triamterene (Dytac) resembles spironolactone in its behaviour, but is not an aldosterone antagonist. Like spironolactone it encourages potassium retention. The usual daily dosage is 100 to 200 mg. It is best combined with a thiazide diuretic.

Amiloride (Midamor) is similar but more potent; 5 mg daily is usually effective. Combinations of the aldosterone antagonists with thiazide preparations are available (see Table 2).

Other less commonly used diuretics.   Mercurial diuretics, which were for many years the only effective diuretic drugs, have now largely been superseded. They seem rather less prone, than some of the modern diuretics, to producing potassium depletion and are therefore favoured by some physicians. Various preparations are available including mersalyl (Salyrgan), mercuramide (Neptal) and mercaptomerin (Thiomerin). These drugs may be given in a dose of 2 ml intramuscularly or, in the case of mercaptomerin, subcutaneously. Toxic reactions are unusual but include hypokalaemia and nephrotoxicity. The drugs should not be used intravenously.

Acetazolamide (Diamox) acts by inhibiting carbonic-anhydrase activity in the renal tubular cells. As a consequence there is an increased excretion of sodium bicarbonate and a retention of hydrogen. This eventually leads to a metabolic acidosis which has the effect of preventing further diuretic action. It is therefore a mild diuretic which can only be used for a few days at a time. The usual dose is 250 to 500 mg daily. It may have a special role in preventing high altitude pulmonary oedema.

Several new diuretics, such as quinethazone, clopamide, mefruside and xipamide have become available, but their place in therapy has yet to be defined.

Diuretic therapy should be employed in virtually all cases of symptomatic heart failure whether or not digitalis is also given. As a rule, thiazide diuretics are indicated in moderate cardiac failure and for long-term maintenance, whereas frusemide, ethacrynic acid or bumetanide are required in acute situations and for patients resistant to thiazide therapy. In resistant cases, particularly if there is hepatic congestion, spironolactone, triamterene or amiloride may be added.

Vasodilator therapy (Table 3)

Constriction of the arteries and veins is a characteristic feature of cardiac failure. In early cardiac failure, the reduction in vascular bed may be beneficial in ensuring an adequate venous return and maintaining the blood pressure, but frequently, particularly in more

Table 3. Some vasodilator drugs

Venous:
Nitrates (Isosorbide Dinitrate) 10–40 mg 4 to 6 hourly orally or 2–7 mg
    per hour intravenously

Arterial:
Hydralazine (Apresoline) 25–50 mg 3 or 4 times daily

Venous and arterial:
Sodium nitroprusside (Nipride) 15–400 μgm/min intravenously
Prazosin (Hypovase) 0.5–5 mg 4 times daily orally
Captopril (Capoten) 25–150 mg 3 times daily orally

Therapy should start with the lowest dosage quoted and be increased cautiously.

advanced failure, the arteriolar constriction imposes an excessive afterload and a venoconstriction too high a preload.

Depending upon the pathophysiology of the individual case, it may be desirable to reduce preload or afterload or both. Generally, in cardiac failure, it has been found that the optimal filling (or end-diastolic) pressure of the left ventricle is between 15 and 20 mmHg. If the pressure is higher than this, pulmonary congestion will result. The administration of a venodilator will cause the filling pressure to fall; a cardiac output which either stays the same or increases. Ideally, before using a venodilator, the left ventricular end-diastolic pressure should be measured indirectly from a pulmonary wedge pressure recording. Venodilator drugs should not be given to patients with filling pressures of less than 15 mmHg; the administration of venodilating drugs should be discontinued when such a pressure has been achieved.

The increased arteriolar resistance that results in excessive afterload imposes a burden on the heart which leads to a fall in cardiac output with or without a rise in end-diastolic pressure. Arteriolar vasodilators usually result in a brisk rise in cardiac output.

Isosorbide dinitrate may be used as a venodilator drug and hydralazine as an arteriolar dilator. A combination of veno- and arteriolar dilatation can be achieved by prescribing both these drugs or by the use of prazosin, captopril or nitroprusside. In addition, there are drugs which combine vasodilatation as a result of the activation of beta$_2$ receptors with a positive inotropic action. These include salbutamol and pirbuterol.

The role of vasodilator therapy in the management of heart failure is still not clearly defined. At present, it would seem wise to restrict it to patients with severe failure. Vasodilators are of considerable value in the management of acute left-sided failure, with pulmonary oedema, and as an adjuvant to other forms of therapy in patients who are severely incapacitated by dyspnoea. It seems unlikely that they will have a major role in early failure.

Mechanical removal of effusions and oedema fluid

Hydrothorax and ascites usually respond well to conventional treatment for cardiac failure. In a few cases, however, they cause considerable discomfort and in these it is appropriate to remove 0.5 to 1.0 litre of fluid. When peripheral oedema is intractable, one may employ peritoneal dialysis or utilize Southey tubes, which are inserted into the oedematous tissues of the legs after the patient has been positioned for several hours with the lower limbs dependent.

The treatment of acute left ventricular failure

Acute left ventricular failure (paroxysmal dyspnoea and acute pulmonary oedema) is an emergency requiring vigorous treatment. Morphine 10 to 20 mg should be given subcutaneously, intramuscularly or intravenously, if it is not contraindicated on the grounds of respiratory failure. Aminophylline 0.25 to 0.5 g administered slowly intravenously often provides relief. The patient should receive oxygen therapy, if possible under slight positive pressure. Venous return may be reduced by the application of tourniquets to three limbs at a time, with the serial removal from one to another extremity every 15 minutes. A diuretic, such as frusemide 20–40 mg intravenously is also of value as is vasodilator therapy.

If there is no contraindication, and more particularly if there is known to be an atrial arrhythmia with a rapid ventricular response, digoxin in a dosage of 0.5 to 1.0 mg may be given intravenously. If severe hypertension is present, it may be treated by labetalol, nitroprusside, or diazoxide (see p. 256).

Acute circulatory failure (shock)

The terms acute circulatory failure and shock are used to describe a syndrome comprising arterial hypotension, cold, moist and cyanosed extremities, a rapid weak pulse, a low urine output and a diminished level of consciousness. This clinical pattern is common to a number of disorders such as severe blood or gastrointestinal fluid loss, burns, trauma, bacteraemia, massive pulmonary embolism and acute myocardial infarction. As yet, physiological studies have not clearly defined the nature of the changes responsible for the clinical syndrome, but a common factor is a sudden fall in cardiac output associated with tissue hypoxia. In a substantial proportion of cases, the fall in cardiac output is a consequence of reduction in blood volume and venous return. Such a situation is exemplified by haemorrhage, the loss of fluids from burns, vomiting and diarrhoea. In another group of cases, the cause of the fall in cardiac output is clearly cardiac in origin and the shock may then be designated 'cardiogenic'.

Although the fall in cardiac output and blood pressure is an essential feature of shock, these abnormalities are insufficient to account for the syndrome. Falls of the same magnitude may be seen in some patients in whom the clinical features of shock are not seen and in whom the prognosis is good.

In the first stage of shock, there is a fall in cardiac output and blood pressure, due to either a diminution in venous return or to an inability of the myocardium to expel an adequate stroke volume. As a consequence of the hypotension, there is a fall in renal blood flow, with oliguria. Reflex tachycardia takes place. Compensatory mechanisms follow, with arteriolar constriction affecting particularly the kidneys, abdominal viscera, muscle and skin. Vasodilatation of the cerebral and coronary vessels permits the maintenance of a relatively good blood flow in these territories. If the vasoconstriction is sufficiently great, the blood pressure may be kept at or close to normal levels but at the expense of producing tissue hypoxia with consequent acidosis. If the underlying process can be corrected quickly, recovery may ensue, but if shock persists untreated for many hours, the stage of irreversibility may be reached. At this time, the correction of the original cause fails to prevent death. The nature of irreversible shock remains undetermined, but has been attributed to the production of endotoxins, and to irreparable cellular changes as a result of hypoxia in the liver, kidney, heart or brain.

When the shock syndrome is due to blood or fluid loss, the situation may be reversed by infusing the appropriate fluid. In the case of cardiogenic shock due to myocardial infarction, there is little evidence that any therapy is effective, unless the cause of shock is an arrhythmia susceptible to treatment but inotropic drugs and intra-aortic balloon pumping provide temporary support.

Further reading

BRAUNWALD, E. (1980) *Heart Disease*. Philadelphia: Saunders.

COHN, J. N. and FRANCIOSA, J. A. (1978) Selection of vasodilator, inotropic or combined therapy for the management of heart failure. *Am. J. Med.*, **65**, 181.

DOHERTY, J. E., de SOYZA, N., KANE, J. J., BISSETT, J. K. and MURPHY, M. L. (1978). Clinical pharmacokinetics of digitalis glycosides. *Prog. Cardiovasc. Dis.*, **21**, 141.

FRAZIER, H. S. and YAGER, H. (1973) The clinical use of diuretics. *New Engl. J. Med.*, **288**, 246.

MARSHALL, R. J. and SHEPHERD, J. T. (1968) *Cardiac Functions in Health and Disease*. Philadelphia: Saunders.

PARMLEY, W. W. and TALBOT, L. (1979) Heart as a pump. In: *Handbook of Physiology — The Cardiovascular System I*. American Physiological Society.

3

The Electrical Activity of the Heart: the Electrocardiogram

Electrical activity is a basic characteristic of the heart and is the stimulus for cardiac contraction. Disturbances of electrical function are common in heart disease. Their registration on an electrocardiogram (ECG) plays an essential role in the diagnosis and management of myocardial infarction, and of rhythm and conduction abnormalities. The ECG also provides important information about the presence of atrial and ventricular enlargement and can contribute to the detection of electrolyte disorders and drug intoxication.

The ECG is best understood by first considering some electrical and chemical features of the myocardial cell. Resting cells have a potassium concentration (about 150 mmol per litre) which is high in comparison with that in the extracellular tissues (abour 5 mmol per litre), whereas extracellular sodium concentration is much greater than intracellular. This ionic disequilibrium between the cell and its environment is maintained by a 'sodium pump' which actively excludes sodium from the cell. The cell membrane is, in fact, relatively permeable to potassium, but this ion is retained within the cell, thus ensuring overall ionic balance. The intra-extracellular potassium gradient results, however, in a difference in electrical potential across the cell membrane so that there is a relative negative potential within the cell of the order of 90 mV — the *transmembrane resting potential*. Cells at rest are therefore 'polarized', and may be regarded as having positive charges on their external surface and negative charges within.

When the cell membrane is injured or electrically stimulated, membrane permeability is increased so that sodium ions enter the cell. This reduces the membrane potential; when this reaches a certain level ('threshold potential'), further changes take place in the membrane permeability that allow a further rapid influx of sodium accompanied by a slower influx of calcium. Extremely rapid depolarization results, the interior of the cell transiently becoming positive relative to the exterior (phase 0). This is followed by a plateau phase, during which the transmembrane potential is close to zero; this is largely dependent on the continued influx of calcium. Repolarization follows until the resting potential is reached.

In a pacemaking or automatic cell (Fig. 6B), diastole is not stable; a

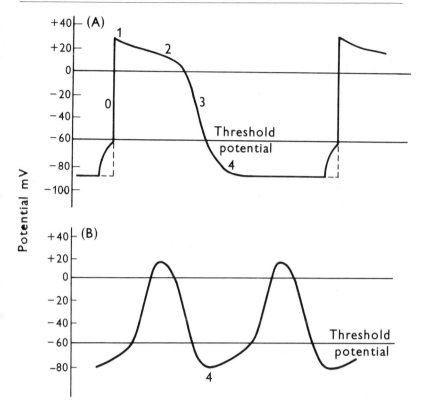

Fig. 6. (A) Transmembrane potential. Phase 0 corresponds with depolarization, and phases 1, 2 and 3 with repolarization. Phase 4 is the period of diastolic rest. When the cell is electrically stimulated, the transmembrane potential is reduced to the threshold potential, after which the process of depolarization is self-perpetuating. (B) Transmembrane potential in a pacemaking cell. In these cells, phase 4 is a period of slow depolarization. When the threshold potential is reached, the cell rapidly becomes depolarized.

slow leak of sodium into the cell during this time produces slow depolarization. When the transmembrane potential reaches its threshold, the cell automatically becomes depolarized. This characteristic forms the basis of automaticity.

The groups of automatic cells, which are present in the sinus node, certain areas of the atria, the junctional tissue in the neighbourhood of the atrioventricular (AV) node, the AV bundle of His, the bundle branches and the Purkinje cells of the ventricles vary, from each other in their rate of spontaneous depolarization. In the normal heart, the cells of the sinus node have the shortest spontaneous depolarization

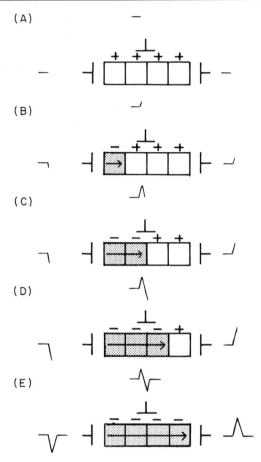

Fig. 7.   The recording produced from electrodes during depolarization of a muscle strip. By convention, an upstroke (a positive deflection) is recorded as depolarization is proceeding towards that electrode, and a negative deflection is obtained from an electrode facing the opposite direction.

time (phase 4) and so have the fastest firing rate. The sinus node dominates the heart because impulses spreading from it discharge the other potential pacemakers before they are ready for spontaneous depolarization. If, however, the sinus node discharge rate is reduced for any reason, or if one of the other areas develops a faster rate, a new and 'ectopic' focus assumes the role of pacemaker.

A single resting cell may be represented by a square with a positive charge on the outside and a negative one within. A muscle strip can be represented diagrammatically as a series of such squares (Fig. 7). If a cell at one end is stimulated, it becomes depolarized and its surface is negatively charged in relation to its fellows. As the electrical impulse spreads from one cell to the next, there is a progressively advancing negative charge. Immediately in front of it is a positive charge of equal magnitude. This combination of negative and positive charges in close proximity is termed a *dipole* with, in this case, the positive charge preceding the negative. The advancing dipole sets up an electrical field which can be detected by an exploring electrode paired with an indifferent electrode. By convention, relative positivity in the exploring electrode is represented by an upright deflection and negativity by a downward one. Therefore, as the positive front of the dipole approaches the electrode, an upright deflection is recorded; as it retreats, the deflection is negative.

The whole heart can be regarded as a large number of muscle strips arranged in a complex fashion. At any one time in the cardiac cycle there are a large number of dipoles moving in many directions; as viewed from a single electrode many of these cancel each other out. The total electrical activity at any one moment in time can be summated and represented by a single electrical force of a certain magnitude and in a certain direction which is termed the *instantaneous vector*. All the instantaneous vectors occurring throughout the cardiac cycle form the *cardiac vector*.

The pathways of conduction

The sinus node is situated in the right atrium close to the entrance of the superior vena cava. The AV node lies in the right atrial wall immediately above the tricuspid valve. The fibres of the AV bundle (of His) arise from the AV node and run along the posterior border of the

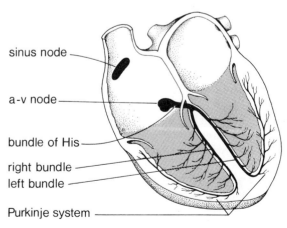

sinus node

a-v node

bundle of His

right bundle

left bundle

Purkinje system

Fig. 8.   The pathways of conduction.

septum between the ventricles (Fig. 8). On reaching the muscular part of the septum, they split into right and left bundle branches and then spread out in the subendocardium of the ventricles as the Purkinje system.

In the usual sequence of events, the electrical impulse arises in the sinus node and spreads across the atria to reach the AV node. It then passes into the rapidly conducting AV bundle and its branches. The right bundle is a slender, compact structure. The left bundle soon splits into two or more divisions or fascicles, one of which proceeds anteriorly, sharing the same blood supply as the right bundle, and another is directed posteriorly.

The first part of the ventricles to be activated is the septum, followed by the endocardium. Finally, the impulse spreads outwards to the epicardium.

The electrocardiogram

Electrodes and leads

A conventional electrocardiogram (ECG) consists of tracings from twelve or more leads. The term 'lead' refers to the ECG obtained as a result of recording the difference in potential between a pair of electrodes.

The bipolar (standard) leads. In these leads, the electrodes are attached to the limbs. In lead I the positive electrode is attached to the left arm and the negative to the right arm. In lead II the positive electrode is attached to the left leg and the negative to the right arm. In lead III the positive is attached to the left leg and the negative to the left arm. They may thus be depicted as:

Lead I = left arm minus right arm (LA–RA)
Lead II = left leg minus right arm (LL–RA)
Lead III = left leg minus left arm (LL–LA)

It can be deduced from these equations that lead II should be equal to the sum of leads I and III.

The position from which the heart is viewed by each of these leads is shown in Fig. 9.

Einthoven regarded each limb used in the recording of the bipolar ECG as an apex of an equilateral triangle, equidistant electrically from the heart at the centre. Although useful, this hypothesis is only approximately true, as it is assumed that the body is a homogeneous sphere, which it clearly is not.

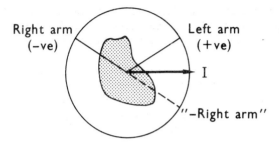

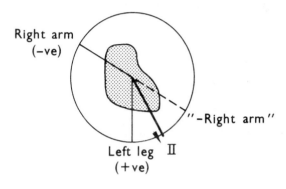

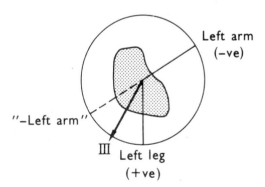

Fig. 9.   Diagram of the effective position of the bipolar (standard) leads. In lead I, the positive electrode is attached to the left arm and the negative to the right arm. In effect, lead I is the sum of the potentials from the left arm with those that would be obtained from an electrode diametrically opposite the right arm. The resultant force is directed mid-way between these two points. Similar principles can be applied to derive effective direction of the leads II and III.

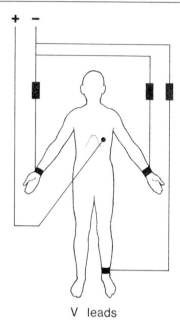

V leads

Fig. 10.   The attachments of unipolar chest leads.

Unipolar leads.   These have an exploring electrode placed on a chosen site linked with an indifferent electrode with a very small potential. In an attempt to obtain a central terminal with 'zero potential', Wilson connected all three limb electrodes through 5000 ohm resistances to form the indifferent electrode.

Unipolar chest leads.   When unipolar leads are recorded from the chest wall, the exploring electrode is connected to the positive pole of the ECG and the negative to the central terminal of Wilson (Fig. 10). By convention, the following sites are normally selected:

V1, the fourth intercostal space just to the right of the sternum.
V2, the fourth intercostal space just to the left of the sternum.
V3, mid-way between V2 and V4.
V4, the fifth intercostal space in the mid-clavicular line.
V5, the left anterior axillary line at the same horizontal level as V4.
V6, the left mid-axillary line at the same horizontal level as V4.

Additional leads can be taken from V3R and V4R, sites on the right side of the chest equivalent to V3 and V4. Occasionally, leads may be taken at higher levels, e.g. the second, third or fourth intercostal spaces or further laterally (V7 and V8).

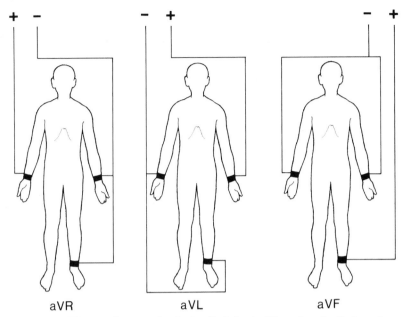

aVR   aVL   aVF

Fig. 11.   The attachment of unipolar limb leads. Note that the limb under study is not attached to the central (negative) terminal.

Unipolar limb leads.   In these leads, the exploring electrode is placed on one limb, and the negative pole is connected to Wilson's central terminal, modified by the omission of the connection from the limb under study to the central terminal (Fig. 11). This modification augments the voltage of the ECG, and the leads so derived are referred to as 'a' leads. They are designated as follows:

aVR, Right arm lead; aVL, Left arm lead; aVF, Left foot lead.

The normal electrocardiogram

The normal electrocardiogram (Fig. 12) shows a series of deflections from the base-line which are designated P, Q, R, S, T and U (Fig. 13). The base-line is referred to as the iso-electric line and the intervals between deflections are described as segments.

Normally, ECGs are recorded at a rate of 25 mm per second and the ECG paper is printed with thin vertical lines 1 mm apart and thick vertical lines 5 mm apart. The interval between the thin lines represents 0.04 sec and that between two thick lines 0.20 sec. If the heart rhythm is regular, the rate can be counted by dividing the number of small squares between two consecutive R waves into 1500. If the rhythm is irregular, one can multiply the number of complexes

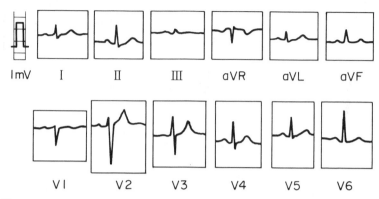

Fig. 12.   Normal 12-lead electrocardiogram. Note the progression in the upright deflection from 'r' over the right ventricle (VI) to an 'R' over the left ventricle (V6).

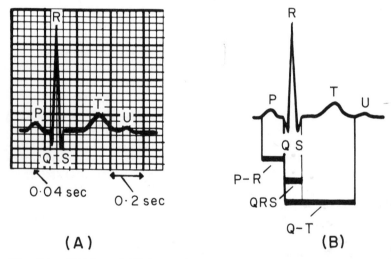

Fig. 13.   (A) Normal ECG complexes. (B) PR, QRS and QT segments.

in 6 sec by 10. Special rulers, which are freely available, simplify the calculation of rate but only if the rhythm is regular.

There are also thin horizontal lines at 1 mm intervals and thick horizontal lines at 5 mm intervals. An ECG recording is standardized so that 1 mV gives a deflection of 10 mm on the paper. The height of a deflection therefore indicates its voltage.

The P wave.   The normal P wave results from the spread of electrical activity across the atria (the activity of the sinus node itself cannot be

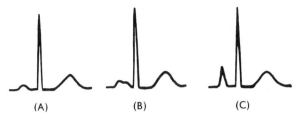

Fig. 14.   (A) Normal P wave. (B) Broadened and notched P wave (P mitrale). (C) Tall peaked P wave (P pulmonale).

detected in the ECG). Because the impulse spreads from right to left, the P wave is upright in leads I, II and aVF, is inverted in aVR and may be upright, biphasic or inverted in lead III, aVL and V1. It should not be higher than 3 mm in the bipolar leads or 2.5 mm in the unipolar leads, or greater than 0.10 sec in duration.

When abnormal, it may be:

1. Inverted (i.e. negative in the leads in which it is usually positive). This indicates depolarization of the atria in an unusual direction, and that the pacemaker is not in the sinus node, but is situated either elsewhere in the atrium, in the AV node or below this; or there is dextrocardia.

2. Broadened and notched, due to delayed depolarization of the left atrium when this chamber is enlarged (P mitrale) (Fig. 14B). In V1, the P wave is then usually biphasic with a small positive wave preceding a deep and broad negative one.

3. Tall and peaked, exceeding 3 mm, as a result of right atrial enlargement (P pulmonale) (Fig. 14C).

4. Absent or invisible due to the presence of junctional rhythm or sinu-atrial block.

5. Replaced by flutter or fibrillation waves.

PR interval.   This is measured from the beginning of the P wave to the beginning of the QRS complex (i.e. to the onset of the Q wave if there is one, and to the onset of the R wave is there is no Q wave). This interval corresponds to the time taken for the impulse to travel from the sinus node to the ventricular muscle. There is an iso-electric segment between the end of the P wave and the beginning of the QRS, whilst the impulse is passing through the AV node and the specialized conducting tissue, an insufficient amount of tissue being electrically stimulated to produce a deflection detectable on the body surface.

The PR interval varies with age and with heart rate. The upper limit in children is 0.16, in adolescents 0.18 and in adults 0.20 sec, although it may be even longer in a few normal individuals. The faster the heart rate the shorter is the PR interval. It is regarded as abnormally short if

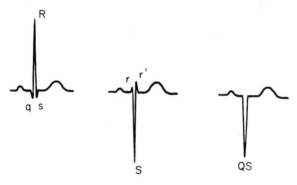

Fig. 15.   Variations in QRS complex (see below).

it is less than 0.10 sec. A shortened PR interval is seen when the impulse originates in the junctional tissue and in the Wolff–Parkinson–White syndrome (see p. 68). The PR interval is prolonged in some forms of heart block (see p. 64).

The QRS complex.   The QRS complex represents depolarization of the ventricular muscle. The components of the ARS complex are defined as follows (Fig. 15):

The R wave is any positive (upward) deflection of the QRS. If there is more than one R wave, the second is denoted R′; an R wave of small voltage may be denoted r.

A negative (downward) deflection preceding an R wave is termed Q, and a negative deflection following an R wave is termed S. If the ventricular complex is entirely negative (i.e. there is no R wave), the complex is termed QS. The whole complex is often referred to as the QRS complex irrespective of whether one or two of its components are absent.

Ventricular depolarization starts in the middle of the left side of the septum and spreads across to the right (phase 1 of ventricular depolarization) (Fig. 16). Subsequently, the main free walls of the ventricles are activated, the impulse spreading from within outwards and from below upwards. Because of the dominating bulk of the left ventricle, the direction of the vector of phase 2 is to the left and posteriorly. Finally, the base of both ventricular walls and the interventricular septum are stimulated. The appearances of the QRS in different leads can be largely explained by the major vectors of these phases as is seen in Fig. 16. In leads facing the left ventricular surface, there is a small Q wave due to septal depolarization and a large R wave due to left ventricular depolarization. On the right side of the heart, as seen from V1, there is usually an r wave due to septal depolarization and a large S wave due to left ventricular forces directed away from the electrode.

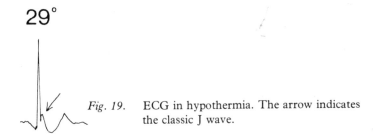

Fig. 19.   ECG in hypothermia. The arrow indicates the classic J wave.

hypothermia there is a prominent J wave (the junction of the S wave and the ST segment) (Fig. 19).

Abnormal ECG patterns

Left ventricular hypertrophy (Fig. 20)

Hypertrophy of the left ventricle increases the amplitude of R waves in left chest leads and S waves in right chest leads. Where there is septal hypertrophy, large but narrow Q waves are seen in left chest leads. When left ventricular hypertrophy becomes advanced, the T wave may become flattened in the leads in which the R wave is tall; eventually ST depression and T wave inversion may occur.

Many efforts have been made to lay down criteria for the diagnosis of left ventricular hypertrophy. None is satisfactory as many factors contribute to the amplitude of ECG waves, including the thickness of the chest wall and the age of the patient. The following criteria have gained wide acceptance:

1. R in V5 or V6 plus S in V1 is greater than 35 mm.
2. R and V5 or V6 is greater than 25 mm.
3. R in aVL is greater than 13 mm or the R in aVF is greater than 20 mm.

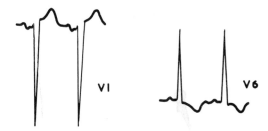

Fig. 20.   Left ventricular hypertrophy, showing tall R waves in V6 and deep S waves in V1, accompanied by ST depression and T wave inversion in V6.

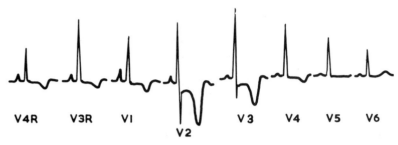

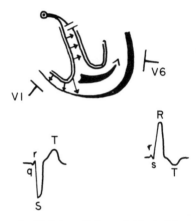

Fig. 21.   Right ventricular hypertrophy showing tall R waves in the right chest leads associated with T wave inversion.

Fig. 22.   The genesis of left bundle branch block. Note that the initial vector is abnormal in being from right-to-left across the septum, thus producing an initial r wave in V6 and a q wave in V1.

These criteria apply only in individuals over 25 years of age. In younger persons, R in V5 or V6 plus S in V1 should exceed 40 mm before the diagnosis of left ventricular hypertrophy can be made.

Right ventricular hypertrophy (Fig. 21)

When the right ventricle becomes hypertrophied, the leads facing the right ventricle (particularly in V1, V3R and V4R) show dominant R waves instead of the usually dominant S wave, i.e. R larger than S, and at least 5 mm tall. As with left ventricular hypertrophy, ST depression and T wave inversion may develop in the leads with tall R waves.

Left bundle branch block (Fig. 22)

When the left branch of the bundle is blocked, the interventricular septum is activated from the right instead of from the left side and the

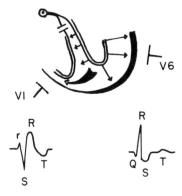

Fig. 23.   Right bundle branch block.

initial vector (phase 1) is directed to the left. Because of this, the normal initial q wave in the left ventricular leads is lost, being replaced by a small r wave. Right ventricular depolarization, which follows, produces an r in V1 and an s in V6. The left ventricle is finally depolarized resulting in an R′ in V6 and a broad S in V1. The QRS duration is increased to 0.12 sec or more.

Right bundle branch block (Fig. 23)

In this disorder, the right branch of the bundle is blocked, but the septum is activated from left to right, as in the normal heart. The left ventricular q wave is preserved, as is the initial r wave over right chest leads. The left ventricle is then depolarized, producing an S wave in right chest leads and an R wave in left chest leads. Finally, depolarization reaches the right ventricle, and so produces an R′ in the right chest leads and a deep broad S wave in the left chest leads. The M pattern is thus seen in the right chest leads, such as V1.

The mean frontal QRS axis

As pointed out on p. 31, the total electrical activity at any one moment of time can be summated and represented by a single electrical force of a certain magnitude and in a certain direction, termed the instantaneous vector. All the instantaneous vectors occurring during the inscription of the QRS complex can be averaged, the direction of the vector so derived being called the mean QRS axis. It is customary

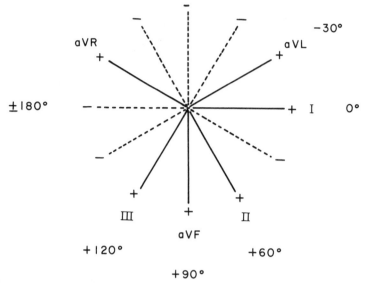

Fig. 24.   Hexaxial reference system.

to measure this only in the frontal plane and any two of the ECG leads which view electrical forces in this plane can be used for this purpose. This can be seen from the so-called hexaxial reference system (Fig. 24).

An approximate method of deriving the mean frontal QRS axis is to find in which of the leads I, II, III, aVR, aVL and aVF, the deflections of the QRS above and below the line are most nearly equal. The mean frontal QRS axis is at right angles to this lead.

To calculate the QRS axis more accurately, one should plot the difference between positive and negative QRS deflections in lead I on the lead I axis and that in lead III on the lead III axis of Fig. 25. By dropping perpendiculars from both points and drawing a line through this intersection from the centre point to the periphery of the curve, the axis may be determined.

Left axis deviation is present when the axis is less than − 30° and right axis deviation when the axis is greater than + 110°.

Calculation of the mean frontal QRS axis is of limited value except in a few conditions such as the differentiation of ostium primum from ostium secundum atrial septal defects (see p. 220).

Left axis deviation is often due to block in the anterior division (fascicle) of the left bundle branch, and when associated with right bundle branch block is a frequent precursor of complete heart block.

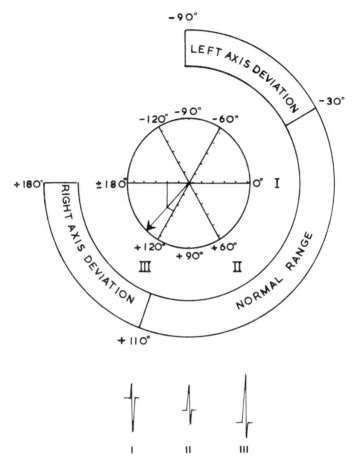

Fig. 25. The measurement of the mean frontal plane axis of the QRS complex. In this example, the sum of Q, R and S in lead I is −2 and in lead III is +2.5. By drawing a line through the intersection of perpendiculars drawn from these points, the axis may be derived.

Right axis deviation commonly accompanies right ventricular hypertrophy, but may be due to block of the posterior fascicle of the left bundle.

Vectorcardiography

Vectorcardiography is a term applied to the technique by which the movement and magnitude of the cardiac vectors are represented by two-dimensional loops rather than by waves and complexes. The derivation of a vector loop is shown in Fig. 24. Vector loops can be

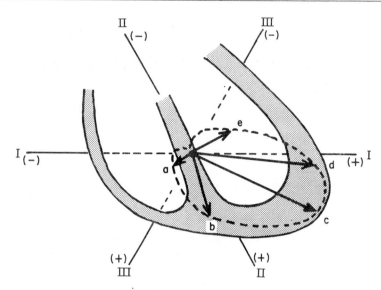

Fig. 26.   The derivation of a vector loop in the frontal plane. Arrows from *a* to *e* indicate the progressive movement of the cardiac vector throughout the inscription of the QRS.

obtained in frontal, horizontal and sagittal planes. Unfortunately, vectorcardiography is technically more complex than conventional (scalar) electrocardiography and, except in the hands of experts, contributes little to clinical cardiology at present.

References

GOLDMAN, M. J. (1976). *Principles of Clinical Electrocardiography*, 10th ed. Los Altos, Calif.: Lange.
NOBLE, D. (1979). The Initiation of the Heartbeat, 2nd ed. Oxford: Clarendon.
SCHAMROTH. L. (1977) *An Introduction to Electrocardiography*, 5th ed. Oxford: Blackwell.

4

Disorders of Rate, Rhythm and Conduction

Introduction

As is discussed in more detail in Chapter 3, there are electrically two types of cell in the myocardium — the automatic and the nonautomatic — the automatic cells having the capacity of self-excitation. The group of automatic cells with the most rapid rate of spontaneous depolarization dominates the heart as the pacemaker. This is normally the sinus node, which is under the control both of the vagus and of the sympathetic nervous system. Ectopic rhythms, in which the heart is activated from a pacemaker other than the sinus node, arise from a variety of mechanisms:

Escape of lower centres.   An increase in vagal activity reduces the rate of spontaneous depolarization of the sinus node and thereby slows the heart; another group of automatic cells may exhibit a rate faster than that of the sinus node and become the pacemaker.

Increased automaticity of other zones.   Increased sympathetic activity increases the rate of discharge not only of the sinus node, but also of other areas, including the ventricles. Ischaemia, digitalis intoxication and electrolyte disorders also enhance ventricular automaticity.

Re-entry.   When there are pathways of conduction with differing refractory periods, an impulse may enter an area which is receptive but cannot activate a zone refractory from the previous cycle (Fig. 27). When this zone recovers, it may then accept the impulse and act as a pathway back to the area that was initially activated. If this area has had time to recover, it can be stimulated again. In order for there to be time for recovery to take place, the re-entrant pathway must either be long (macro re-entry) or conduction through it must be extremely slow. Re-entry in small areas of atrial or ventricular muscle (micro re-entry) probably also requires that the refractory period is abnormally short. This process can lead to single or repetitive ectopic activity. Supraventricular arrhythmias are frequently associated with

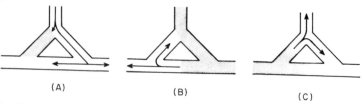

(A)   (B)   (C)

Fig. 27.   The re-entry phenomenon. In (A) the impulse cannot enter a zone which is still in the refractory phase. In (B) this zone has become receptive as adjacent muscle becomes refractory. In (C) the impulse leaves the newly activated zone and re-enters the same tissue as was activated in (A) which has now recovered.

anatomically abnormal pathways. The most distinctive variety occurs in the Wolff–Parkinson–White syndrome, in which a slender bundle of myocardium forms a bridge between the atria and the ventricles, bypassing the atrioventricular node.

Disturbances of sinus rate and rhythm

Sinus tachycardia is sinus rhythm at a rate faster than is normal. In adults, this is commonly defined as being greater than 100 per minute. In children the heart rate, even at rest, frequently exceeds 100 per minute, and in infants may exceed 150 per minute. Sinus tachycardia occurs in normal individuals when sympathetic activity is increased, as by emotion or exercise, or when vagal tone is inhibited. Amongst factors associated with disease which cause sinus tachycardia are anaemia, hyperthyroidism and fever. It also occurs as a reflex response to a fall in blood pressure, as in shock, or to a rise in venous pressure, as occurs in heart failure. It may be provoked by such drugs as adrenaline, isoprenaline, ephedrine, propantheline, atropine and thyroxine. Sinus tachycardia is seldom harmful and may be a compensatory mechanism.

The patient with sinus tachycardia may complain of palpitation which is of gradual and explicable onset, unlike the abrupt and unexpected appearance of the symptom in paroxysmal tachycardia. The diagnosis is usually obvious when there is a regular pulse at a rate of more than 100 per minute. Frequently, the tachycardia subsides during the examination as anxiety diminishes. Carotid sinus pressure causes little slowing in contrast to its usually dramatic effect in atrial tachycardia or atrial flutter. The ECG shows P waves having a normal relationship to QRS complexes. The J point may be depressed; the ST then slopes upward (see Fig. 18).

Sinus tachycardia does not require treatment.

Sinus bradycardia describes a slow heart in sinus rhythm. This term is commonly applied to heart rates of less than 60 per minute, although

Fig. 28.   Sinus arrhythmia. Note the gradual change in RR interval, with each QRS complex being preceded by a similar P wave.

such rates are frequently seen in healthy elderly people, and in the highly trained athlete. Sinus bradycardia occurs when there is increased vagal tone and can be provoked by carotid sinus or eyeball pressure. Other causes are myxoedema, hypothermia, raised intracranial pressure and certain drugs including digitalis, reserpine, and the β-adrenergic blocking agents such as propranolol.

Sinus bradycardia seldom gives rise to symptoms or undesirable haemodynamic effects but, occasionally, in the elderly and in acute myocardial infarction, cardiac failure or hypotension may develop if the stroke output cannot be increased to compensate adequately for the slow rate. The heart can be accelerated by atropine 0.6 mg subcutaneously or intravenously, by ephedrine given orally in a dosage of 15 to 30 mg three times a day or by long-acting isoprenaline 15 to 30 mg three or four times daily. Sinus bradycardia is a component of the *sick sinus syndrome*, a condition that occurs transiently in acute myocardial infarction and persistently in some elderly people. The bradycardia may be complicated by paroxysms of atrial arrhythmias (tachycardia, flutter or fibrillation), in which the ventricular rate is very rapid. Syncope may result either from too slow or too fast a heart rate. Treatment is difficult; it may necessitate the combined use of a pacemaker and anti-arrhythmic drugs.

Sinus arrhythmia (Fig. 28)

Normally, the sinus node does not discharge with absolute regularity owing to variations in vagal tone. These variations are related to respiration, and it is characteristic in the young to find acceleration of the heart during inspiration with slowing during expiration. This phasic change in the rhythm of the heart is known as sinus arrhythmia. It is seldom clinically obvious in adults, but is occasionally seen in the healthy old person. It is of no clinical importance, but it must be differentiated from the other types of arrhythmia. Its relationship to respiration usually makes this easy.

Supraventricular arrhythmias

A variety of rhythm disturbances can arise in the atria and AV junctional area (that is, the AV node and adjacent specialized tissues). These may result from either increased automaticity or re-entry.

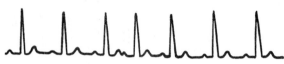

Fig. 29.   Atrial ectopic beat. Note the premature P wave followed by a QRST of normal appearance.

Atrial ectopic beats (atrial extrasystoles, atrial premature beats)

Atrial ectopic beats are common in normal individuals, but seldom give rise to symptoms, apart from an awareness of heart irregularity from time to time. They cause an occasional irregularity in an otherwise normal pulse, and are usually abolished by exercise. The diagnosis is readily confirmed from the ECG (Fig. 29) which shows a premature beat occurring earlier than the next anticipated sinus beat. The P wave differs in configuration from that of a sinus beat, because depolarization of the atria takes place in an abnormal direction. The accompanying QRST complex is usually similar to that of previous beats of sinus origin because the pathway of ventricular depolarization is normal. Occasionally, the QRST complex is abnormally broad ('aberrant') because the impulse passes down only one of the bundle branches, the other still being refractory from the preceding beat. It then simulates the appearance of bundle branch block or a ventricular ectopic beat (see p. 62).

Atrial ectopic beats may presage the appearance of other atrial arrhythmias but they require no treatment.

Junctional nodal ectopic beats (Fig. 30)

Ectopic beats deriving from the junctional tissue are quite common and, like atrial ectopic beats, usually benign. They are responsible for an occasional irregularity in an otherwise regular pulse and cannot be

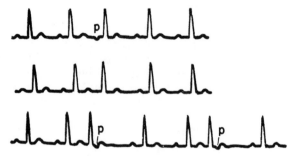

Fig. 30.   Junctional ectopic beats. Note that the P wave may precede, follow or coincide with the QRS complex.

Fig. 31. Supraventricular tachycardia showing QRS complexes of normal width at a rapid rate and with regular RR intervals.

diagnosed without an electrocardiogram, which shows the same features as with atrial ectopic beats except that the P wave is inverted in lead II and is either buried in the QRS complex, or precedes or follows it by a very short interval.

Junctional nodal rhythm

In this condition the junctional tissue is acting as the pacemaker of the heart and the ECG appearance is that of a succession of junctional ectopic beats. It is usually a transient condition resulting from a depression of sinus node activity. It occurs in some normal individuals and may be provoked by digitalis or ischaemic heart disease. The heart rate is usually in the region of 50 to 60 per minute and no treatment is required. If the heart rate is undesirably slow, it can be accelerated by the use of atropine.

Supraventricular tachycardias (Fig. 31)

Tachycardias which arise in atrial or AV junctional tissue can be described collectively as supraventricular. They share certain characteristics — starting abruptly, usually being regular at a rate of 140 to 220 per minute, and being associated with narrow QRS complexes, closely resembling those seen in sinus rhythm. Aberrant conduction may, however, occur as may rates above and below those quoted. Atrial tachycardias are often the consequence of an accelerated automatic focus in the atria, whereas junctional tachycardia is usually due to a re-entry mechanism — the commonest form involving dual pathways within the AV node which have different rates of conduction and refractoriness.

There is usually normal atrioventricular (AV) conduction. The attacks may last only seconds, but they often persist for minutes or hours or, much less commonly, for days. They may occur frequently or be separated from one another by weeks, months or even years. It is sometimes possible to identify provoking factors such as tobacco, coffee, alcohol, emotion and exercise. Supraventricular tachycardia is a frequent complication of the Wolff–Parkinson–White syndrome (see p. 68).

Paroxysms are most often encountered in otherwise normal people in whom they give rise to palpitation, but no serious haemodynamic effects. These tachycardias can, however, produce failure and hypotension in the presence of heart disease because of the increased workload of the heart and the inadequate filling time during diastole.

The patient usually complains of attacks of rapid regular palpitation of abrupt onset, sometimes accompanied by dizziness or even syncope. When the attack is prolonged or when it occurs in those with heart disease, there may be dyspnoea and ischaemic chest pain.

The episodes are often so brief and infrequent that no doctor ever sees them; if the patient is observed at the time, the pulse is found to be regular at a rate between 140 and 220. Carotid sinus massage frequently terminates the attack, but if it fails to do so, it has no effect upon the pulse rate. The ECG usually reveals QRST complexes of normal or near normal configuration occurring rapidly and regularly (Fig. 31); P waves, if they can be seen, often appear abnormal. They may precede, coincide with, or follow the QRS. In some instances, the QRST complexes are abnormally broadened and conform to a bundle branch block pattern, the appearances simulating ventricular tachycardia. Differentiation may often be made on the basis of the reaction to carotid sinus stimulation to which ventricular tachycardia does not respond, or to the identification of P waves preceding each QRS complex, for in ventricular tachycardia the P waves usually occur independently of, and at a much slower rate than, the ventricular complexes.

The ECG between attacks is usually normal, but the appearances of the Wolff–Parkinson–White syndrome, the Lown–Ganong–Levine syndrome (short PR, normal QRS), or other abnormalities of conduction may be seen.

Because of the repetitive paroxysmal nature of the tachycardia, prevention is often of greater importance than the treatment of the individual attack. When possible, a provoking factor such as strong coffee or tobacco should be identified and avoided. Some patients are satisfied by reassurance that there is no serious heart disease, but in those in whom anxiety is important both as a causative factor and as a symptom of the paroxysms, a sedative such as diazepam (Valium) 2 to 5 mg orally, thrice daily is helpful. When the attacks are prolonged or if they complicate organic heart disease, either disopyramide (100 to 150 mg thrice daily), a beta-adrenergic blocking drug, or digoxin in the usual doses may be of value. Occasionally, it may be necessary to use quinidine.

In the treatment of the individual attack, the patient may be taught to carry out the Valsalva manoeuvre and the doctor can use carotid sinus massage. If this is not effective, sedation is often all that is necessary. If the patient is in great distress, treatment is more urgent. Verapamil (2 to 10 mg slowly), digoxin or a beta-adrenoceptor blocking drug may be administered or electrical shock applied.

Atrial tachycardia with block (Fig. 32)

This resembles paroxysmal atrial tachycardia of the type previously described in that there is an ectopic atrial focus discharging at a rate of

Table 4. *Diagnosis of tachycardias*

	Ventricular rate	Ventricular complexes (QRST)	Relation of atrial (P) to ventricular complexes (QRST)	Atrial rate	Atrial complexes (P)	Effect of carotid sinus massage	Additional clues
Sinus tachycardia (p. 50)	Seldom more than 130 at rest	Unchanged	Normal relationship	Seldom more than 130	Normal	Slight slowing	Gradual changes in rate
Atrial tachycardia with block (p. 54)	70–220 Usually half atrial	Usually unchanged	Long PR or dropped beats	140–220	Abnormal	Increases block, slows ventricle	P waves seen best in V1
Supraventricular tachycardia (p. 53)	140–220 Same as atrial	Usually unchanged, may be bizarre	Normal or P superimposed on QRS or ST	140–220	Abnormal	Abolishes arrhythmia or has no effect	Sudden onset
Atrial flutter (p. 56)	Usually 140–160 regular	Usually unchanged	2 or more atrial (f) waves to each QRS	Usually 280–320	'Saw-tooth'	Increases block, slows ventricle	Suspect when pulse regular at 150
Atrial fibrillation (p. 57)	Usually 100–150 irregular	Usually unchanged	No relationship	300+	Irregular	Slight slowing of ventricle	—
Ventricular tachycardia (p. 60)	140–220 regular	Broad and bizarre	P waves usually regular and independent of QRS complexes	60–100	Normal	None	Preceding ventricular ectopic beats

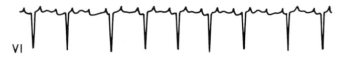

VI

Fig. 32.   Atrial tachycardia with block. This is often most easily recognized in V1. Commonly there are two P waves to each ventricular complex, but greater or lesser degrees of block may occur. It may be difficult to identify those P waves which are superimposed on T waves.

140 to 220 per minute; it differs in that there is some degree of AV block. It is rare in the absence of serious organic heart disease, and is usually due to advanced digitalis intoxication. There is nearly always cellular potassium depletion, but the serum potassium is not necessarily low.

The ventricular rate is dependent upon the degree of AV block. Commonly, this is 2:1 and there are no adverse haemodynamic effects as the ventricular rate is about 80 to 100 per minute. Sometimes the only manifestation of block is a long PR interval; in this case the ventricular rate is fast and cardiac failure is aggravated.

The clinical recognition of this rhythm disturbance is virtually impossible as it may give rise to no symptoms and no obvious physical signs. The diagnosis must be made from the electrocardiogram (Fig. 32), in which P waves are seen to occur at a rate of 140 to 220 per minute; there is either a prolongation of the PR interval or some of the P waves are not followed by QRS complexes. The P waves are usually only slightly abnormal and do not have the saw-tooth appearance of atrial flutter. Carotid sinus pressure produces a transient increase in the atrioventricular block with a corresponding fall in the ventricular rate — a response quite unlike that of paroxysmal atrial tachycardia without block (see p. 54).

Atrial tachycardia with block is seldom dangerous in itself but is associated with a high risk of death from digitalis intoxication. As soon as the arrhythmia is recognized, digitalis should be stopped and potassium supplements given; if the ventricular rate is fast, it may be slowed by diphenylhydantoin or a beta-adrenoceptor blocking drug used. When digitalis poisoning is not responsible, digitalis is the drug of choice. Electrical shock should not be used unless it is certain that digitalis intoxication is not responsible, as it may induce more serious arrhythmias.

Atrial flutter (Fig. 33)

In this arrhythmia, the atria beat regularly at a rate of 250 to 350 per minute — usually close to 300 per minute. The exact mechanism of atrial flutter remains unclear. The theory of circus movement proposes that the excitation wave moves in a circular fashion around the orifices

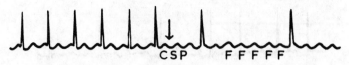

Fig. 33. Atrial flutter. Note that flutter waves are difficult to discern until carotid sinus pressure is applied.

of the superior and inferior venae cavae and is therefore self-perpetuating (macro re-entry).

It is rare for all the atrial impulses to be conducted to the ventricles and varying degrees of atrioventricular block may be present. In most instances of atrial flutter, the ventricular rhythm is regular because of a 2:1, 3:1 or 4:1 response to the regular atrial activity, but it is irregular in some patients in whom the degree of block varies from cycle to cycle. The commonest variety is that of 2:1 block with a ventricular rate of 140 to 160.

Atrial flutter is almost always a complication of serious organic heart disease. The most common association is with rheumatic heart disease, but it is seen in hyperthyroidism, ischaemic heart disease, myocarditis and other disorders. Atrial flutter may be persistent or occur in paroxysms which are usually self-limited to hours or days, but it may progress to atrial fibrillation. The symptoms resemble those of atrial tachycardia, with palpitation, dizziness or syncope. The arrhythmia often provokes cardiac failure.

The pulse is usually regular at a rate of 140 to 160 per minute. It may be possible to see venous 'flutter' waves in the neck. Carotid sinus massage leads to an increase in the atrioventricular block, with a slowing of the ventricular rate as long as the pressure is maintained.

The electrocardiogram is diagnostic with 'flutter' waves of a sawtooth appearance, best seen in leads II and III occurring at approximately 300 per minute (Fig. 33). The sawtooth nature of the complexes may be obscured by the QRS complexes when there is 2:1 block, but it is readily revealed when carotid sinus massage is applied.

As mentioned, atrial flutter is usually self-terminating, but because of its deleterious effects, treatment should be initiated without delay. Digitalis increases the AV block, brings the heart rate under control, and sometimes abolishes the arrhythmia. Treatment should be started with this drug, but electric shock is indicated if immediate correction is necessary and is almost invariably effective (see p. 71). In the patient liable to paroxysms of atrial flutter, digitalis should be continued indefinitely.

Atrial fibrillation (Fig. 34)

In this arrhythmia, irregular atrial impulses occur at rates over 300 per minute. The mechanism of atrial fibrillation, like that of atrial flutter, remains uncertain. It may be that there are multiple foci of ectopic

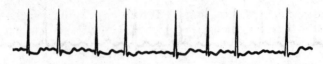

Fig. 34.   Atrial fibrillation, with complete irregularity of atrial and ventricular rhythms.

activity or that wavelets of excitation follow variable courses through the atrial myocardium depending upon the location of patches of excitable and refractory muscle. If there are multiple areas of the atrium with different refractory periods, one can conceive of re-entry as a permanently self-perpetuating process. Some degree of AV block is invariable; the ventricular rhythm is slower than the atrial but it is also irregular.

There is usually an obvious organic lesion, most often rheumatic mitral valve disease. Other causes include ischaemic heart disease, especially acute myocardial infarction, thyrotoxicosis, hypertension, acute infections, particularly when these affect the lungs, and cardiopulmonary surgery. It is a rare complication of many other types of heart disease. In about 5% of patients, no evidence of organic heart disease can be found — 'lone' atrial fibrillation.

The presence of atrial fibrillation suggests that there has been either a pathological process involving the atria, such as atrial infarction or rheumatic fever and its sequelae, or that there has been a rise in pressure with atrial dilatation secondary to mitral valve or left ventricular disease.

Atrial fibrillation may be paroxysmal, with attacks lasting for a few minutes or hours. This is particularly likely in acute myocardial infarction, in chest infections, and in the early stages of thyrotoxicosis and mitral valve disease. In rheumatic cases, the arrhythmia usually becomes established and persists for the rest of the patient's life.

Atrial fibrillation leads to untoward effects for three major reasons. First, the ventricular response is usually so fast that there is inadequate time for diastolic filling and the cardiac output falls. Second, the atrial contribution to ventricular filling is lost. Third, stasis in the ineffectively contracting atrium encourages thrombosis. As a consequence, embolism is common, particularly in patients with mitral valve disease. Emboli from the right atrium produce pulmonary artery obstruction; those from the left atrium may lodge in cerebral, renal or other peripheral vessels.

The first symptom may be that of irregular palpitation, but in many patients atrial fibrillation leads to the sudden development of left ventricular failure and pulmonary oedema. The onset may also be insidious with gradually increasing dyspnoea.

The diagnosis is usually easy because the arterial pulse is irregular.

The ventricular response to atrial fibrillation is random and it is not possible to define any pattern in the pulse. Because of the varying times available for filling of the ventricles, the output of the heart and the volume of the pulse alter from beat to beat. This chaotic pulse serves to differentiate atrial fibrillation from atrial or ventricular ectopic beats, which are the arrhythmias most likely to be confused with it. In these latter conditions some periods of regularity are usually observed, and often the irregularity will be noted to occur every second, third or fourth beat. The venous pulse in atrial fibrillation is also irregular. The heart rate at the apex ('the apex rate') is higher than in the radial pulse because the heart expels so little blood in some beats that no pulsation can be appreciated in the peripheral arteries.

In the electrocardiogram, the P wave disappears but atrial activity produces an irregular undulation of the base line (Fig. 34). The QRST complexes are totally irregular in timing, except in the rare situation of atrial fibrillation complicated by complete heart block. In most cases of untreated atrial fibrillation, the ventricular rate lies between 100 and 160 per minute, but rates above or below this are not uncommon.

Although patients with the arrhythmia may survive for many years with few symptoms, atrial fibrillation is frequently a serious complication because of the risks of heart failure and embolism.

There are three components of the treatment of atrial fibrillation: the control of ventricular rate, the restoration of sinus rhythm and the prevention of embolism. The control of the ventricular rate comes first because it is the fast ventricular rate that is deleterious, rather than the atrial fibrillation per se, and also because the arrhythmia may terminate spontaneously. Depending upon the severity of the clinical situation, digoxin or one of the other cardiac glycosides may be given intravenously or orally. In most cases, oral administration is satisfactory, and brings the heart rate under control within 2 or 3 hours. When full digitalization has been achieved, the ventricular rate at rest should be held at about 70 to 80 per minute. If the heart rate cannot be reduced to this level, a beta-adrenoceptor blocking drug or verapamil may be added.

When atrial fibrillation has developed recently in a patient with mitral valve disease, heparin should be given as the risk of embolism is particularly high at this time; oral anticoagulants should be continued subsequently for at least a year.

When atrial fibrillation has been present for many years, and there is associated and untreatable severe heart disease, there is little to be gained by trying to restore normal rhythm because this is not likely to be maintained. Even if it is, the atrial muscle has usually atrophied and is functionally ineffective. When the arrhythmia is of relatively recent onset, and particularly when the heart disease has been alleviated, or some complicating condition such as thyrotoxicosis or pulmonary infection corrected, the patient is likely to benefit from its termination.

Therefore, if sinus rhythm has not returned within a few days; but it seems probable that it would be maintained were the atrial fibrillation terminated, electric shock therapy (p. 71) should be employed. This is effective in most instances, at least initially. However, there is a considerable relapse rate within the succeeding months whether or not prophylactic drugs, such as quinidine, are used. Because of this, it is advisable in most instances to keep the patient on digitalis therapy after restoration of sinus rhythm, as a subsequent recurrence of atrial fibrillation may be associated with a dangerously fast ventricular rate.

Ventricular ectopic rhythms

Ventricular ectopic beats (extrasystoles, premature beats)

An ectopic focus in the ventricles may arise because of ventricular escape, enhanced automatic activity, or re-entry. Ventricular ectopic beats are not uncommon in normal individuals but are encountered frequently in organic heart disease, especially in myocardial infarction. If they occur every second beat (pulsus bigeminus or 'coupling') they are usually due to digitalis therapy.

Patients are seldom aware of ventricular ectopic beats, but may complain of the heart seeming to stop briefly, or of an occasional heavy beat. The diagnosis may be suspected from an irregularity of the pulse interrupting an otherwise regular rhythm, but cannot be made without an ECG, in which there are bizarre and broadened QRS complexes followed by T waves pointing in the direction opposite to that of the main QRS component (Fig. 35). The QRST complexes are not preceded by a P wave and are usually succeeded by a long period (the compensatory pause) before the next sinus-activated beat appears.

The importance of ventricular ectopic beats depends upon their context. In normal individuals they are virtually of no consequence. They are associated with an impaired profusion in ischaemic heart disease but it is not established that the outlook is improved by their suppression (see pp. 143 and 159).

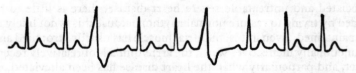

Fig. 35.   Ventricular ectopic beats. Note bizarre pattern of QRST, and succeeding compensatory pause.

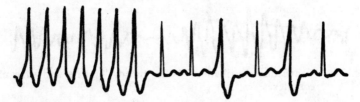

Fig. 36.   Ventricular tachycardia. Note broad bizarre QRS complexes, resembling the ventricular ectopic beats seen after termination of the ventricular tachycardia.

Ventricular tachycardia (Fig. 36)

In this condition a tachycardia arises in the ventricles at a rate of 120 to 220 per minute; the atria usually remain under the control of the sinus node. It may be a consequence of either re-entry or enhanced automaticity of ventricular pacemaker cells. It is nearly always a complication of serious heart disease, although occasionally seen in an otherwise normal individual. The attacks are liable to occur in paroxysms lasting for seconds or minutes, but may continue for several hours. Ventricular tachycardia frequently causes or aggravates heart failure and the shock syndrome.

As with supraventricular tachycardia, the first symptom may be that of rapid and regular palpitation, but because of the more serious effects on the circulation, acute breathlessness and ischaemic chest pain tend to be more severe. On examination there is a rapid, regular but small pulse. The independent atrial activity may be responsible for dissociated 'a' waves in the venous pulse and a variation in the intensity of the first heart sound, but these physical signs are difficult to elicit. The clinical diagnosis depends largely on the recognition of the rapid regular pulse and its lack of response to carotid sinus pressure. The ECG shows rapidly occurring broad QRS complexes resembling those of bundle branch block (Fig. 36). P waves may be identified at a rate different from that of the ventricles. The RR intervals are usually equal, but may vary by up to 0.03 sec from one another. The lack of response to carotid pressure assists in the differentiation from atrial tachycardia with bundle branch block (see also p. 63).

In the patient with good underlying heart function, urgent treatment may not be necessary. Most instances of ventricular tachycardia, however, call for immediate action, particularly in the presence of acute myocardial infarction. Lignocaine (lidocaine), 50 to 100 mg may be given intravenously and repeated if necessary. Alternative therapy includes disopyramide, mexiletine or the beta-adrenergic blocking drugs. If these drugs fail to control the arrhythmia, electric shock may be used.

The drugs mentioned above may be used to prevent recurrences.

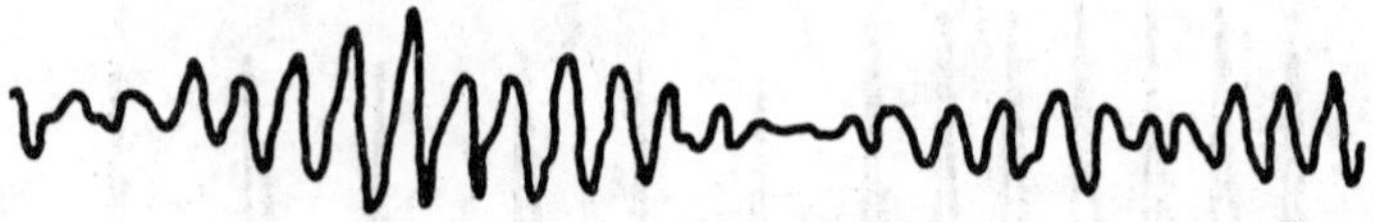

Fig. 37.   Ventricular fibrillation. Note broad, bizarre and irregular complexes.

Ventricular fibrillation (Fig. 37)

In this condition there is a chaotic electrical disturbance of the ventricles, with impulses occurring irregularly at a rate of 300 to 500 per minute. Ventricular contraction is uncoordinated and no time is available for ventricular filling or emptying. The cardiac output falls precipitously to zero.

Ventricular fibrillation is a common complication of acute myocardial infarction and ischaemia, and may also result from drowning, electrocution and overdosage by drugs including digitalis, adrenaline and isoprenaline. Self-terminating episodes are rare but may complicate complete heart block.

Because of its catastrophic effects, ventricular fibrillation gives rise to the clinical features of cardiac arrest, with sudden disappearance of arterial pulses, cessation of respiration, loss of consciousness and dilatation of the pupils. Although it cannot be diagnosed clinically, it is to be suspected in any patient dying with apparent suddenness, particularly in the context of acute myocardial infarction. On the electrocardiogram, there is a chaotic rhythm with ventricular complexes of varying amplitude and rate (Fig. 37). The attack may commence with rather tall and relatively regular complexes, which later become flattened. Eventually asystole ensues.

Ventricular fibrillation is almost invariably fatal, and immediate treatment is necessary if death is to be prevented. As with other forms of cardiac arrest, an effective circulation and ventilation must be obtained within 4 minutes if irreversible brain damage is not to occur. If the patient is receiving intensive care, sinus rhythm and consciousness can be promptly restored by applying a defibrillating electric shock within seconds. If an electrical defibrillator is not immediately available, the standard treatment of cardiac arrest should be started with closed-chest cardiac compression and artificial ventilation (see p. 72). Electrical defibrillation should be carried out as soon as possible. Acidosis, which develops quickly, should be corrected by giving 50 to 75 mmol of sodium bicarbonate intravenously.

Recurrences of ventricular fibrillation should be prevented in the same way as ventricular tachycardia.

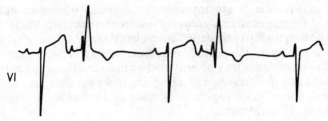

Fig. 38. Supraventricular ectopic beats with aberration. Note that the ectopic beats are preceded by a P wave.

The differentiation of supraventricular from ventricular ectopic rhythms

It may be difficult to differentiate supraventricular (atrial or junctional) from ventricular ectopic rhythms even with an ECG.

Ectopic beats

The QRS complexes of ectopic beats of atrial or junctional origin are usually identical to those of preceding sinus beats. However, they may be broad and bizarre due to *aberration* (Fig. 38). Conduction through the bundle branches is aberrant if one branch is still refractory from the preceding beat, when the other has recovered. Usually, the right bundle takes longer to recover than the left and the aberrant beat has the appearance of right bundle branch block. Aberration should be suspected when the ectopic beat is preceded by a P wave different from that of normal sinus beats, or if it is of right bundle branch block type (RSR' in VI), or when the initial part of the QRS is the same in the ectopic beat as it is in the normally conducted beats.

Tachycardias

It may be possible to determine the nature of a tachycardia clinically because the activity of the atria is usually dissociated from that of the ventricles in ventricular tachycardia. There may be irregular cannon waves in the jugular veins (see p. 92) and variation in the intensity of the first heart sound. In junctional tachycardia, cannon waves may occur with every beat.

The response to carotid sinus stimulation is even more diagnostic, for this manoeuvre frequently abolishes supraventricular tachycardia but leaves ventricular tachycardia unaffected. However, one should delay applying this test if possible until an ECG is available, as one may otherwise miss the opportunity of verifying the nature of the arrhythmia by obtaining a graphic record.

Supraventricular tachycardia can be diagnosed easily on the ECG if the QRS complexes resemble, as they usually do, those that the patient exhibited during sinus rhythm. Difficulty arises when supraventricular tachycardia is accompanied by aberrant bizarre complexes. Carotid sinus pressure may quickly resolve this problem, but if it does not, the diagnosis largely depends on identifying P waves. If these are dissociated from the QRS, ventricular tachycardia is probable. Additional evidence may be provided by the occurrence and nature of ectopic beats in previous tracings. Sometimes the diagnosis requires the insertion of electrodes into the heart to determine the origin and spread of the arrhythmia.

The carotid sinus and arrhythmias

The carotid sinus is situated at the bifurcation of the common carotid artery and is sensitive to changes in arterial pressure. Impulses arising from the stretch receptors in the carotid sinus pass to the medulla and reflexly slow the heart by stimulating the motor nucleus of the vagus nerve and by inhibiting cardiac sympathetic action. Usually, external pressure on the carotid sinus leads to a slight slowing of the heart rate by reducing the activity of the sinus node. In some individuals in whom the carotid sinus is hypersensitive, external pressure leads to extreme bradycardia and hypotension with resulting syncope.

Carotid sinus pressure plays an important part in the recognition and management of cardiac arrhythmias. It is best to locate the carotid artery on one side first and then to stroke it gently, but firmly. If this is ineffective, the manoeuvre should be repeated on the other side. Carotid sinus massage causes only slight slowing of the ventricular rate in patients with sinus tachycardia and with atrial fibrillation. If it has any effect in the patient with supraventricular tachycardia, it causes an abrupt termination of the arrhythmia. In atrial flutter and in atrial tachycardia with block, it produces an increase in atrioventricular block, temporarily decreasing the ventricular rate which rises again when the massage is discontinued. It has no effect in ventricular tachycardia. It is best to carry out carotid sinus massage with ECG control, as excessive bradycardia and even ventricular arrhythmias may result from this procedure. Other dangers include reflex hypotension and cerebrovascular insufficiency.

Disorders of conduction

Sinu-atrial block and sinus arrest

In sinu-atrial block, an impulse from the sinus node fails to activate the atria. This results in a dropped beat; on the electrocardiogram a complete PQRST complex is absent, but the next sinus beat comes in at the predicted time (Fig. 39). It is of little clinical importance except that it may be a manifestation of intoxication by digoxin or other anti-arrhythmic drugs. It may be a component of the sick sinus syndrome

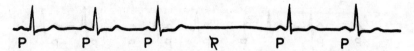

Fig. 39. Sinu-atrial block. Note complete absence of PQRST, with the next beat coming in at the predicted time.

(see p. 51). If it is prolonged, syncope occurs. In sinus arrest, the sinus node fails to initiate an impulse; after a pause, junctional or ventricular escape occurs. Its significance is similar to that of sino-atrial block.

Atrioventricular (heart) block

The term atrioventricular (AV) block implies that there is some defect in conduction of the impulse from the atria to the ventricles. In first-degree AV block, all the impulses reach the ventricles but they are delayed in their passage and the PR interval exceeds 0.20 sec (Fig. 40). In second-degree block, some impulses reach the ventricles while others fail to do so (Fig. 41). In complete heart block, no impulses reach the ventricles from the atria, and the ventricles are under the control of a lower pacemaker situated in the junctional tissue, bundle of His, the bundle branches or Purkinje tissue (Fig. 42). In bundle branch block, AV conduction is maintained through one branch, the other being blocked.

First-degree AV block (Fig. 40). First-degree AV block occurs occasionally in normal individuals, is a characteristic feature of the carditis of acute rheumatic fever, but is most commonly due to digitalis overdosage. It cannot be diagnosed clinically and its recognition depends on observing a PR interval of greater than 0.20 sec in the ECG. Its only importance is as an index of digitalis intoxication and as a precursor of the more advanced degrees of AV block.

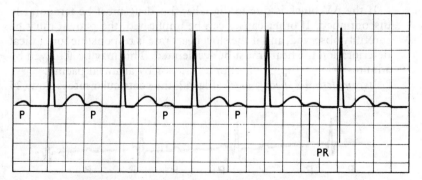

Fig. 40. First-degree heart block. The PR interval is prolonged to 0.36 sec, but each sinus impulse is conducted to the ventricles.

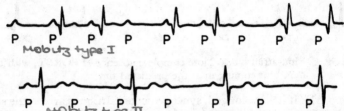

Fig. 41.   (A) Partial heart block of the Wenckebach type. Note that the PR interval increases from beat to beat until a beat is dropped, following which the cycle restarts. (B) Second-degree heart block — 2:1 block. Note that only every second P wave is followed by a QRS.

Second-degree AV block.   One of the commonest varieties of second-degree block is the Wenckebach pehnomenon in which the PR interval becomes progressively more prolonged from beat to beat until one P wave is not succeeded by a QRS complex (Fig. 41A). The next atrial complex is followed at a normal or near normal interval by a QRS complex and the cycle of events recurs. The pulse is correspondingly irregular. In 2:1 block, every second atrial beat is followed by a ventricular complex. This may be suspected clinically by a regular slow ventricular rhythm and is confirmed on the electrocardiogram (Fig. 41B). The Wenckebach phenomenon is frequently the result of digitalis intoxication, but both this and the other varieties of second-degree heart block are often due to ischaemic heart disease, particularly myocardial infarction, and to many other types of cardiac disease. The main significance of second-degree heart block lies in the liability of the patient to develop complete heart block and the Adams–Stokes syndrome. However, if the ventricular rate in second-degree heart block is sufficiently slow, cardiac failure or hypotension may be precipitated.

If the AV block is due to digitalis, this drug must be temporarily discontinued. If other causes can be implicated, the patient must be carefully observed, and if the slow heart rate is responsible for clinical deterioration the heart must be accelerated. This may be achieved by administering atropine or isoprenaline, or by artificial pacing.

In *complete AV (heart) block* (Fig. 42) the ventricular rate is slow (25

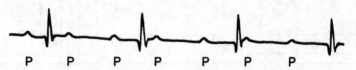

Fig. 42.   Complete heart block. Note that both P waves and QRS complexes are regular, but have no fixed relationship to one another.

to 50 min). There are cannon waves in the venous pulse (see p. 92) and a varying first heart sound (see p. 98).

Acute complete heart block is most commonly a complication of acute myocardial infarction, but may also result from cardiac surgery and myocarditis. In acute myocardial infarction, it usually follows occlusion of the right coronary artery which is responsible for the blood supply of the junctional tissue and bundle of His (see also p. 125). The severely damaged heart may not be able to compensate adequately for the bradycardia by increasing its stroke volume and heart failure and hypotension may ensue. There is also a considerable risk of ventricular asystole. The bradycardia may be controlled by infusing isoprenaline in a dose of 2 to 5 mg in 500 ml of 5% laevulose or dextrose, or by an artificial pacemaker (see p. 70). If the patient survives, normal AV conduction is usually restored within a week.

In most cases of chronic complete heart block there is fibrosis of both bundle branches of unknown cause. This variety is most commonly seen in the elderly. A congenital form occurs either as an isolated finding or in association with other congenital heart defects. It can also complicate rheumatic or ischaemic heart disease, or follow trauma to the conducting tissue at surgery. A proportion of patients with chronic complete heart block survive for years with no symptoms, but once heart failure or syncopal attacks of the Adams–Stokes variety develop, the expectation of life is usually only a few months. For this reason, treatment is indicated when symptoms arise. The heart rate may be accelerated by the use of long-acting isoprenaline (Saventrine) in a dosage of 15 to 60 mg three or four times a day. This therapy is satisfactory in some cases, but is apt to provoke ventricular arrhythmias which may themselves be dangerous. Most physicians now recommend the use of artificial pacemakers in all patients with symptoms (see p. 70).

The Adams–Stokes attack

In an Adams–Stokes attack the patient loses consciousness for a period of some seconds because of transient cardiac arrest. It usually occurs in patients with second-degree or complete heart block who develop sudden loss of ventricular activity. It is particularly common during the progression from second-degree to complete heart block because the ventricular pacemaker necessary for survival may not have become firmly established. In some cases, the Adams–Stokes attack is due not to ventricular asystole but to a short burst of ventricular tachycardia or fibrillation.

The presenting symptom is syncope with or without a preceding period of dizziness. The attack usually lasts some 10 to 30 sec and convulsions may occur. During the attack the patient is pulseless, pale or cyanosed. Consciousness returns rapidly with reappearance of the heart beat, the patient then flushing as blood courses through capillaries dilated by the hypoxia of the attack. Attacks of the Adams–Stokes variety may be separated from one another by a number of months, but occasionally a series occurs over a period of minutes or hours. Sooner or later, the patient is likely to die of ventricular asystole or ventricular fibrillation.

The diagnosis should be considered in any patient presenting with syncope, but is unlikely to be the explanation in the absence of bundle branch block, second-degree block, or complete AV block between the episodes.

During an attack a blow over the cardiac apex may restore the heart action, but if it does not do so, the usual therapy for cardiac arrest should be undertaken (p. 72) with closed-chest cardiac compression and artificial ventilation. Adams–Stokes attacks can be prevented by an artificial pacemaker.

Bundle branch block

In this condition, either the right or the left branch of the bundle of His is not conducting impulses.

Block of the right bundle branch gives rise to a characteristic electrocardiographic appearance (Figs. 23 and 43). This is often an isolated congenital lesion of no importance but may be associated with other congenital heart defects, particularly atrial septal defect; in middle or advanced age, it is usually due to ischaemic heart disease or idiopathic fibrosis. Right bundle branch block may be partial, with QRS width of less than 0.12 sec, or complete, in which the QRS is of 0.12 sec duration or more. It may be suspected clinically because the block leads to a delayed activation, and therefore contraction, of the right ventricle. This results in late closure of the pulmonary valve which can be recognized by a wide splitting of the second heart sound (p. 98). Right bundle branch block is of little clinical significance, except as an indicator of possible heart disease and as a precursor of complete heart block (especially if associated with left or right axis deviation).

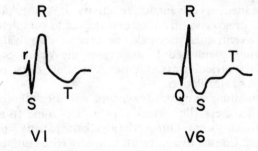

Fig. 43.   Right bundle branch block.

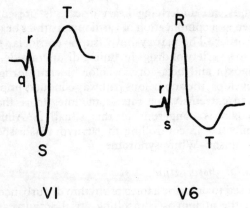

Fig. 44. Left bundle branch block.

Left bundle branch block is rare in the otherwise normal individual and is most commonly seen in ischaemic heart disease. It is difficult to recognize clinically, although there may be reversed splitting of the second heart sound (p. 98); it is readily identified on the ECG (Figs. 22 and 44). Because it is associated with severe ventricular disease (usually ischaemic) it carries a more serious prognosis than right bundle branch block, but patients with this lesion may survive for many years.

Neither form of bundle branch block requires treatment.

Pre-excitation (Wolff–Parkinson–White syndrome)

In this condition, an anomalous conduction pathway bypasses the AV node. This permits the abnormally early activation of part of one ventricle, the remaining ventricular muscle receiving its impulse normally. This leads to a short PR interval (less than 0.11 sec) and a widened QRS (Fig. 45).

The normal and abnormal conduction pathways are able to form part of a re-entry circuit. This facilitates the occurrence of supraventricular tachycardia. The combination of pre-excitation and supraventricular tachycardia constitutes the Wolff–Parkinson–White syndrome.

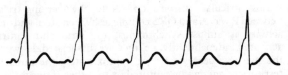

Fig. 45. Pre-excitation (Wolff–Parkinson–White syndrome). Note short PR interval, and broad QRS complex with notch (delta wave) on the upstroke.

In most cases, no underlying heart disease is present, but it is sometimes seen as a complication of cardiomyopathies or other forms of cardiac disorder. The paroxysms of supraventricular tachycardia may respond to a variety of drugs including disopyramide, verapamil, quinidine, digoxin and beta-adrenoceptor blocking drugs. If atrial fibrillation develops, the anomalous pathway conducts impulses to the ventricles at an extremely fast rate (sometimes more than 250 per minute). Digoxin is dangerous in this situation. Amiodarone is particularly effective in controlling the arrhythmias associated with the Wolff–Parkinson–White syndrome.

Atrioventricular dissociation

This term is used to describe a form of rhythm disturbance in which a pacemaker in the atrium is controlling atrial activity and another pacemaker situated in the junctional tissue or the ventricle is controlling the ventricular activity. Although there is dissociation of atria and ventricles in complete heart block, AV dissociation occurs in the absence of any abnormality of conduction. It is always secondary to some other abnormality, with either slowing of the sinus node or acceleration of a lower pacemaker, or a combination of the two. When the two pacemakers are initiating impulses almost synchronously the territory of one is refractory to stimulation from the other. Sooner or later, the two foci cease to fire at the same time; the territory of one is then captured by the other (Fig. 46). It is a not uncommon complication of digitalis therapy and of acute myocardial infarction. It is important to differentiate this from organic heart block as it carries a much less sinister prognosis and requires no specific therapy.

Electrical therapy

When a brief electrical shock of high energy is applied to the heart, all parts of the heart are usually simultaneously depolarized; the sinus

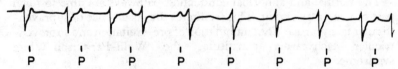

Fig. 46.   Atrioventricular dissociation. Note the varying relationship between P waves and QRS complexes. When atrial and ventricular activity is almost synchronous, the atria and ventricles are activated independently, i.e. they are dissociated. However, when the two foci cease to fire at approximately the same time, the territory of one can be captured by the other. Thus the third atrial complex (P wave) is followed by a QRS complex and the atrium has 'captured' the ventricle. Subsequently, there is a return to atrioventricular dissociation.

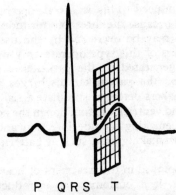

P   QRS T

Fig. 47. The vulnerable period of ventricular repolarization is illustrated by the hatched area. Electrical impulses of sufficient magnitude occurring during the upstroke of the T wave may initiate ventricular fibrillation.

node subsequently recommences cardiac rhythmicity. If, however, the shock falls during the 'vulnerable' period of ventricular repolarization (i.e. on the T wave), depolarization of the ventricles is incomplete, the re-entry phenomenon (p. 49) may occur and lead to ventricular tachycardia or fibrillation (Fig. 47).

Electrical pacing

Control over the electrical activity of the heart may be obtained by the use of an artificial pacemaker (Fig. 48). If pacing is to be maintained for only a short period of time, an external power source is used; if long-term pacing is necessary, the pulse generator is implanted.

Electrical pacemaking is potentially hazardous. If the electrical impulse is of sufficient magnitude and falls during the period of ventricular repolarization, i.e. on the T wave of the ECG, ventricular

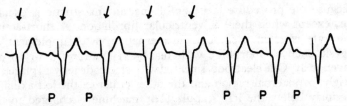

P   P   P P P

Fig. 48. Electrical pacing. A thin vertical pacing impulse, indicated by the arrow, immediately precedes the broad QRS resulting from ventricular stimulation. The P waves continue independently, due to heart block.

fibrillation may be induced. This is a considerable risk in acute myocardial infarction because the threshold for inducing ventricular fibrillation is low. It may be overcome by the use of a 'demand' pacemaker. Pacemakers of this type operate only when there is no ventricular complex generated by the patient's own heart. In the absence of a complex, the pacemaker discharges after a selected interval. Some pacemakers detect or stimulate atrial activity as well; these allow the atria and ventricles to function in the normal sequence. Other hazards of pacemaking include infection and failure of the components of the pacemaking unit, such as batteries, circuitry and electrodes.

When pacing is employed in the treatment of heart block in acute myocardial infarction, it is customary to introduce the electrode through a peripheral vein and to position its tip in the apex of the right ventricle. The other end of the electrode is attached to a portable battery-operated demand pacemaker. The electrode is withdrawn when the risks of atrioventricular block seem to have disappeared.

In chronic heart block, an electrode of a similar type is positioned with its tip in the right ventricle, but with its proximal end attached to a pacemaker buried under the skin of the axillary region or the anterior chest. Alternatively, electrodes may be placed upon the surface of the myocardium at the time of a thoracotomy or laparotomy and the wires passed subcutaneously to a pacemaker positioned in the sheath of the rectus abdominis. Pacemakers should have a life of more than 10 years but regular checking for battery or other failure is necessary.

Direct current (dc) shock therapy

Alternating current (ac) shock can be used to terminate arrhythmias, but dc shock is more reliable and less likely to produce myocardial damage and ventricular fibrillation. The dc shock must be timed to avoid the vulnerable period and it is customary to arrange for the defibrillator to discharge 0.02 sec after the peak of the R wave. A synchronized discharge of this kind is not possible when there is ventricular fibrillation.

Because the procedure is a painful one, an anaesthetic is usually given, except when there is ventricular fibrillation. A short-acting barbiturate is often used, but an alternative is to supplement an analgesic such as morphine with diazepam (Valium) 5 to 10 mg intravenously. One electrode, smeared with electrode jelly, is placed in the right parasternal region and the other either in the left axilla or posteriorly below the left scapula. The machine is charged to the chosen level and discharged by pressing a button on the electrode. For the treatment of ventricular fibrillation, a shock of 200 to 400 Watt seconds (Ws) is usually necessary, but for other arrhythmias it is best to start with a small shock such as 50 or 100 Ws. This may be increased until 400 Ws is reached, but if four or five shocks are ineffective it is unlikely that sinus rhythm will be restored by further shocks.

Apart from slight skin burns, the procedure is usually free from undesirable effects. However, there is a danger of producing serious arrhythmias in the patient with digitalis intoxication, and it is wise to discontinue this drug for one or two days prior to electric shock administration if possible.

The indications for electric shock therapy are discussed under the individual arrhythmias, but in general it may be stated that electric shock therapy is almost invariably effective for all types of tachycardia including the supraventricular tachycardia, atrial flutter, atrial fibrillation, ventricular tachycardia and ventricular fibrillation. Some cases of chronic atrial fibrillation are resistant. Electric shock should not be given if it is thought that the arrhythmia is digitalis- or quinidine-induced.

Cardiac arrest

Cardiac arrest may be defined as the sudden cessation of cardiac function due to either ventricular asystole or ventricular fibrillation. It may result from a large number of different factors, and in any case more than one factor may be involved. The commonest cause of cardiac arrest is acute myocardial infarction and ischaemia. Anaesthesia is also important, particularly if there has been underventilation or an obstruction to ventilation. Further problems associated with anaesthesia arise from endotracheal intubation which may cause strong vagal reflexes, and the use of anaesthetic drugs such as cyclopropane and chloroform. Disturbances of electrolytes, particularly potassium and calcium, may be responsible, as may drugs including digitalis, adrenaline, isoprenaline and quinidine. Other causes include drowning, hypothermia and electrocution.

Cardiac arrest usually occurs suddenly and without warning. The most important finding is absence of arterial pulsation. Consciousness is soon lost and respiration ceases. After a short interval the pupils dilate. The combination of unconsciousness and loss of pulse should be sufficient for the diagnosis.

Treatment should be started immediately; irreversible brain damage will occur if there is circulatory arrest for more than 4 minutes. A blow over the cardiac apex will sometimes restart the heart; if this fails, external cardiac massage should be combined with artificial ventilation. For external cardiac massage, the patient must be lying on a firm surface, either on the floor or on a board placed behind his chest. The heel of one hand should be placed on the lower part of the sternum and the heel of the other hand placed immediately on top of it. The sternum is then rhythmically depressed by about 3 to 5 cm 60 times or more per minute. The action should be forceful and must be applied only to the sternum. Pressure by the fingers or the hand on the ribs leads to fractures which may cause serious respiratory embarrassment, or damage the liver and spleen. If the cardiac compression is effective, pulses can be felt in the carotid or femoral arteries, and the pupils become smaller. Occasionally, open-chest massage may be more effective than closed-chest, but this technique is only suitable for use by surgeons.

At the same time that external cardiac compression is commenced, ventilation must be ensured. First of all, the neck is extended and the jaw pulled forward. If no apparatus is available, mouth-to-mouth or mouth-to-nose breathing is employed. A Brook airway which has mouthpieces for both patient and resuscitator is a useful method of giving direct ventilatory assistance. Various bags and masks are available for artificial ventilation, but ideally an endotracheal tube should be introduced by someone skilled in the technique as soon as possible and ventilation achieved with oxygen.

Severe acidosis develops rapidly and should be corrected by giving 50–75 mmol of sodium bicarbonate intravenously. Further therapy should be determined by the result of arterial pH estimations. Other drugs may occasionally be necessary, including isoprenaline and calcium chloride for the treatment of asystole. Electrical defibrillation is almost always necessary for terminating ventricular fibrillation.

The patient needs to be observed carefully after recovery from cardiac arrest as further episodes may occur. If there has been cerebral damage, hypothermia and corticosteroids may be helpful. Renal failure is not uncommon if cardiac arrest has been prolonged. Respiratory function may also be depressed and mechanical ventilation may be needed for some days.

The results of treating cardiac arrest are good provided it has been recognized immediately and the underlying cardiac disease is not severe. Thus, in the operating theatre, nearly all cases are resuscitated, but after myocardial infarction, the prognosis is less good, particularly if cardiac failure or shock have been present.

Anti-arrhythmic drugs

Anti-arrhythmic therapy is used to:
  1. Suppress or prevent ectopic rhythms.
  2. Slow the ventricular response to supraventricular arrhythmias.
  3. Increase cardiac rate when this is abnormally slow.

Drugs used to suppress or prevent ectopic rhythms

There are four main classes of anti-arrhythmic drug action.
  1. 'Membrane-stabilizing' drugs, which also have a local anaes-

thetic action, block the inflow of sodium into the cell and, therefore, the rate of depolarization. This has the effect of reducing the automaticity of ectopic pacemaker foci.

2. 'Anti-sympathetic' drugs — notably those which block beta-adrenoceptors.

3. Drugs which prolong action potential. Amiodarone (Cordarone) is the only available drug whose main action is of this type.

4. Drugs which block the inflow of calcium into the cell. This affects the activity of certain cells, particularly those of the atrioventricular node, which are dependent more on the calcium inflow than on sodium. Verapamil (Cordilox, Isoptin) belongs to this group.

Membrane-stabilizing drugs

Quinidine. This drug has been used for more than 50 years in the prevention and termination of atrial and ventricular ectopic rhythms. When given in adequate doses it is an effective anti-arrhythmic agent, but frequently produces nausea, vomiting, headache, tinnitus and diarrhoea. More serious are its cardiotoxic effects, including heart block and asystole, and the provocation of ventricular tachycardia and ventricular fibrillation. Other rarer toxic effects include respiratory depression, thrombocytopenia and skin rashes. Because of its toxicity, quinidine has been largely replaced by dc shock and by other anti-arrhythmic drugs. However, it remains of value in preventing recurrences of supraventricular tachycardia, flutter and fibrillation, and ventricular tachycardia and fibrillation, particularly when such therapy is required over long periods of time.

Quinidine is usually given orally as the sulphate in tablets containing 0.2 g or 0.3 g. The dose required for maintenance varies from 0.2 g thrice daily to 0.4 g 4-hourly. A sustained action preparation (Kinidin Durules) may be used in a dosage of 0.25 to 0.50 g twice daily. The dosage required to suppress or prevent arrhythmias varies considerably from patient to patient and therapy must be individualized, preferably with estimation of blood levels of the drug.

Quinidine produces a variety of ECG effects including a prolonged QT interval, depression of the ST segment and T wave inversion. These do not necessarily indicate overdosage, but the appearance of conduction defects or ventricular arrhythmias implies cardiac toxicity and the drug should be discontinued.

Procainamide (Pronestyl). The actions of procainamide are similar to those of quinidine, but it is less effective in the treatment of atrial arrhythmias and is less toxic when used intravenously.

Procainamide may be administered intravenously, intramuscularly and orally. When given intravenously, it may produce a marked hypotensive effect, but this can be avoided with care. It should be given at a rate not exceeding 100 mg per minute; an ECG should be recorded and the blood pressure taken every minute. Further procainamide should not be given if the systolic pressure falls below 90 mmHg, or if the QRS complex becomes more than 25% wider than it had been, or if the arrhythmia has been controlled. If parenteral treatment with procainamide is necessary, but there is no urgency, procainamide can be given by the intramuscular route in doses of 250 to 500 mg 6-hourly.

By the oral route, a total daily dose of some 3 g, which may be 500 mg 4-hourly or in a long-acting preparation (Durules) 1 g thrice daily is required. Long-term oral procainamide therapy may lead to depression of the bone marrow, skin rashes and a syndrome simulating systemic lupus erythematosus.

Lignocaine (lidocaine, Xylocaine). This drug resembles quinidine and procainamide in its mode of action, but is relatively ineffective in controlling atrial arrhythmias and has virtually no myocardial depressant effect in therapeutic doses. It is therefore much safer to give intravenously than the other two drugs. However, it should not be given in the presence of AV block, which it may aggravate. At present, the drug is used mainly intravenously, and by this route its duration of action is only 10 to 20 minutes. Initially, a dose of 50 to 100 mg (i.e. 5 to 10 ml of the 1% solution) can be given over a period of 1–2 minutes and repeated, if necessary, two minutes later. This may be followed by an intravenous infusion of 4 mg per minute for 30 minutes, 3 mg per minute for a further 30 minutes and thereafter 2 mg per minute for 24 to 48 hours, if necessary.

Serious toxic effects from lignocaine are unusual, but include confusion, convulsions, respiratory depression and coma.

Disopyramide (Rythmodan, Norpace). Disopyramide resembles procainamide in its anti-arrhythmic effects but has atropine-like actions which cause a dry mouth and urinary retention and, rarely, glaucoma. It has a negative inotropic effect and should be avoided in cardiac failure. The oral dosage is 100 to 150 mg three to four times daily. Intravenously it may be given in a dosage of 0.5 mg/kg.

Mexiletine (Mexitil). Mexiletine resembles lignocaine in its structure and actions but is well absorbed orally and is therefore useful in the chronic treatment of ventricular arrhythmias. Toxic effects include nausea, vomiting and tremor. The oral dosage is usually 200–250 mg thrice daily.

Phenytoin (diphenylhydantoin, Epanutin, Dilantin). This drug is moderately effective in combating ventricular arrhythmias, but is of particular value if they are digitalis-induced. Up to 1 g may be given

Table 5. Beta-adrenoceptor blocking drugs

Drug	Tablet size (mg)
Non-selective:	
Propranolol (Inderal)	10, 40, 80, 160
Oxprenolol (Trasicor)	20, 40, 80, 160
Sotalol (Beta-Cardone, Sotacor)	40, 80, 160
Nadolol (Corgard)	40, 80
Pindolol (Visken)	5
Timolol (Blocadren)	10
Selective:	
Acebutolol (Sectral)	100, 200
Atenolol (Tenormin)	100
Metoprolol (Lopresor, Betaloc)	50, 100
Alpha- and beta-adrenergic blockade	
Labetalol (Trandate)	100, 200

intravenously, if this is given slowly in doses not exceeding 100 mg in 5 minutes. Intravenous diphenylhydantoin is relatively safe, but occasionally produces hypotension or conduction disorders.

Beta-adrenoceptor blocking drugs (see Table 5)

Beta-adrenoreceptor blocking drugs oppose the effects of catecholamines on the beta-adrenoceptors.

Some appear to block the receptors in the heart selectively (β_1-receptor blocking agents). Others also block receptors in the bronchi and peripheral vessels. Consequently, they may induce bronchospasm in susceptible subjects and impair the circulation to the limbs.

Propranolol and similar drugs antagonize the ability of sympathetic substances to increase the rate and contractility of the heart. These drugs are sometimes effective in abolishing ventricular and atrial arrhythmias and are of value in slowing the ventricular response to atrial arrhythmias.

There is little to choose between propranolol and the other beta-adrenergic blocking drugs except in their effect on the bronchi. A selective preparation should be used for patients with airways obstruction. Intravenous preparations of most of these drugs are available; they must be used with great caution.

Unwanted effects of beta-adrenergic blocking drugs include cardiac failure, bronchospasm, nightmares, impotence, cold extremities and rashes. These drugs are also used to prevent angina and to treat hypertension. For these conditions, laeger doses may be required.

Amiodarone. This drug prolongs the action potential and the refractory period; it is therefore of value in blocking re-entrant pathways. It has proved particularly effective in the Wolff–Parkinson–White syndrome, but also in many resistant supraventricular and ventricular arrhythmias. Its toxic effects have precluded its widespread use. It causes corneal deposits, but these appear to be benign and reversible and seldom give rise to symptoms. Other side-effects include a bluish discoloration of the skin and thyroid disorders, especially thyrotoxicosis. Oral amiodarone may not exert its anti-arrhythmic action for up to a week and on stopping the drug it may take several weeks for the effects to disappear. The usual dosage is 200 mg thrice daily for a week, gradually reducing thereafter to 200 mg daily.

Verapamil. This calcium antagonist, when used intravenously in a dosage of 2–10 mg is almost always effective in abolishing supraventricular tachycardias in individuals with normal hearts. It must be administered slowly and should be avoided in those receiving beta-blocking drugs, and given cautiously to patients with compromised ventricular function.

Oral verapamil (40–120 mg three times a day) is useful in slowing the ventricular rate in atrial fibrillation.

Drugs used to slow the ventricular response to atrial arrhythmias

Digitalis and allied drugs. These are the mainstay of therapy designed to slow the ventricular response to atrial arrhythmias such as atrial flutter and atrial fibrillation. They are considered in detail in Chapter 2.

Beta-adrenergic blocking drugs. Of value in combination with digoxin when it alone slows the heart rate inadequately (see above) Verapamil is also of value in this context, but should not be given with beta-blockers.

Further reading

HOFFMAN, B. F. and RASEN, M. R. (1975) Electrocardiography and pharmacology of cardiac arrhythmias. *Amer. Heart J.* **89**, 804; **90**, 117.
KNIKLER, D. M. and GOODWIN, J. F. (Eds) (1975) *Cardiac Arrhythmias*. London: Saunders.
OPIE, L. H. (1980) Drugs and the heart. *Lancet*, **i**, 693, 806, (also Lancet Press).

5

The Symptoms of Heart Disease

Dyspnoea

Dyspnoea — difficulty with breathing — is the commonest symptom of heart failure. The term implies discomfort in the act of respiration, a consciousness of laboured breathing. It is, of course, also a symptom of respiratory disease and occurs in normal individuals on exercise.

No single explanation so far advanced accounts for all cases of dyspnoea. Furthermore, because it is subjective the degree of distress depends, in part, upon the personality of the patient. Thus some patients do not complain of breathlessness in spite of obviously laboured respiration, whereas others claim to be short of breath although their capacity for exercise is normal.

Mechanisms

The dyspnoea of cardiac disease may be due to the following factors:

Increased work of breathing

It is probable that in most cases of cardiac failure the discomfort arises in overworked respiratory muscles. In left-sided cardiac failure, engorgement of the pulmonary veins and capillaries occurs; if the pulmonary capillary pressure exceeds 25 mmHg, fluid may exude into the alveolar walls or even into the alveoli. These changes make the lung more rigid (less compliant) and require more respiratory work for a given volume of air inspired.

Reduced vital capacity

This is due to pulmonary venous congestion and, occasionally, to hydrothorax or ascites.

Reflex hyperventilation

The pulmonary stretch receptors may be abnormally stretched by congestion of the lungs.

Bronchial narrowing

Bronchial narrowing by spasm or fluid may occur in cardiac failure and adds to the work of breathing.

Hypoxaemia and carbon dioxide retention

These may both contribute to dyspnoea. They are seldom important factors in patients with left-sided heart failure, in whom the carbon dioxide tension is normal or low as a result of hyperventilation, and there is little hypoxaemia except when there is pulmonary oedema. In cyanotic congenital heart disease, hypoxaemia is severe.

Clinical features

The patient with cardiac dyspnoea breathes rapidly and shallowly. This pattern contrasts with that of the anxious individual who has deep and sighing respiration, and 'is unable to take a deep breath' or 'fill his lungs with air'. It also differs from the deep breathing of patients with diabetic keto-acidosis or renal failure.

Dyspnoea in patients with cardiac disease is usually slowly progressive, although it may be suddenly exacerbated by the onset of atrial fibrillation or the occurrence of pulmonary infarction or infection. At first it occurs only on effort, but as the disease process advances, less and less exercise is required to provoke breathlessness until it may eventually be present at rest.

Orthopnoea.   This is dyspnoea when lying flat. There are several possible explanations for its occurrence in left heart failure:

1. When an individual lies flat there is increased venous return, which in the patient on the verge of failure may increase pulmonary venous congestion, and thereby decrease pulmonary compliance and vital capacity.

2. The vital capacity is reduced in the recumbent posture by the relatively high position of the diaphragm, which may be further displaced upwards by ascites or an enlarged liver.

Orthopnoea usually occurs when there is already a considerable limitation of exercise tolerance, but is occasionally an early symptom. Many patients learn for themselves that they are more comfortable propped up by three or four pillows.

Paroxysmal dyspnoea

In patients with left-sided cardiac failure, attacks of dyspnoea may develop without an obvious precipitating cause. They are most apt to occur during sleep (paroxysmal nocturnal dyspnoea). The mechanism is probably the same as that of orthopnoea, but the sensory unawareness of the sleeping state prevents the patient from correcting the situation by sitting up. The victim wakes up intensely short of breath and frightened. He sits on the side of the bed or struggles to the window. The attack may pass off spontaneously within a few minutes, or progress to acute pulmonary oedema.

Acute pulmonary oedema

In this condition, fluid accumulates in the alveoli as a result of a high pulmonary capillary pressure. Such attacks occur in patients with mitral stenosis, acute myocardial infarction and other left-sided cardiac lesions. There is often a provoking factor such as an arrhythmia, respiratory infection or parturition.

The patient is intensely dyspnoeic with noisy breathing, cough and frothy sputum which is often blood-tinged. The skin is usually moist, cold and cyanosed. The pulse is fast and may be irregular. Crepitations may he heard throughout the chest in a severe attack. In some patients, rhonchi, due to fluid in the bronchi, predominate and the clinical picture may resemble bronchial asthma. Pulmonary oedema is usually visible on a chest radiograph (see p. 112).

Cheyne–Stokes respiration

In Cheyne–Stokes respiration, there is a periodic waxing and waning in the depth of respiration, over a period of about one minute. As William Stokes wrote in 1854:

> It consists in the occurrence of a series of inspirations, increasing to maximum, and then declining in force and length, until a state of apparent apnoea is established. In this condition the patient may remain for such a length of time as to make his attendants believe that he is dead, when a low inspiration, followed by one more decided marks the commencement of a new ascending and then descending series of inspirations.

This pattern of breathing is seen during sleep in some normal individuals, but its occurrence in the conscious patient suggests advanced left ventricular failure. It also occurs in patients with cerebral vascular disease, particularly if they have received morphine.

The causation of Cheyne–Stokes breathing is not yet established, but it seems likely that the prolonged lung-to-brain circulation time disturbs the normal feedback mechanisms for respiratory control.

Cardiac pain

There are two major causes of cardiac pain: myocardial ischaemia and pericarditis.

Myocardial ischaemia and infarction (see also Chapter 8)

A transient and reversible inadequacy of the coronary circulation gives rise to that type of chest pain known as angina pectoris. If the reduction in coronary blood flow is such as to cause death of an area of myocardium (myocardial infarction), the pain is usually more severe and prolonged.

The term angina pectoris was adopted by William Heberden, who described the characteristics of the syndrome in 1768. He wrote:

> There is a disorder of the breast marked with strong and peculiar symptoms, considerable for the kind of danger belonging to it, and not extremely rare which deserves to be mentioned more at length. The seat of it, and the sense of strangling, and anxiety with which it is attended, may make it not improperly called angina pectoris.
>
> They who are afflicted with it, are seized while they are walking (more especially if it be uphill, and soon after eating) with a painful and most disagreeable sensation in the breast, which seems as if it were to extinguish life, if it were to increase or continue; but the moment they stand still, all this uneasiness vanishes.
>
> In all other respects the patients are, at the beginning of this disorder, perfectly well, and in particular have no shortness of breath, from which it is totally different. The pain is sometimes situated in the upper part, sometimes in the middle, sometimes at the bottom of the os sterni, and often more inclined to the left than to the right side. It likewise very frequently extends from the breast to the middle of the left arm.

Heberden clearly described the four cardinal features of angina pectoris, namely its location in the retrosternal region and its radiation particularly to the left arm, its relationship to exertion, its relatively short duration (usually 1 to 10 minutes), and the strangling quality. For more details of the clinical characteristics of angina pectoris, see p. 134.

Angina pectoris most commonly occurs in response to exercise in patients with coronary artery disease. The same symptom can be provoked by paroxysmal tachycardia, when there is insufficient time during diastole for the coronary arteries to fill and meet the increased oxygen demands of the tachycardia. Angina is a frequent symptom in aortic stenosis because of the inability of the coronary circulation to match the oxygen requirements of extreme left ventricular hypertrophy. Other conditions which may cause or exacerbate angina pectoris are coronary arterial spasm, aortic regurgitation, syphilitic aortitis, anaemia, hyperthyroidism and mitral stenosis.

There seems little doubt that the cause of angina pectoris is myocardial hypoxia secondary to inadequate coronary blood flow. The site of angina appears to be the myocardium; the stimulus to the pain has not been determined but may be due to a chemical substance related to oxygen lack or to a phenomenon analogous to cramp. The impulses arising in the myocardium pass through afferent sympathetic fibres to reach the upper thoracic sympathetic ganglia and are then directed to the upper four or five thoracic spinal nerves. In this way, the same segments of the spinal cord receive sensations from the heart as receive sensory impulses from the anterior chest wall and the inner aspect of the arm, forearm and hand. The pain is perceived as arising in the territory supplied by the corresponding spinal somatic nerves, rather than in the organ itself.

The pain of myocardial infarction is similar to that of angina pectoris in its location and character, but its duration is longer (usually more than 30 minutes), it is usually more severe, and it has no relationship to exertion. Its mechanism is presumably similar.

Pericarditis (see also Chapter 9)

Pain is a characteristic feature of pericarditis, and appears to arise in the parietal pericardium, the visceral pericardium being insensitive. It is usually sharp, but may be of an aching nature. It is situated in the retrosternal region, and radiates to the neck, back or upper abdomen, but rarely the arms. It may be exacerbated by inspiration, swallowing and by lying down flat.

Palpitation

Palpitation may be defined as an awareness of the heart beat. It takes several different forms including a thumping sensation in the chest, a throbbing in the neck, a consciousness of missed or extra beats, or a racing of the heart. Anxious individuals are often distressed by the sinus tachycardia associated with emotion. Even normal individuals may be disagreeably conscious of their heart action when lying on the left side. Palpitation is, therefore, a common symptom in those without heart disease, but it is also an important complaint in patients with arrhythmias or abnormal heart action. Ectopic beats frequently give rise to the sensation of jumping of the heart, missed beats or extra beats. Patients with supraventricular tachycardia are aware of the sudden onset of regular beating of the heart, whereas those with atrial fibrillation may be conscious of its irregularity.

Patients with a vigorous cardiac action due, for example, to thyrotoxicosis or aortic regurgitation, may feel the forceful beating of their hearts.

Oedema

Oedema — the accumulation of fluid in the interstitial tissues — is an important but relatively late manifestation of cardiac failure. It does not usually occur except in the presence of a raised venous pressure, and salt and water retention. Oedema is preceded by a gain in body weight of some 3 to 5 kg due to an increase in the extracellular fluid.

Normally, fluid exudes into the tissues at the arterial ends of capillaries because the hydrostatic pressure of approximately 30 mmHg exceeds the colloid osmotic pressure of 25 mmHg. Fluid is reabsorbed at the venous ends because the hydrostatic pressure at this point is approximately 12 mmHg. Oedema occurs when there is inadequate reabsorption of fluid from the tissues. A high venous pressure alone can, by increasing the hydrostatic force at the venous ends of the capillaries, cause oedema, as it does, for example, in vena caval obstruction. Raised venous pressure is nearly always a factor in cardiac oedema, but seldom seems to be the sole explanation, for salt and water retention almost invariably antedates the appearance of the oedema.

The location of oedema in cardiac failure is determined by local factors, particularly gravity. In the ambulant patient, it occurs bilaterally in the lower legs and feet; in those kept in bed, it accumulates in the sacral area. When the oedema is very great, it may affect the whole of the lower limbs, the genitalia, the abdominal and chest walls and even the face (anasarca).

In the oedema of cardiac failure, the tissues dimple ('pit') when pressure is applied to them by the thumb.

Ascites

The intraperitoneal accumulation of fluid is a manifestation of advanced heart disease, it usually occurring later than peripheral oedema but for similar reasons. In some conditions, however, such as tricuspid valve disease and constrictive pericarditis, ascites may be even more evident than oedema and is probably then, in part, a consequence of portal hypertension secondary to cardiac cirrhosis of the liver.

Cyanosis

Cyanosis, a blue discoloration of the skin or mucous membranes, is more a sign than a symptom of heart disease and is often first noticed by relatives when the affected individual exercises or is exposed to cold temperatures. It is usually due to a large proportion of reduced haemoglobin in the superficial capillaries and venules. It has been observed that cyanosis appears when the amount of reduced haemoglobin in the blood of the vessels exceeds 5 g per 100 ml. Cyanosis results either from oxygen desaturation of the arterial blood or from an unusually large extraction of oxygen in the peripheral tissues. When

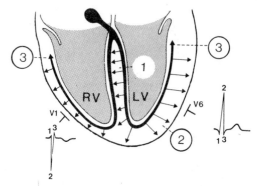

Fig. 16.   Genesis of QRS complex. Note that the first phase, directed from left to right across the septum, produces a Q wave in V6 and an R wave in V1. The second phase, due mainly to depolarization of the left ventricle from endocardium to epicardium, results in a tall R wave in V6 and a deep S wave in V1. Finally, depolarization of the basal parts of the ventricles, may produce a terminal S wave in V6 and a terminal R wave in V1.

As mentioned, small, narrow Q waves are normally to be found in leads facing the left ventricle, e.g. lead I, aVL, aVF, V5 and V6. These Q waves do not normally exceed 2 mm in depth, or 0.03 sec in width. It should be noted that QS waves are normal in aVR, and are common in V1 and V2. Abnormally broad and deep Q waves are often a feature of myocardial infarction (see p. 148). Q waves in lead III are difficult to evaluate but can be ignored if there are no Q waves either in lead II or in aVF, or if they do not exceed 0.03 sec. Usually, a 'normal' Q wave in lead III diminishes or disappears on deep inspiration because of an alteration in the position of the heart, whilst the 'pathological' Q wave of infarction persists.

The QRS complex should not exceed 0.10 sec in duration, and usually is in the range 0.06 to 0.08 sec. Broad QRS complexes occur in bundle branch block (p. 44), in ventricular hypertrophy and in ventricular ectopic beats.

The T wave.   The T wave is due to repolarization of the ventricles. If repolarization (the T wave) occurred in the same direction as depolarization (the QRS complex) the T wave would be directed in an opposite way to that of the QRS (Fig. 17). In fact, depolarization takes place from endocardium to epicardium, whereas repolarization takes place from epicardium to endocardium. Because of this, the T wave usually points in the same direction as the major component of the QRS complex. Thus, the T wave is normally upright in leads I and II as well as in V3 to V6, is inverted in aVR, and may be upright or inverted in lead III, aVL, aVF and V1 and V2.

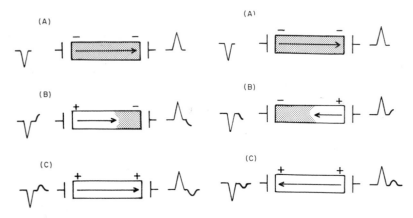

Fig. 17.   The genesis of the T wave. (A) shows the situation at the end of depolarization. Repolarization produces a negative deflection in the electrode towards which it is proceeding. Thus, as illustrated on the left, if depolarization occurs in the same direction as repolarization, the T wave is negative. If, as is usual, repolarization occurs in the reverse direction to depolarization, an upright T wave is inscribed, as illustrated on the right.

The T waves are usually not taller than 5 mm in standard leads and 10 mm in precordial leads. Unusually tall and peaked T waves are seen in the presence of hyperkalaemia and also in some patients with myocardial ischaemia and infarction. Flattened T waves are seen when the voltage of all complexes is low, as in myxoedema, as well as in hypokalaemia and in a larger number of other conditions in which it may be regarded as a non-specific abnormality. Slight T wave inversion is also often non-specific, and may be due to such influences as hyperventilation and smoking. More important causes of T wave inversion are myocardial ischaemia and infarction, ventricular hypertrophy and bundle branch block. Detailed descriptions of T wave changes will be found in the subsequent section on abnormalities of the ST segment, and also under the subheadings dealing with ventricular hypertrophy, bundle branch block and myocardial infarction.

The U wave.   The U wave is a broad, low-voltage wave present in most normal ECGs. Its cause is unknown; it may become unusually prominent in hypokalaemia and with digitalis therapy.

The QT interval.   The QT interval represents the total time from the onset of ventricular depolarization to the completion of repolarization. It is measured from the beginning of the Q wave (or the R wave if there is no Q wave) to the end of the T wave. Its duration varies with heart

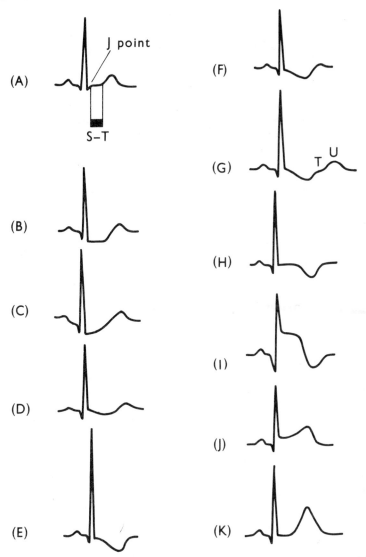

Fig. 18. Normal and abnormal ST segments and T waves. (A) Normal ST segment with J point. (B) Horizontal ST depression in myocardial ischaemia. (C) ST segment sloping upwards in sinus tachycardia. (D) ST sagging in digitalis therapy. (E) Asymmetrical T wave inversion associated with ventricular hypertrophy. (F) Similar pattern sometimes seen without voltage changes in hypertrophy-'strain'. (G) ST sagging and prominent U waves of hypokalaemia. (H) Symmetrically inverted T wave of myocardial ischaemia or infarction. (I) ST elevation in acute myocardial infarction. (J) ST elevation in acute pericarditis. (K) Peaked T wave in hyperkalaemia.

rate, becoming shorter as the heart rate increases. In general, the QT interval at heart rates between 60 and 90 per minute does not exceed in duration half the preceding RR interval. The measurement of the QT interval is often difficult as the end of the T wave cannot always be clearly identified, and the relationship between heart rate and duration of the QT interval is a complex one. Tables are available in textbooks of electrocardiography giving the normal QT intervals. In practice, the main importance of a prolonged QT interval is that it is associated with a risk of ventricular tachycardias and sudden death. A long QT is sometimes an inherited abnormality but may result from such drugs as quinidine, procainamide, disopyramide and tricyclic antidepressants.

The ST segment. The ST segment is that part of the electrocardiogram between the end of the QRS complex and the beginning of the T wave (Fig. 18). The point of junction between the S wave and the ST segment is known as the J point. The ST segment occurs during a period of unchanging polarity in the ventricles, corresponding with phase 2 of the action potential (see Fig. 6). The normal ST segment is situated on the iso-electric line but curves upwards.

Displacements of the ST segment and variations in its shape are of great importance in electrocardiographic diagnosis. The characteristic abnormalities of the ST segment are illustrated in Fig. 18. In some normal individuals, particularly young Negroes, slight ST elevation is seen. This may be up to 1 mm in standard leads and 2 mm in the right precordial leads. Depression of more than 0.5 mm is abnormal. When ST elevation occurs in normal individuals, it is often preceded by a slight notch on the downstroke of the R wave. In acute myocardial infarction, the ST segment is elevated with a curve which is convex upwards in the leads facing the infarct. At a later stage ST segment elevation becomes less pronounced as T wave inversion develops. These changes are considered in more detail in Chapter 8, p. 149. In pericarditis there is also ST elevation, but the ST segments are concave upwards and the changes are widespread rather than localized as in myocardial infarction. Digitalis therapy depresses the ST segment, particularly in leads II and III, so that there is a gentle sagging, but the T wave remains upright or flattened. In left and right ventricular hypertrophy, ST segment depression may occur in leads facing the relevant ventricle and be accompanied by asymmetrical T wave inversion. This contrasts with the symmetrical T wave inversion seen in myocardial infarction and ischaemia. In acute myocardial ischaemia the ST segment is horizontally depressed or slightly downward sloping from the J point onwards. In sinus tachycardia there may be ST depression which slopes upwards from the J point. In the cyanosis is due to arterial oxygen desaturation, it is considered to be 'central' in origin because it is caused by a disorder in the heart or lungs. When the cause of the cyanosis is high oxygen extraction in the tissues, it is said to be 'peripheral'.

Cyanosis of the 'central' type is due either to blood bypassing the lungs as it is shunted from the venous side of the circulation to the arterial, as a result of congenital heart disease, or to inadequate oxygenation of the blood in the lungs, as in some varieties of lung disease. Clubbing of the digits is a common accompaniment of cyanotic congenital heart disease.

Peripheral cyanosis, a consequence of diminished blood flow through the skin and mucous membranes, occurs in normal people when they are cold, and in patients with a low cardiac output due to such conditions as mitral stenosis and acute circulatory failure.

The differentiation of central from peripheral cyanosis is usually not difficult. In peripheral cyanosis the skin is cold, and the cyanosis does not affect the warm mucous membranes such as those of the tongue. Furthermore, peripheral cyanosis can be abolished by warming the skin. The central origin of the cyanosis can be confirmed by measuring the arterial oxygen saturation which is usually less than 85%.

Rarely, central cyanosis may be due not to arterial oxygen desaturation but to methaemoglobinaemia or sulphaemoglobinaemia as a result of taking certain drugs.

Haemoptysis

The expectoration of blood is not uncommon in patients with heart disease. Several mechanisms are involved; examination of the sputum may help to determine which of them is responsible.

Frank haemoptysis — the coughing up of pure blood — occurs in mitral stenosis, probably due to the rupture of pulmonary or bronchial veins, or to pulmonary infarction. Of course, patients with heart disease may also have haemoptysis due to other types of lung disease such as tuberculosis, bronchiectasis and bronchial neoplasm. When there is pulmonary infection, the sputum may be purulent or rusty in appearance.

In pulmonary oedema, the sputum is frothy, and may be pink or streaked with blood.

Syncope

Syncope is a transient loss of consciousness due to inadequate cerebral blood flow or perfusion pressure. Cerebral blood flow and perfusion pressure depend upon the cardiac output, the arterial blood pressure and the resistance of the cerebral circulation. Cerebral arteries are relatively uninfluenced by the autonomic system but are dilated by carbon dioxide.

The commonest type of syncope is that of the simple faint (*vasomotor* or *vasodepressor syncope*). It is often a response to emotion, but various physical factors such as blood loss, debility after infection and pain may contribute to its occurrence. It is believed to result mainly from dilatation of the arterial resistance vessels in the muscles. The fall in blood pressure causes a diminished perfusion pressure in the brain and loss of consciousness. Fainting of this kind usually develops when standing, rarely when sitting and virtually never when lying or walking. The first symptom is usually a sense of weakness, accompanied by yawning or sighing, sweating, nausea and 'a sinking feeling' in the stomach. After seconds or minutes, unconsciousness ensues; this is transient because the subject usually falls flat on the ground and this posture leads to an improvement in cerebral blood flow. In a severe attack, the face is pale, the pupils are dilated and respiration is slow. The heart rate is usually diminished and the radial pulse difficult to feel, although carotid artery pulsation can be detected without difficulty.

Micturition syncope occurs in adult men with nocturia. Consciousness is lost immediately after passing urine. It is particularly likely after considerable alcohol consumption. It may be due to reflex vasodilation secondary to sudden relief of distension of the bladder combined with the vasodilator effects of alcohol and a warm bed.

Heart disease may be responsible for syncope. A catastrophic fall in cardiac output may result if the heart rate is either extremely slow or very fast. In supraventricular and ventricular tachycardias the ventricular rate sometimes exceeds 180 per minute, leaving insufficient time for adequate filling of the heart. A more important and dangerous form of syncope is the *Adams–Stokes attack,* which is a brief episode of cardiac arrest due to either asystole or ventricular fibrillation. This characteristically occurs in patients with heart block in whom either the ventricular pacemaker suddenly fails, or in whom ventricular arrhythmias are superimposed on the heart block. In most cases, effective cardiac action returns in 10 to 15 sec, but if the attack is more prolonged convulsions may occur. The return of consciousness is accompanied by flushing as flood flows once more through vessels dilated by hypoxia.

Syncope on exertion. This is a characteristic feature of severe aortic stenosis (see p. 205), and may be due to an inability of the heart to supply an adequate blood flow in the face of the increased demands of the muscles. Patients with aortic stenosis are also susceptible to syncope due to heart block or ventricular arrhythmias.

Carotid sinus syncope. This is a rare condition occurring in elderly individuals in whom light pressure on the carotid sinus produces extreme cardiac slowing or reflex hypotension.

When a normal individual stands up, pooling of blood in the legs is prevented by arteriolar and venous constriction, and there is an acceleration of the heart rate together with an increase in plasma catecholamine levels. *Postural syncope*, due to orthostatic hypotension, occurs in patients with autonomic disorders, including diabetic neuropathy and tabes dorsalis, as well as in some otherwise normal elderly individuals in whom these compensatory mechanisms do not function. Some hypotensive agents, particularly anti-adrenergic drugs such as guanethidine, lead to orthostatic hypotension.

Syncope of cardiac origin also occurs in other conditions in which there may be a sudden fall in cardiac output such as massive pulmonary embolism, acute myocardial infarction and mitral valve obstruction due to left atrial myxoma or ball-valve thrombus.

Functional capacity

On the basis of recommendations of the New York Heart Association, patients may be divided into four classes depending upon the severity of their symptoms.

In class 1, the patients, although they have heart disease, can withstand normal physical activity without symptoms. If the patient develops symptoms on moderate or severe exertion but not at rest or with mild exertion, then he is classified as class 2. In class 3, symptoms are present even on mild exertion. In class 4 it is impossible to undertake any physical activity without distress, which may be present even at rest.

Such a classification is of value provided its limitations are borne in mind. Thus, many patients with severe heart disease have few or no complaints, whereas those who have an anxiety neurosis, or are anaemic or pregnant may have dyspnoea in the absence of heart disease.

Further reading

Criteria Committee of the New York Heart Association (1964) *Diseases of the Heart and Blood Vessels (Nomenclature and Criteria for Diagnosis).* Boston: Little, Brown.

6

The Physical Signs of Heart Disease

The arterial pulse

The elastic structure of the aorta and its major branches enables them to act as both reservoirs and conduits. As a consequence, they are able to convert the highly pulsatile discontinuous blood flow from the ventricles into a more continuous flow in the peripheral vessels. The pressure pulse recorded a short distance above the aortic valve shows a sharp upstroke, produced by the rapid ejection of blood from the left ventricle, followed by a slower downstroke, as the rate of flow into peripheral arteries exceeds that from the left ventricle into the aorta (Fig. 49). This descending limb of the pulse wave is interrupted by the *dicrotic notch*, as the column of blood, briefly retreating towards the ventricle at the onset of diastole, is halted by aortic valve closure. As the main wave of the pulse travels peripherally, secondary waves are produced at the points of branching of the arteries. These are reflected backwards and summate with the main wave. Consequently, the peak systolic pressure in a peripheral artery may be higher than that in the central aorta.

When the arterial pulse is examined, the following characteristics should be noted: rate, rhythm, amplitude and quality or wave form. It is customary to feel the right radial artery to determine the rate and rhythm of the heart, but the amplitude and quality of the pulse is better appreciated in the carotid arteries. One should also search for pulsation in the radial, brachial, carotid, femoral, dorsalis pedis and posterior tibial arteries on both sides.

The *rate* of the pulse, if regular, can be calculated by multiplying the number of beats in 15 seconds by 4. If it is irregular, the number of beats in 30 seconds should be doubled. The pulse rate in normal resting adults ranges from 60 to 100 per minute. A rate of less than 60 per minute is most commonly due to sinus bradycardia (see p. 51), but may also be due to junctional rhythm or heart block. Rates in excess of 100 per minute (tachycardia) are most often due to sinus tachycardia associated with emotion or exercise. If the rate exceeds 120 per minute at rest in adults, some form of arrhythmia is likely (see Chapter 4).

The normal pulse is regular or exhibits sinus arrhythmia. An

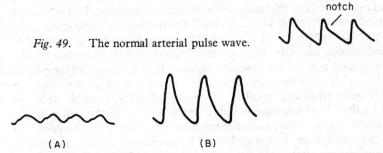

Fig. 49. The normal arterial pulse wave.

Fig. 50. (A) The pulse of severe aortic stenosis. (B) The rapidly rising and collapsing pulse of aortic regurgitation.

occasional irregularity in an otherwise regular pulse suggests ectopic beats, and a coupling of beats (pulsus bigeminus or bigeminy) is due to the alternation of normal and ectopic beats. A totally irregular pulse suggests atrial fibrillation.

The *amplitude* of the pulse depends on the pulse pressure, i.e. the difference between the systolic and diastolic pressures. The pulse is of small volume when the pulse pressure is small. This is the case when there is a low stroke volume and peripheral vasoconstriction as occurs in acute myocardial infarction, the shock syndrome, mitral stenosis and constrictive pericarditis. In aortic stenosis, the pulse is small and prolonged and has a slow upstroke. This is sometimes called the *anacrotic* pulse because the wave has a notch on its upstroke (Fig. 50), but an anacrotic notch is difficult to recognize and is a sign of little practical value. A similar criticism applies to the term *pulsus bisferiens* which is used to describe a pulse of moderate or large volume in which a double beat can be felt. This sign suggests a combination of aortic stenosis and regurgitation but is not diagnostic.

Pulses of large volume, which are produced by large stroke volumes, occur in aortic regurgitation, anaemia, pregnancy and thyrotoxicosis. When a large volume pulse rises rapidly and collapses suddenly (Fig. 50) it is described as a *collapsing* pulse. This type of pulse is encountered when there is a rapid runoff of blood during diastole as in aortic regurgitation, persistent ductus arteriosus and arteriovenous fistulae. It is best felt by placing the palm of the hand on the patient's vertically elevated forearm, thereby increasing the retrograde flow of blood during diastole.

A reduction in systolic pressure of up to 10 mmHg may occur on inspiration in normal people, probably because the capacity of the pulmonary vascular bed enlarges and reduces the return of blood to the left ventricle. This is partly compensated for by simultaneous increase in right ventricular output. A more substantial inspiratory fall, which occurs in obstructive airways disease, especially asthma, and pericardial constriction, produces *pulsus paradoxus*. In obstructive lung disease the reduction in arterial pressure is the consequence of the increased negativity of the intrathoracic pressure. In pericardial constriction, the right ventricle may be unable to compensate for the augmented pulmonary vascular capacity by increasing its output.

In *pulsus alternans*, the beats are evenly spaced in time but are alternately large and small in volume. This is most readily detected when the blood pressure is being measured, for as the cuff is being deflated only alternate beats are heard at first. After a fall of a further 5 or 10 mmHg, every beat is audible. The mechanism of pulsus alternans is not well understood, but is usually associated with left ventricular failure.

The *absence* of a peripheral pulse indicates an anatomical aberration, or narrowing or occlusion of the artery proximal to it. In coarctation of the aorta, pulsation of the femoral arteries is delayed compared with that of the radial arteries.

Blood pressure recording

Precise recording of blood pressure can be obtained only by intra-arterial catheterization but a sufficiently accurate estimate may be made using a sphygmomanometer. This instrument consists of a manometer linked to an inflatable bag, surrounded by an inelastic cuff. The size of bag and cuff is of importance in ensuring accuracy, large cuffs being required for the obese and small for children. The cuff must fit around the arm snugly, being neither loose nor touching any article of clothing. It should be applied about 2 cm above the antecubital space with the rubber bag over the medial aspect of the arm.

Manometers are of two types: mercury and aneroid. The mercury type requires care in ensuring that there is no loss or oxidation of mercury and that the air vent at the top of the tube is open. Aneroid manometers are as accurate as mercury instruments, provided they are calibrated regularly.

It is best for the patient to be reclining comfortably, but the blood pressure can be taken satisfactorily with the patient sitting or standing provided the limb is supported and at the same level as the heart. Using a mercury manometer, one's eye should be in line with the top of the meniscus.

For a thorough evaluation of the severity of hypertension it may be desirable to record 'basal' blood pressures, necessitating bed rest for hours or days and, perhaps, sedation. However, for most purposes, 'casual' blood pressures are satisfactory provided certain conditions are observed. The patient should be warm, comfortable and in a quiet environment. He should have stayed in the same position for 5 minutes before the blood pressure recording and, if there is any reason to suppose that the patient has been anxious, several recordings should be made.

The cuff should be inflated until the pulsations of the brachial artery can no longer be felt. The pressure is then raised by a further 20 mmHg and released at a rate of about 2 mmHg a second. As the pressure falls, sounds are heard as blood begins to pass through the artery which has been occluded. At first these are faint and tapping; then a swishing quality is noted. The sounds become crisper and more intense and, as the pressure falls further, there is an abrupt muffling (fourth phase) and, finally, the sounds disappear altogether (fifth phase). Sometimes there is a period of silence between the first appearance of the sounds and their final disappearance, known as the ausculatory gap, which is particularly common in the presence of hypertension.

The systolic pressure is that at which the sounds are first heard. There has been much controversy as to whether the true diastolic pressure is better represented by the fourth phase or the fifth phase. Intra-arterial pressure recordings suggest that the fifth phase is usually more accurate but in some individuals, particularly if they are vasodilated, the sounds may never disappear; this is sometimes due to overextension of the elbow. To avoid inconsistency between different observers and repeated observations, the pressures both at muffling and disappearance should be noted.

When blood pressure measurements are taken in the leg, the patient should be lying on his abdomen, with a large cuff covering the mid-thigh region, and the stethoscope placed in the popliteal fossa.

Certain circumstances make blood pressure estimations difficult. In the shock syndrome, blood pressure readings from a sphygmomanometer may be grossly inaccurate. In atrial fibrillation and other arrhythmias, the blood pressure may vary from beat to beat; the average of a number of beats should be taken for both the systolic and diastolic pressures.

The venous pulse and pressure (Fig. 51)

Inspection of the internal jugular veins is an essential but often neglected part of cardiac diagnosis. There are normally three peaks, 'a' corresponding to atrial systole, 'c' occurring at the time of tricuspid valve closure, and 'v' at the time of tricuspid valve opening. The 'x' trough corresponds to the descent of the tricuspid valve ring as the right ventricle contracts, and the 'y' trough represents the fall in pressure as blood flows into the right ventricle. As it is usually not possible to see the 'c' wave in the jugular pulse, the normal venous pulse in the neck is composed of two positive and two negative waves (Fig. 51).

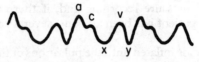

Fig. 51.   The venous pulse. Note the 'a' wave due to atrial systole and the 'c' wave occurring at the time of tricuspid valve closure. The upstroke of the 'v' wave occurs as the atrium is passively filling during ventricular systole, and the descent from the peak of 'v' to 'y' occurs as blood flows from the atrium to the ventricle after tricuspid valve opening.

It is essential to observe both the *waveform* and *pressure level* of the jugular venous pulse. The pressure should not be determined until the characteristics of the wave form have been identified. The patient should be reclining with the chest, head and neck at 45°, and with the muscles of the neck relaxed. In differentiating venous from arterial pulsation the following points are important: the venous pulse normally shows two positive pulsations in each cardiac cycle compared with the single pulsation in the arteries; the venous pulse cannot usually be felt, although it can be readily seen, whereas the arterial pulsation is more easily felt than seen; the venous pulse wave can be obliterated by light pressure at the root of the neck. Pressure on the abdomen, by increasing venous return to the thorax, increases the venous pressure in the neck transiently and permits it to be visualized more easily. If venous pulsation cannot be seen with the patient at 45°, he should be placed more horizontally until it can.

With the patient in the semi-recumbent position, the vertical height of the top of the venous column above the sternal angle is observed. In normal individuals, this does not exceed 2 cm; it is increased by factors which augment venous return including pregnancy, anxiety, exercise and anaemia. If these causes cannot be invoked, raised venous pressure is usually due to right-sided cardiac failure; it is important to exclude non-pulsating engorgement due to obstruction of the superior vena cava.

The timing of venous waves may be difficult; it is essentially either to feel the carotid artery pulsation on the other side of the neck or to listen for the first heart sound in order to allow identification of the 'a' wave which precedes these two events.

Giant 'a' wave (Fig. 52). This develops when the right atrium contracts forcefully against the increased resistance provided by a stenotic tricuspid valve, or hypertrophied right ventricle.

Cannon waves. These are large venous pulsations due to atrial contraction against a closed tricuspid valve. They occur intermittently in complete heart block and in ventricular tachycardia when atrial and

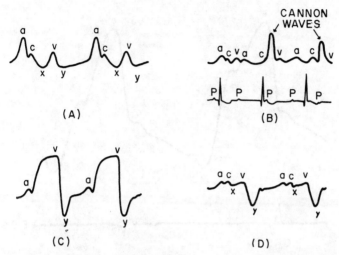

Fig. 52. (A) The giant 'a' wave. (B) Intermittent cannon waves in complete heart block, occurring at the time of synchronous atrial and ventricular contraction. (C) The systolic venous pulsation of tricuspid regurgitation. (D) The venous pulse in pericardial constriction, showing the rapid 'y' descent, followed by a plateau.

ventricular systoles coincide (Fig. 52B) (see p. 66). In junctional rhythms, atrial and ventricular contractions are synchronous and cannon waves occur with every heart beat.

Systolic venous pulsation ('cv' wave).   This is due to blood regurgitating into the venous system during ventricular systole and is characteristic of tricuspid regurgitation (Fig. 52C).

In pericardial constriction, the venous pressure is greatly raised, and there is a sharp 'y' descent as blood rushes into the right ventricle in the early part of diastole (Fig. 52D). Another feature of this condition is elevation of venous pressure during inspiration because the increase in venous return at this time cannot be accommodated by the constricted right ventricle.

Inspection of the chest

Abnormalities of the thorax and lungs may cause changes in the position of the heart; they may also result from or cause heart disease. Funnel chest (pectus excavatum) and kyphoscoliosis may lead to displacement of the heart. Cardiac enlargement associated with advanced congenital heart disease in childhood may cause deformity of the sternum and ribs.

The rate and pattern of breathing should be noted. The respiratory

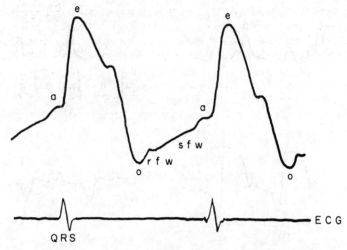

Fig. 53.   The apex cardiogram. Note 'a' due to atrial systole, 'e' as the ventricle rotates forward with left ventricular systole, the fall from 'e' to 'o' as the ventricle empties, the early rapid filling wave (rfw) in the ventricle, followed by a slow filling wave (sfw).

rate is often increased in left ventricular failure. The characteristically prolonged expiration in obstructive airways disease should suggest the possibility of pulmonary heart disease.

The cardiac impulse is frequently visible, particularly when there is heart disease. It is often possible to see the exaggerated apical impulse of left ventricular hypertrophy, the displaced apex of left ventricular dilatation, the left parasternal pulsation of right ventricular hypertrophy or the abnormal pulmonary arterial pulsation in the second and third left interspaces in pulmonary hypertension.

Palpation of the chest

In the normal individual, the maximal thrust of the left ventricle — the apex beat — can be felt at or just internal to the mid-clavicular line in the fifth intercostal space. If it is displaced, one should determine whether this is due to abnormalities of the thoracic cage or lungs. After the apex beat has been located and assessed, the whole precordium should be explored with the palm of the hand in the search for abnormal pulsation.

The graphic record of the movements of the apex beat shows a characteristic pattern — the *apex cardiogram* (Fig. 53). This commences with an 'a' wave as atrial systole causes ventricular distention. The next wave, which is the major one in the cardiac cycle, corresponds to the forward rotation of the apex due to left ventricular systole. The apex beat starts to retract as soon as the aortic valve opens and continues to do so until the 'o' point is reached, at which time the mitral valve opens and the ventricle distends rapidly. This process then slows and there is little change before the next atrial systole. Normally, only the ventricular systolic component is detectable by palpation, but in left ventricular hypertrophy, the 'a' wave can sometimes be felt immediately before ventricular systole, producing a double impulse. More rarely, one can feel an impulse at the end of rapid filling, corresponding with the third heart sound (see below).

The ventricular impulse may be abnormal in three different ways:

1. Left ventricular hypertrophy produces a sustained heaving or thrusting apex beat.
2. Left ventricular dilatation displaces the apex downwards and outwards. If there is a large left ventricular stroke volume, as in aortic regurgitation, the impulse is vigorous, but when myocardial contractility is impaired as by ischaemic heart disease, it may be diffuse and feeble.
3. In mitral stenosis, the apex beat often has a characteristic abrupt tapping quality due to the vibrations associated with the loud first sound.

Following myocardial infarction affecting the anterior wall of the heart, there is often an outward movement of the non-contracting area of the left ventricle during systole between the apex and the left sternal edge.

The right ventricular impulse in the left parasternal region is not usually palpable in health, except in children and thin adults. In right ventricular hypertrophy, as occurs in pulmonary stenosis and pulmonary hypertension (particularly secondary to mitral stenosis) there is a sustained lifting impulse along the left sternal edge. When there is right ventricular dilatation associated with a high right ventricular output (as in atrial septal defect), the impulse is vigorous but less sustained. In severe mitral regurgitation, systolic pulsation of the enlarged left atrium may also cause a left parasternal heave.

Pulmonary arterial pulsation can quite often be felt in the second left intercostal space when there is pulmonary hypertension or high pulmonary blood flow. Occasionally, the pulsation of an aneurysm can be detected in the aortic area.

Vibrations may be felt over the precordium corresponding to audible sounds and murmurs. When they are associated with heart sounds, they may be described as 'shocks'. Shocks may accompany any loud heart sound.

'Thrills' are the tactile equivalent of murmurs. They do not occur in the absence of loud murmurs and have no significance beyond that possessed by the murmur. Thrills are usually best felt by the palm of the hand when the patient is sitting upright and holding his breath in full expiration. The commonest thrills are the following:

An apical systolic thrill corresponding with the loud systolic murmur of mitral regurgitation.

A systolic thrill between the apex and the left sternal edge in ventricular septal defect.

A systolic thrill in the second right intercostal space, occasionally over the sternum and the third or fourth left intercostal space, in aortic stenosis. This is often associated with a systolic thrill over the carotid arteries.

A systolic thrill in the second or third left intercostal spaces in pulmonary stenosis.

Diastolic and presystolic thrills at the apex in mitral stenosis.

A continuous systolic and diastolic thrill below the left clavicle in persistent ductus arteriosus.

It is rare for the murmurs of aortic or pulmonary regurgitation to be accompanied by a thrill.

Percussion of the heart

A crude estimate of the size of the heart may be made by percussion, but this is much less accurate than radiology and it has little place in diagnosis. It is sometimes of value in the diagnosis of pericardial effusion, as in this condition the area of cardiac dullness may be extended to the right of the sternum and to the second left intercostal space. In emphysema, the area of cardiac dullness may be reduced.

Auscultation: heart sounds and murmurs

Vibrations within the heart give rise to sounds which are loud enough to be audible through a stethoscope and to be registered graphically by a phonocardiogram. If the noise is brief and transient, it is termed a heart sound; if more prolonged, it is a murmur. Careful auscultation, combined with the other methods of physical examination, provides information about the heart which even the most sophisticated modern techniques of investigation can scarcely match. A phonocardiogram is useful, however, in timing murmurs and sounds and is of value in differentiating the various types of added sounds such as the opening snap and the third heart sound.

The physician should always use a stethoscope with which he is familiar. The earpieces should fit comfortably; the tubing should be short (not greater than 30 cm) and thick-walled. Both types of endpiece (diaphragm and bell) are necessary. The rigid diaphragm is best for hearing high-frequency sounds and murmurs such as the second heart sound and the diastolic murmur of aortic regurgitation. The bell pressed *lightly* on the chest is superior to the diaphragm for the low-pitched third and fourth heart sounds and the mid-diastolic and presystolic murmurs of mitral stenosis. Because of the usual apical location of the low-pitched sounds, one must always use the bell when listening to the mitral area; the diaphragm should be used for listening in all the cardiac areas.

Traditionally, there are four areas of auscultation: aortic (right second intercostal space), pulmonary (left second intercostal space), tricuspid (lower sternal) and mitral (apex beat), where it is commonly believed that noises arising in the related valves are best heard. These designations are misleading, especially with regard to the aortic valve, because aortic murmurs (especially if diastolic) are often maximal at the left sternal edge at the level of the fourth intercostal space. The opening snap of mitral stenosis is also best heard in this area. Auscultation should never be restricted to the traditional areas; one should start on one side of the precordium and gradually move the stethoscope towards the other areas. One may begin in the pulmonary area in order to identify the first and second heart sounds, palpating the carotid artery whose pulsation occurs just after the first heart sound. The aortic area may be listened to next, before moving obliquely across the sternum to the lower left sternal edge, thence to the tricuspid area, to the mitral area and into the axilla. One should then listen particularly in the aortic, pulmonary and lower left sternal edge areas with the patient sitting up and holding his breath in full expiration. The apical area should be listened to with the patient rotated into the left lateral position. If mitral stenosis is suspected, the patient should exercise by sitting forward and backwards several times, and lie down again in the left lateral position.

Success in auscultation depends upon listening selectively for individual sounds and murmurs. Initially, the first heart sound should be identified and assessed before turning one's attention to the second heart sound and to any additional sounds. Having noted any normal or abnormal sounds, one should then listen for systolic and, later, for diastolic murmurs.

The heart sounds

The first sound

The first sound occurs at the time of closure of the atrioventricular valves. Although some have attributed the sound to the impact of closure, it seems more likely that it is due to the tensing of the cusps as they are projected into the atrium at the beginning of ventricular systole. Both tricuspid and mitral valves contribute to the sound. As these valves close slightly asynchronously, the first heart sound, in health, may be narrowly split. As the mitral component is louder, the first heart sound is usually best heard at the apex.

The intensity of the first heart sound is related to the extent of upward movement of the cusps when the ventricles contract. In the normal resting heart the valve cusps come into light contact with each other before the onset of ventricular systole which, therefore, projects them only a short distance. If the cusps are well down in the ventricular chamber, ventricular systole forces them rapidly upwards and causes a loud sound. This situation arises when the atrium contracts immediately before the ventricle (short PR interval) and when the left atrial pressure is abnormally high, as in mitral stenosis. In complete heart block, the relationship between atrial and ventricular systole changes from cycle to cycle, and the first sound varies in intensity accordingly. When the cusps are rigid, as in calcific mitral valve disease, the first sound is soft or inaudible.

The second sound

The second heart sound is related to the closure of the semilunar valves. Normally, it is single on expiration but splits into its aortic and pulmonary components during inspiration (Fig. 54). This phenomenon is accounted for by the prolongation of right ventricular systole associated with the increased flow into the right side of the heart occurring with inspiration (see p. 8). Splitting is best heard in the second left intercostal space. Abnormally wide splitting of the second sound, due to delay in pulmonary valve closure, occurs when the right ventricle is overburdened by either a volume load (as in atrial septal defect) or a pressure load (as in pulmonary stenosis), or when there is a delay in electrical activation of the right ventricle (as in right bundle branch block). In atrial septal defect, there is usually 'fixed' splitting of the second heart sound because the increase in venous return on inspiration affects the filling of both ventricles.

When there is left bundle branch block and when the left ventricle is overburdened, as by systemic hypertension or aortic stenosis, the aortic component of the second sound may be delayed. This produces

I exp. 2   I insp. ɑp

Fig. 54.   Normal splitting of the second heart sound during inspiration, with the aortic component preceding the pulmonary.

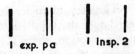

Fig. 55. 'Reversed' splitting of the second sound. Due to delay in left ventricular emptying, the aortic component follows the pulmonary component of the second sound on expiration. On inspiration, the pulmonary component is, as usual, delayed and is superimposed on the aortic component.

'reversed' splitting; the sound being single on inspiration and split on expiration (Fig. 55).

The intensity of the second heart sound may be increased by systemic or pulmonary hypertension, but this is not a reliable sign. The aortic component of the second sound may be reduced or inaudible in aortic stenosis, particularly if the aortic valve is calcified, and the pulmonary component may be soft or absent in pulmonary stenosis. Both first and second sounds may be soft when the heart is separated from the chest wall by fat, pericardial effusion or emphysematous lung, or when the cardiac output is low as in shock.

The third sound (Fig. 56A)

The third sound occurs at the end of the period of rapid filling of the ventricles. It is probably due to sudden tensing of the valve structures and ventricular walls at this time. It is usually generated in the left ventricle and is best heard at or internal to the apex. The sound is low-pitched and distant, and is often heard only with the lightly applied stethoscope bell. Although normal in the young, it is a pathological finding in the middle-aged and elderly. Its presence implies either left ventricular failure or abnormally rapid filling of the ventricle, as in

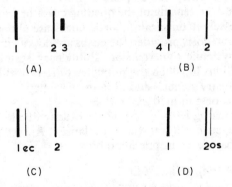

Fig. 56. (A) The third heart sound. (B) The fourth or atrial sound. (C) The ejection click (ec). (D) The opening snap.

mitral regurgitation, pregnancy or anaemia. Occasionally, a third heart sound can be heard over the right ventricle in right ventricular failure. In pericardial constriction, there is a very early third heart sound of higher frequency associated with the sudden limitation to ventricular filling.

The fourth or atrial sound (Fig. 56B)

This sound resembles the third heart sound in being low-pitched and best heard at the apex, and probably has a similar mechanism. In this instance, the ventricular distension results from atrial contraction; the fourth sound immediately precedes the first heart sound. It is not heard in health, and is usually a sign of either ventricular failure or hypertrophy. Thus, a fourth heart sound is heard over the left ventricle in some cases of aortic stenosis, hypertension and ischaemic heart disease. A right ventricular fourth heart sound may be heard at the left sternal edge in pulmonary stenosis and pulmonary hypertension.

Both third and fourth heart sounds occur only when there is rapid flow from atrium to ventricle. Their presence precludes the diagnosis of severe mitral stenosis if the sounds derive from the left ventricle, or of tricuspid stenosis if they derive from the right ventricle.

Gallop rhythm

This term is applied to a cadence of three heart sounds which may be heard in the presence of tachycardia. It may be due to a third heart sound, to a fourth heart sound or to the superimposition of the two ('summation gallop').

Additional sounds in systole

Early systolic sounds (ejection sounds or clicks) occur at the time of aortic and pulmonary valve opening (Fig. 56C). Whether the clicks arise from sudden tensing of the opening cusps or from distension of the great vessels is uncertain. Aortic clicks are almost invariable in valvar aortic stenosis provided the cusps are not calcified, and may be present in systemic hypertension. Pulmonary systolic clicks occur under conditions in which the pulmonary artery is dilated, as it is in valvar pulmonary stenosis and in pulmonary hypertension. They are usually heard best in held expiration.

Clicks occurring later in systole are usually due to ballooning of a mitral valve cusp (mitral valve prolapse). A systolic clicking or crunching may occur in pneumothorax.

The opening snap (Fig. 56D)

This is one of the most important signs in auscultation and is virtually diagnostic of mitral stenosis. It occurs at the time of mitral valve

Table 6. The differentiation of splitting of the second heart sound, the opening snap, and the third heart sound (of the left ventricle)

	Splitting of second sound (normal)	Splitting of second sound (fixed)	Splitting of second sound (reversed)	Opening snap	Third heart sound
Interval between first component of second sound and 'extra' sound	0–0·05 sec (on inspiration)	0·03–0·08 sec (at all phases)	0·01–0·03 sec (on expiration)	0·03–0·12 sec	0·10–0·16 sec
Effect of inspiration	Widens	Unaffected	Narrows	None	None
Character	Abrupt — heard best with diaphragm			'Snap' heard best with diaphragm	Low-pitched heard best with bell
Site of maximal intensity	Second left intercostal space			Lower left sternal edge	At apex
Radiation	Left sternal edge			All cardiac areas	Localized (usually)

opening and is presumed to be due to sudden tension of stenosed but pliant cusps. It is soft or absent if the mitral valve is rigid from fibrosis or calcification. It is heard best at the left sternal edge in the fourth intercostal space or between this point and the apex beat and has a snapping quality. Unlike splitting of the second sound and the third heart sound with which it may be confused, it can often be heard widely over the precordium (see Table 6).

Heart murmurs

Murmurs appear to result from vibrations set up by turbulent blood flow. Turbulence is encouraged by high velocity of flow, by abrupt change in the calibre of a vessel or chamber and by reduced blood viscosity. Murmurs therefore develop when there is rapid flow through a valve, valvar narrowing, or anaemia.

The following features of a murmur should be noted: its timing in the cardiac cycle, its location and radiation, its intensity and its quality.

Murmurs may occur either in systole or in diastole; they may continue from one into the other.

Murmurs are usually best heard at the place on the chest wall closest to their place of origin or in the direction in which the flow of blood is occurring. Thus, the murmur of aortic stenosis may be best heard over the aortic valve (the third left intercostal space), or in the second right intercostal space, or in the neck. On the other hand, the diastolic murmur of aortic regurgitation is often loudest at the fourth left intercostal space and is less well heard in the 'aortic area'.

The intensity of murmurs is usually classified in six grades.

Grade 1	Only just audible, even under good auscultatory conditions
Grade 2	Soft
Grade 3	Moderately loud
Grade 4	Loud
Grade 5	Very loud but not audible with the stethoscope away from the chest
Grade 6	So loud as to be audible with the stethoscope lifted from the chest wall

The quality of a murmur may be 'blowing', 'rumbling', 'harsh' or 'musical'. These are poor descriptions of what is heard; only with experience can one appreciate what is meant by such terms. Murmurs may also be described as low, medium or high-pitched.

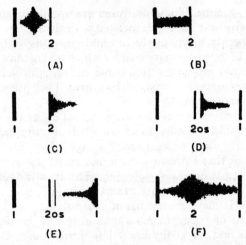

Fig. 57. (A) A midsystolic murmur. (B) A pansystolic murmur. (C) An early diastolic murmur. (D) A mid-diastolic murmur, following an opening snap in mitral stenosis. (E) The presystolic murmur of mitral stenosis. (F) The continuous murmur of a persistent ductus arteriosus.

Systolic murmurs

These are usually midsystolic or pansystolic (holosystolic) in timing.

Midsystolic murmurs start after the opening of the aortic and pulmonary valves, increase in intensity to a maximum in midsystole and decrease and disappear before the second heart sound (Fig. 57A). Because of their configuration, they are sometimes called 'diamond-shaped', and are also termed 'ejection' because they arise during ejection of blood from the ventricles into great arteries. Murmurs arising at the aortic and pulmonary valves are characteristically midsystolic.

The murmur of aortic stenosis, which is often harsh, is usually best heard in the second right intercostal space, although sometimes it is maximal at the lower left sternal edge or even at the apex. It frequently radiates to the neck. The murmur of subaortic stenosis is loudest at the lower left sternal edge. The murmur of pulmonary valve stenosis is maximal at the second left intercostal space; that of infundibular pulmonary stenosis is most intense at the third or fourth left intercostal space. The murmurs of aortic and pulmonary stenosis are often loud and accompanied by thrills.

A systolic murmur due to high flow in the pulmonary artery is characteristic of atrial septal defect but also occurs in conditions associated with a high cardiac output such as pregnancy, thyrotoxicosis and anaemia. These murmurs are usually of no more than grade 3 intensity and are not associated with thrills.

Quite frequently, particularly in children, midsystolic murmurs may be heard in the pulmonary area for which no organic cause can be found. These may be termed 'functional' or 'benign'. Such murmurs are neither intense nor accompanied by a thrill. They usually vary with position and respiration.

Pansystolic (holosystolic) murmurs persist from the first to the second heart sound and only occur as a result of mitral regurgitation, tricuspid regurgitation or ventricular septal defect, for it is only in these conditions that a pressure difference exists across the defective valve or septum throughout systole (Fig. 57B). In mitral regurgitation, the murmur is maximal at or just internal to the apex beat, and radiates into the axilla. It may be maximal in late systole.

The murmur of tricuspid regurgitation is usually loudest in the xiphisternal region, or at the lower left sternal edge. It frequently radiates to the apex and may therefore be readily confused with that of mitral regurgitation, but differs in becoming louder on inspiration, due to the increase in venous return at this time.

The murmur of ventricular septal defect is usually loud and is maximal at the lower left sternal edge.

Murmurs may be confined to early or late systole; those associated with a prolapsed mitral cusp characteristically follow a midsystolic click.

Assessing the significance of a systolic murmur

One can usually determine the cause of a systolic murmur by taking into account its location and radiation, its intensity, its character and its association with other abnormal findings. The duration of the murmur is also of value if one can be certain whether it is midsystolic or pansystolic, but even those with extensive experience are often unsure on this point.

In aortic stenosis, there is usually a loud murmur at the lower left sternal edge and aortic area which is associated with a thrill, a small flat pulse and left ventricular hypertrophy. If the valve cusps are not calcified, there is usually an early systolic ('ejection') click; if the stenosis is severe, there may be reversed splitting of the second sound. In pulmonary stenosis, the loud murmur in the pulmonary or lower left sternal area is accompanied by right ventricular hypertrophy, a soft and late pulmonary component of the second sound and a systolic thrill.

In mitral regurgitation, the apical systolic murmur, which is well heard from cardiac apex to axilla, is usually accompanied by left ventricular enlargement, a third heart sound and a mid-diastolic murmur. In tricuspid regurgitation, the murmur in the tricuspid area is usually increased by inspiration, and is associated with systolic pulsation in the jugular veins.

It is of particular importance to determine whether a systolic murmur is of the 'benign' variety, for the misinterpretation of such a murmur as organic may lead to unwarranted cardiac invalidism. Benign systolic murmurs are seldom of more than grade 2 intensity, are never pansystolic, are usually best heard in the pulmonary area and are not associated with cardiac enlargement or with abnormal heart sounds. Similar murmurs are encountered in pregnancy, thryotoxicosis and anaemia, and these conditions should be excluded before a murmur is accepted as being of no significance. The pulmonary systolic murmur of atrial septal defect resembles a benign systolic murmur but is accompanied by wide splitting of the second heart sound, and often by a mid-diastolic murmur due to high flow across the tricuspid valve. One can usually be confident of the benign nature of a murmur on physical examination alone. Only if there are other features such as cardiomegaly or abnormal sounds is further investigation with ECG, radiography and echocardiography necessary.

Diastolic murmurs

Diastolic murmurs are of three main varieties: early diastolic, mid-diastolic and presystolic.

Early (immediate) diastolic murmurs

These murmurs occur shortly after closure of the aortic or pulmonary valves at the beginning of diastole (Fig. 57C). They are due to regurgitation through one or other of these valves when pressure in the aorta or pulmonary artery exceeds that of the related ventricle. The murmur decreases in intensity as diastole continues. The murmur is usually soft, high pitched and blowing, and is best heard by using the diaphragm chest piece with the patient sitting forward, in full expiration. The murmur of aortic regurgitation is usually loudest at the third or fourth left intercostal space close to the sternum, but is occasionally maximal in the second right intercostal space.

The uncommon early diastolic murmur of pulmonary regurgitation (the Graham Steell murmur) is best heart in the left second, third and fourth intercostal spaces. It is similar in character to that of aortic regurgitation but is increased by inspiration and is accompanied by signs of pulmonary hypertension.

Mid-diastolic murmurs

Mid-diastolic murmurs are associated with flow through the atrioventricular valves and necessarily start an appreciable time after the second heart sound. The most important cause is mitral stenosis, in which there is a low-pitched murmur maximal in a localized area at or internal to the apex beat. The murmur is most easily heard with the bell of the stethoscope and with the patient lying in the left lateral position, preferably after exercise (Fig. 57D). It is frequently associated with an opening snap, a presystolic murmur and a loud first heart sound.

In tricuspid stenosis, a murmur due to a similar mechanism occurs, but in this condition it is maximal in the xiphisternal or lower left sternal region. This murmur is often of a rather scratchy character and is accentuated by inspiration. Mid-diastolic murmurs may also be caused by increased flow through unstenosed tricuspid valves. Such flow murmurs in the mitral area occur in association with mitral regurgitation, ventricular septal defect and persistent ductus arteriosus. A high-flow tricuspid murmur occurs in atrial septal defect. Another mid-diastolic murmur is that due to rheumatic valvulitis (the Carey Coombs murmur). A mid-diastolic murmur may also be heard, in the absence of mitral valve disease, in patients with severe aortic regurgitation (the Austin Flint murmur). This may be due to the aortic regurgitant flow pushing the aortic cusp of the mitral valve across the mitral valve orifice, thereby causing turbulence as blood is also flowing simultaneously from the left atrium to the left ventricle.

Presystolic murmurs

Presystolic murmurs are produced when atrial systole propels blood through narrowed mitral or tricuspid valves. The presystolic murmur of mitral stenosis leads up to the loud first sound of that condition (Fig. 57E); it is most easily heard with the patient lying in the left lateral position with the bell of the stethoscope placed at or internal to the apex beat. The presystolic murmur of tricuspid stenosis is maximal in the xiphisternal region or at the lower left sternal edge and is accentuated by inspiration.

Continuous murmurs

The term 'continuous' is applied to a murmur which starts during systole and continues into diastole; it is not necessarily continuous throughout the cardiac cycle. The commonest types are the venous hum and the murmur of persistent ductus arteriosus.

The venous hum is common in childhood, but may be heard in anaemic or pregnant adults. It is due to high blood flow in the jugular veins and can therefore be diminished or abolished by lying the patient flat, or by constricting the veins by pressure. It is usually loudest in the neck, but may be audible over the upper chest.

The murmur in persistent ductus arteriosus is caused by the flow of blood from the high-pressure aorta into the low-pressure pulmonary artery. It is maximal in the left second intercostal space or under the left clavicle. It increases in intensity throughout systole, is maximal at the time of the second heart sound, and diminishes during diastole (Fig. 57F). It often has a 'machinery' or whirring quality. Similar murmurs are caused by systemic, pulmonary and coronary arterio-venous fistulae, and by rupture of an aneurysm of a sinus of Valsalva (see p. 257).

Pericardial friction (or rub)

As roughened visceral and parietal layers of pericardium slide over one another, they produce a harsh creaking sound which may be likened to the noise made by two pieces of sandpaper rubbing together. As the movement occurs during ventricular systole, ventricular diastole and atrial systole, the rub may be present at one or all of these times. It may be heard all over the precordium, or only at a localized site. It usually sounds superficial and can be accentuated by leaning the patient forward or by pressing the stethoscope diaphragm firmly on the chest. It can occur in acute pericarditis of any cause, as well as in uraemic pericarditis and during the course of acute myocardial infarction. In the latter condition, it is often evanescent, lasting for only a few minutes or hours.

Further reading

AHA Committee Report. Recommendations for human blood pressure determination by sphygmomanometers (1980) *Circulation* **62**, 1145A.

FINLAYSON, J. K., KENMURE, A. C. F. and SHORT, D. S. (1978) Cardiac signs for students. *Brit. med. J.*, **1**, 1471.

LEATHAM, A. (1979) *Introduction to Examination of the Cardiovascular System*, 2nd ed. London: Oxford University Press.

7

Radiology and Other Techniques of Investigation

Radiological examination of the heart is an essential part of the full cardiological assessment as are the newer non-invasive investigations. These techniques include plain radiography, fluoroscopy, angiocardiography, radionuclide studies and echocardiography.

Plain chest radiography and fluoroscopy

Plain radiographs are usually taken in postero-anterior and lateral views; oblique positions are sometimes used.

In the postero-anterior projection, the patient faces the X-ray cassette. In this view (Fig. 58) the right border of the heart consists (from above downwards) of the superior vena cava, the ascending aorta, the right atrium, and the inferior vena cava. The left border of the heart is formed by the aortic arch, the pulmonary artery and its left main branch, and the left ventricle. Between the left ventricle and the diaphragm, there may be a small triangular shadow due to an epicardial fat pad. In this view, the maximum transverse diameter of the heart does not usually exceed 50% of the chest, measured from the inner aspects of the ribs, although 'cardiothoracic ratios' greater than this are sometimes seen in normal individuals.

In the lateral view (Fig. 59), the anterior border of the heart is formed by the pulmonary artery and right ventricle and the posterior border by the left atrium and left ventricle.

Enlargement of the left ventricle, which is most frequently due to hypertension, ischaemic heart disease, aortic valve disease and mitral regurgitation, produces depression and elongation of the cardiac apex (Fig. 60). Left ventricular enlargement is better seen in the lateral view. A normal left ventricle may be displaced posteriorly by an enlarged right ventricle.

Right ventricular enlargement, usually the consequence of pulmonary hypertension or pulmonary stenosis, produces an elevation of the cardiac apex in the postero-anterior view, and in the lateral views

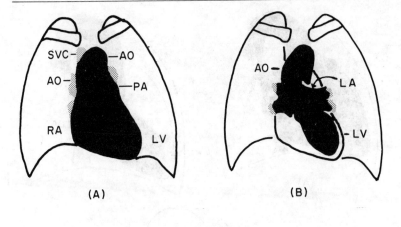

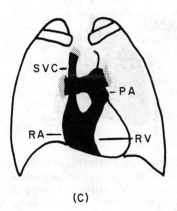

Fig. 58.   The postero-anterior view. (A) The normal chest radiograph. (B) Appearances of the left side of the heart, after injection of radio-opaque material into the left atrium, showing the positions of the left atrium (LA), the left ventricle (LV) and the aorta (AO). (C) Appearances of the right side of the heart after injection of radio-opaque material into the superior vena cava (SVC). The positions of the right atrium (RA), the right ventricle (RV), and the pulmonary artery (PA), are shown.

of the heart makes the normally straight anterior border of the heart bulge towards or impinge on the sternum.

The body of the left atrium enlarges posteriorly and to the right, but its appendage protrudes to the left. Thus, in the postero-anterior view, the left atrial appendage is seen on the left border of the heart between the pulmonary artery and the left ventricle (Fig. 61), whereas the main body of the left atrium forms a dense shadow within the right atrial border, or protrudes to the right above the right atrium on the right

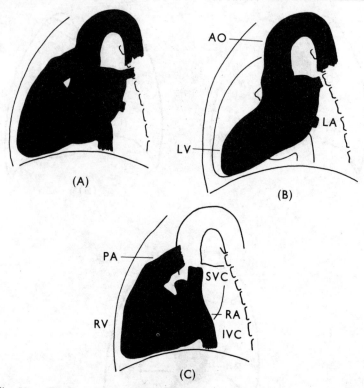

Fig. 59.   The lateral view. (A) Normal chest radiograph. (B) Appearances of the left side of the heart, after injection of radio-opaque contrast medium into the left atrium, showing the positions of the left atrium (LA), left ventricle (LV) and aorta (AO). (C) Appearances of the right side of the heart after injection of contrast medium into the right atrium showing positions of superior and inferior venae cavae (SVC, IVC), right atrium (RA), right ventricle (RV) and pulmonary artery (PA).

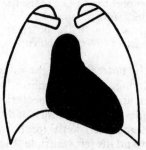

Fig. 60.   Depression and elongation of the cardiac apex in left ventricular enlargement.

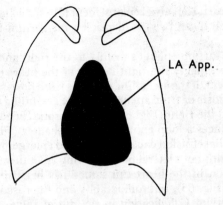

Fig. 61.   The bulge produced by the left atrial appendage (LA App) is seen on the left border of the heart between the positions of the pulmonary artery and left ventricle.

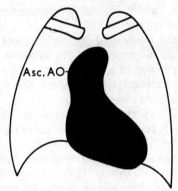

Fig. 62.   Dilatation of the ascending aorta (Asc AO), visible on the right upper cardiac silhouette, in aortic stenosis.

Fig. 63.   The appearances of an 'uncoiled' aorta.

side of the heart. Left atrial enlargement is best diagnosed in the lateral view in which it can be seen displacing the barium-filled oesophagus posteriorly.

The right atrium enlarges mainly to the right and, in the postero-anterior view, makes the right border of the heart more prominent.

Enlargement of the ascending aorta, as from post-stenotic dilatation in aortic stenosis or from aneurysm of the ascending aorta, is seen as a projection to the right (Fig. 62). The sclerotic 'uncoiled' aorta of the elderly produces a loop above the heart shadow (Fig. 63).

A pericardial effusion causes generalized enlargement of the cardiac silhouette, with both lateral borders being smoothly convex (Fig. 64).

Calcification in the heart can sometimes be suspected on a plain radiograph (Fig. 65), but tomography and fluoroscopy are necessary for confirmation. Calcification in the mitral valve, which is usually rheumatic, is best visualized in the lateral view in which it is seen in the posterior third of the cardiac mass. The aortic valve is located more in the centre of the heart; in the postero-anterior view it is situated just to the left of the spine. Calcification of the pericardium is best seen in a penetrated lateral view (Fig. 66).

Fluoroscopy of the heart is of particular value in showing valve calcification, abnormal movements of the pulmonary artery and aorta, and the systolic expansion of a ventricular aneurysm.

The plain chest radiograph is of great value in demonstrating abnormalities of the pulmonary circulation.

Pulmonary venous hypertension, as occurs in left ventricular failure and mitral stenosis, is revealed by dilatation of the pulmonary veins, particularly those draining the upper zones.

Oedema of the lungs is at first interstitial and causes haziness around the vascular shadows, with thin horizontal lines at the bases (Kerley's lines), due to fluid in the interlobular septa and distended lymphatics. Alveolar oedema produces a fluffy opacification spreading out from the hilar region, often providing a 'butterfly' appearance. Occasionally, pulmonary oedema is predominantly unilateral.

In moderate pulmonary arterial hypertension, the main right and left pulmonary arteries are enlarged, although the more peripheral arteries may be normal. In severe pulmonary hypertension, the major pulmonary arteries, which are greatly dilated, contrast with narrowed peripheral pulmonary arteries; the major arteries appear to be 'cut off'.

When there is increased pulmonary blood flow, as in atrial septal defect, ventricular septal defect and persistent ductus arteriosus, both main and peripheral pulmonary arteries are dilated (Fig. 67). Fluoroscopy may show a vigorous pulsation (the 'hilar dance').

When the pulmonary blood flow is decreased, as in pulmonary stenosis, the pulmonary arteries are poorly seen. However, the main and left pulmonary arteries may be dilated by the jet of blood emerging from the stenosis (Fig. 68).

Fig. 64.   The appearances of a pericardial effusion.

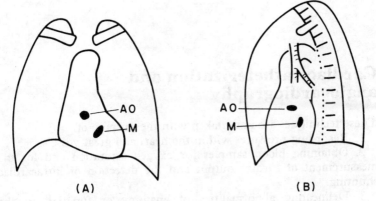

Fig. 65.   The position of the aortic (AO) and mitral (M) valve calcification in: (A) the postero-anterior view and (B) the lateral view.

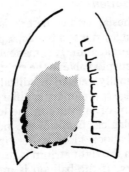

Fig. 66.   Calcification of the pericardium, outlining the ventricles, in the lateral view.

Fig. 67.   Radiological appearances in atrial septal defect, showing enlarged pulmonary arteries and right side of the heart.

Cardiac catheterization and angiocardiography

These techniques are undertaken with the purpose of:
1. Recording pressures within the heart and great vessels.
2. Obtaining blood samples for oxygen saturation and for the measurement of cardiac output and the detection of intracardiac shunting.
3. Delineating abnormalities of anatomy or function in the cardiovascular system by the injection of radio-opaque substances.

See Table 7 for normal cardiovascular pressures.

Right heart catheterization

Under local anaesthesia, a catheter is usually introduced percutoneously or by cutdown into a basilic, saphenous or femoral vein, and advanced to the right atrium. It is manoeuvred with fluoroscopic control through the tricuspid valve to the right ventricle, thence to the pulmonary artery and finally wedged in a distal pulmonary artery. The pulmonary arterial wedge (pulmonary capillary) tracing so obtained is an indirect measurement of pressure in the left atrium.

If appropriate radiological facilities are not available, a catheter (Swan–Ganz) with a balloon close to its tip may be used. If the balloon is inflated when the right atrium is reached, the tip will 'float' into a pulmonary artery. If the balloon is impacted in the artery, a pulmonary artery wedge tracing is obtained.

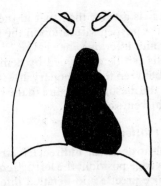

Fig. 68.   Dilatation of the main and left pulmonary artery in pulmonary valve stenosis.

Table 7.   Normal cardiovascular pressures (mmHg)

	Mean	Range
Right atrium — mean	4	0–8
Right ventricle		
systolic	25	15–30
end diastolic	4	0–8
Pulmonary artery		
systolic	25	15–30
diastolic	10	5–15
mean	15	10–20
Pulmonary artery wedge — mean	10	5–14
Left atrium — mean	7	4–12
Left ventricle		
systolic	120	90–140
end diastolic	7	4–12
Aorta		
systolic	120	90–140
diastolic	70	60–90
mean	85	70–105

If there is a septal defect, the catheter may be passed through this into the left side of the heart; if there is a persistent ductus arteriosus, this may be traversed.

As the catheter is withdrawn from the pulmonary artery, blood samples can be obtained from each vessel and chamber. When a left-to-right shunt is present, the blood is found to be more oxygenated in the affected chamber and beyond than it is in the great veins. In a persistent ductus arteriosus the oxygen saturation in the left pulmonary artery exceeds that in the right ventricle, whereas in a ventricular septal defect, the oxygen saturation in the right ventricle and pulmonary artery is greater than that in the right atrium. In an atrial septal defect, the oxygen saturation in the right atrium exceeds that in the superior and inferior venae cavae.

Pulmonary stenosis can be confirmed by demonstrating a systolic pressure difference between the pulmonary artery and right ventricle; in tricuspid stenosis the diastolic pressure in the right atrium is higher than that in the right ventricle.

Left heart catheterization

Although it is possible to obtain an indirect left atrial pressure from the pulmonary arterial wedge position, the left atrium and ventricle must be entered when more precise and detailed information is required about the left side of the heart. There are several techniques which can be used:

Trans-septal technique.   A catheter containing a special needle is advanced from the femoral or saphenous vein to the right atrium. The needle is used to perforate the inter-atrial septum. Subsequently, the catheter is advanced over the needle into the left atrium and manoeuvred into the left ventricle.

Retrograde aortic technique.   A catheter is introduced into the femoral or brachial arteries and advanced retrogradely until it reaches the aortic valve. In most cases it is possible to pass the catheter through the aortic valve into the left ventricle.

Direct left ventricular puncture.   The left ventricle is punctured directly by a needle inserted through the chest wall.

Angiocardiography

By the injection of contrast medium it is possible to demonstrate the anatomy of the chambers of the heart and the great arteries, and to observe the patterns of blood flow. Two techniques are used:

Ciné radiography.   High-speed ciné films are taken at 50 to 150 frames per second in one or two planes.

Rapid film changer.   From two to twelve full-sized chest radiographs can be obtained by a film changer in one or two planes in a period of 2 to 6 sec.

Ciné radiography has the advantage of showing the dynamic changes in the circulation, and is invaluable in demonstrating intracardiac shunts and valvar regurgitation.

The contrast medium is injected at the site most appropriate for the delineation of the suspected abnormality. Therefore, in ventricular septal defect and mitral regurgitation, the injection is made into the left ventricle; in aortic regurgitation it is made into the aorta. When coronary angiography is performed, selective injections are made into each of the two main coronary arteries (see p. 136).

Indications for and risks of cardiac catheterization and angiocardiography

Cardiac catheterization and angiocardiography are procedures which require considerable skill and experience on the part of the physician and entail some discomfort and hazard for the patient. They should be carried out only in a department equipped with facilities for multichannel pressure recording, blood gas estimations, and both ciné and large film angiocardiography. Anaesthetic and resuscitation apparatus must be immediately available.

Right heart catheterization entails little danger, although arrhythmias may be provoked when the catheter tip is in the right ventricle. Left heart catheterization imposes a greater risk both from arrhythmias and from perforation of the myocardium by a transthoracic or trans-septal needle, which may produce haemopericardium and tamponade. The injection of radio-opaque contrast medium in angiocardiography often provokes transient ventricular arrhythmias and, occasionally, ventricular fibrillation. Apart from the mortality of the procedures, there is a morbidity due to complications which include thrombosis of the catheterized artery or vein, pulmonary and systemic embolism, haemorrhage from puncture sites and toxic reactions to the contrast medium.

The natural anxiety of patients prior to the procedure is best allayed by previous preparation and explanation, combined with the use of a sedative. Anaesthesia may have to be employed in children, but should be avoided if possible because of its effects on haemodynamics and blood gases.

Cardiac catheterization and angiocardiography are carried out for two main purposes:

1. To establish a precise diagnosis.
2. To estimate the severity of the lesions.

These techniques are mainly used to evaluate the nature and extent of the heart disease prior to cardiac surgery, but they are also of value when doubt exists as to the nature of a murmur, or the cause of chest pain. Cardiac catheterization and angiography are required in most cases of congenital heart disease and in the majority of instances of rheumatic heart disease other than pure mitral stenosis.

The severity of a stenotic lesion is best determined by measuring both the pressure difference and the blood flow across the valve. This requires the simultaneous recording of pressures on both sides of the valve and the estimation of cardiac output. Thus, measurements must be obtained in the left ventricle and aorta in aortic stenosis, and in the left atrium (or pulmonary artery wedge position) and left ventricle in mitral stenosis. The severity of regurgitation is best evaluated by ciné-angiography at the appropriate site.

The measurement of cardiac output

The cardiac output can be measured by one of two techniques: the Fick principle and the indicator-dilution method.

The Fick principle. Fick pointed out that:

1. The quantity of blood traversing the lungs in a given period of time equals the cardiac output.
2. The change in oxygen (O_2) concentration between pulmonary arteries (PA) and pulmonary veins (PV) depends upon the O_2 uptake in the lungs, and the volume of blood into which it is absorbed, i.e. the cardiac output (CO).
   Therefore,

$$PVO_2 - PAO_2 = \frac{O_2 \text{ uptake}}{CO} \quad \text{and} \quad CO = \frac{O_2 \text{ uptake}}{PVO_2 - PAO_2}$$

Oxygen uptake is derived from the analysis of expired air. Blood samples are obtained by catheterization, arterial blood being used instead of pulmonary venous blood.

Indicator-dilution method. This is based on a similar principle, namely that the concentration of an injected substance in the blood is dependent upon the amount of that substance injected and the volume of blood in which it is diluted.

Currently, the most popular technique is to use cold saline and to measure the change in temperature with a thermistor attached to a catheter tip. An injection of cold saline, of known volume and temperature, is injected into a vein or the right atrium and the temperature is sampled in the pulmonary artery (Fig. 69).

Other indicators are used, including isotopes and cardiogreen, which can be detected by an isotope rate counter or densitometer respectively. These indicators have the disadvantage that they recirculate and so affect the terminal part of the indicator-dilution curve. Formulae can be used to calculate the area under this curve ignoring the recirculated indicator.

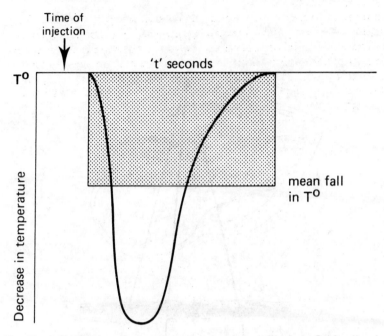

Fig. 69. Cardiac output measurement by thermodilution. Cold saline is injected into the right atrium. The decrease in blood temperature is detected by a thermistor catheter in the pulmonary artery. A special-purpose computer is used to calculate cardiac output from a formula based on the known quantity of saline at a known temperature which produces a mean fall in temperature over 't' seconds at the sampling site.

Radionuclide studies

It has now become possible to carry out radionuclide studies on the heart in most hospitals as the facilities required for this are similar to those needed for radionuclide investigation of other systems. Nuclear imaging is of value in two major contexts which particularly relate to ischaemic heart disease: the demonstration of abnormalities of myocardial perfusion and the evaluation of left ventricular function.

Myocardial perfusion studies

Certain radiopharmaceuticals, of which thallium-201 is the one most commonly used, are taken up into the myocardium in proportion to the regional blood flow. They therefore do not concentrate in areas of ischaemia or fibrosis. Thallium imaging has been found to be of

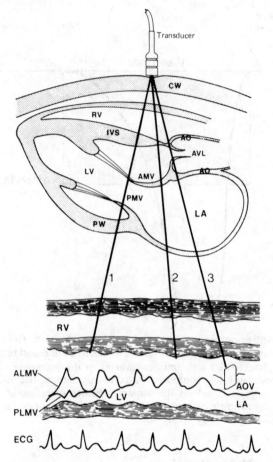

Fig. 70A   The transducer is angled in different directions to permit study
of the various cardiac structures. (1) The beam traverses the
right ventricle (RV), interventricular septum (IVS), and
anterior and posterior leaflets of the mitral valve (ALMV and
PLMV). These leaflets separate abruptly as the blood flows
rapidly from the left atrium to the left ventricle. As the flow
decreases they approximate only to be separated again when
atrial contraction propels more blood into the ventricle. (2)
Provides good views of the RV, septum, ALMV and left atrium.
(3) Shows separation of the aortic valve cusps in systole.

greatest value in the detection of transient myocardial ischaemia in
patients with suspected angina pectoris. If the radio-isotope is injected
intravenously during an exercise at the time when the patient develops
chest pain or ST depression, a 'cold spot' will be seen corresponding to

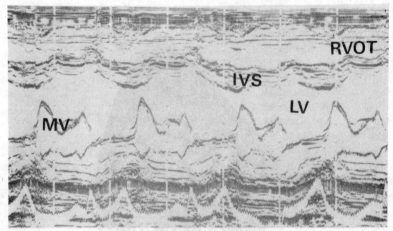

Fig. 70B. Normal echocardiogram, corresponding to 70A, view (1), showing right ventricular outflow tract, interventricular septum, both cusps of the mitral valve, and the left ventricular cavity. RVOT = right ventricular outflow tract. IVS = interventricular septum. MV = mitral valve. LV = left ventricle.

the area of ischaemia, while the rest of the myocardium will take up the isotope. If nuclear imaging is repeated some four hours later, when no ischaemia is present, the 'cold spot' will be seen to have disappeared. This is a relatively sensitive and specific test, but unfortunately the cost of thallium and the degree of skill and experience necessary for optimal interpretation limits its application.

Radionuclide ventriculography

The most common technique for the imaging of left ventricular function involves the use of technetium-labelled red cells so that the pool of blood in the left ventricle can be detected. By using the ECG to 'gate' the images ('gated pool scan'), segments of the cardiac cycle from successive beats can be superimposed. By obtaining 20 or more exposures during each cardiac cycle, it is possible to record the radionuclide equivalent of a ciné-angiogram. This technique allows the evaluation of several aspects of left ventricular function including contractility of the ventricle, end-systolic and end-diastolic volumes and the detection of regional wall abnormalities including ventricular aneurysms.

Echocardiography

When an ultrasonic beam encounters a boundary between structures of different acoustic densities, some of the waves are reflected. These can be detected and used to provide an electrical signal. The procedure

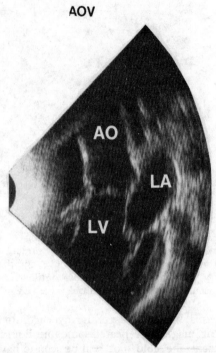

AOV

AO

LA

LV

Fig. 71.   Cross-sectional long axis parasternal view of a normal heart showing the aortic root, aortic valve, mitral valve, left ventricle and left atrium. LV = left ventricle, AO = aorta, LA = left atrium.

of echocardiography exploits this principle to identify many cardiac structures and to study their movements (Fig. 70A and B).

A piezo-electric crystal which acts both as transmitter and receiver, is used to generate high frequency pulses of very short duration. These travel through body tissues at known velocity: the 'echoes' which occur from interfaces are detected by the transducer, amplified and then displayed either on an oscilloscope or on a strip-chart recorder. Bone and lung both interfere with ultrasonic transmission, so that the views that can be obtained of the heart are limited.

The transducer is usually placed in the fourth left intercostal space close to the sternal edge. As can be seen in Fig. 70A and B, by rotating the probe a sweeping view of many of the intracardiac structures may be obtained.

In cross-sectional (two-dimensional, 2D) echocardiography, an ultrasonic beam is moved rapidly across the heart (or a series of ultrasonic elements are fired in sequence) to allow a real-time recording of changes in cardiac shape and movement, which are displayed on a videotape (Fig. 71).

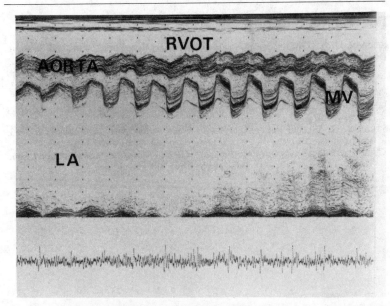

Fig. 72. Severe mitral stenosis — an M-Mode parasternal echocardiogram. The left atrium is hugely enlarged and the mitral valve shows the characteristic slow diastolic closure rate. RVOT = right ventricular outflow tract. MV = mitral valve. LA = left atrium.

Echocardiography has proved particularly valuable in studying disorders of the mitral valve. In the normal valve, the cusps open rapidly in early diastole and return quickly towards the closed position, being further propelled downwards by atrial systole before finally moving upwards before closure. In mitral stenosis, the diastolic closure rate is slow and the posterior cusp, instead of moving away from the anterior cusp during diastole, moves forward with it (Fig. 72). Other abnormalities which may be detected are multiple echoes suggesting calcification, and abnormal movements of the leaflets during systole, indicating prolapse of the cusps.

Although calcification of the aortic valve may be readily demonstrated, other abnormalities of this valve are less diagnostic. However, a useful indicator of aortic regurgitation is the fluttering of the mitral valve which may be produced by the regurgitant jet during early diastole.

Another major diagnostic use of echocardiography is the detection of pericardial effusion. Echo-free spaces may be demonstrated in front of and behind the heart.

The technique is also useful in detecting abnormalities in many varieties of congenital heart disease and in demonstrating such abnormalities as an atrial myxoma.

Further reading

BERMAN, D. S. (1982) *Clinical Nuclear Cardiology*. New York: Grune and Stratton.

DOW, J., PEARSON, M. and STEINER, R. E. (1980). The cardiovascular system. In: *A Textbook of Radiology and Organ Imaging*, ed. D. Sutton, 3rd ed. Edinburgh: Churchill Livingstone.

FEIGENBAUM, H. (1981) *Echocardiography*, 3rd ed. Philadelphia: Lea and Febiger.

JEFFERSON, K. and REES, S. (1980) *Clinical Cardiac Radiology*, 2nd ed. London: Butterworth.

STRAUSS, H. W. and PITT, B. (1979) *Cardiovascular Nuclear Medicine*, 2nd ed. Philadelphia: Mosby.

VEREL, D. and GRAINGER, R. G. (1978) *Cardiac Catheterization and Angiocardiography*, 3rd ed. Edinburgh: Churchill Livingstone.

8

Diseases of the Coronary Arteries

The coronary circulation

There are two major coronary arteries — right and left (Fig. 73). The right coronary artery arises from the right coronary sinus of Valsalva and runs down in the groove between the right atrium and the right ventricle. In most hearts, its branches supply the sinus node, the atrioventricular node and bundle, the right ventricle and the inferior part of the left ventricle. The left coronary artery, which arises from the left coronary sinus of Valsalva, soon divides into two large branches: the anterior descending branch which runs down between the two ventricles anteriorly, and the left circumflex branch which passes around in the groove between the left atrium and the left ventricle. The anterior descending artery supplies the interventricular septum and the anterior wall of the left ventricle. The circumflex supplies the lateral and posterior aspects of the left ventricle. The major vessels traverse the external surface of the myocardium, sending branches perpendicularly into the muscle mass. There are normally many small anastomoses between the coronary arteries, but these are of no functional importance. When an area of the heart becomes ischaemic, the anastomoses enlarge and then provide a collateral blood supply to the affected muscle which is often vital for its survival.

The arteries divide to form arterioles and capillaries similar to those elsewhere in the body, and the venules and veins join to form larger venous channels. Virtually all the blood from the left coronary artery eventually drains into the coronary sinus; that from the right coronary artery drains mainly into the anterior cardiac veins. From these veins the blood passes into the right atrium.

The blood flow in the coronary arteries resembles that in other regions in being dependent on the blood pressure and on the vascular resistance of the arteries and arterioles. A distinctive feature of the coronary circulation is that the arteries are compressed by the contracting myocardium during systole so that the resistance to flow at that time is sharply increased. Consequently, coronary blood flow occurs mainly during diastole. Flow is largely determined by the calibre of the coronary arteries themselves. Certainly, the aortic

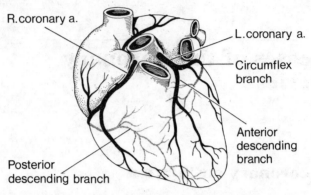

R.coronary a.

L.coronary a.

Circumflex
branch

Anterior
descending
branch

Posterior
descending branch

Fig. 73.   The anatomy of the coronary arteries (see text).

diastolic pressure is also a determinant of coronary flow; but according to Poiseuille's equation, flow is dependent directly on pressure differences but related to the fourth power of the radius. Therefore, a doubling of aortic diastolic pressure doubles coronary flow, whereas a doubling of the radius of the coronary arteries leads to a sixteen-fold increase in flow. In health, variations in coronary blood flow are mainly due to changes in impedance in the small coronary arteries; these dilate in response to a fall in tissue oxygen tension. Variations in tone also occur in the large coronary arteries but these affect blood flow only if these vessels are narrowed by disease or they are extreme (spasm).

In the normal resting heart, almost all the oxygen is extracted during its passage through the capillaries; coronary sinus blood is therefore almost completely desaturated. Unlike other organs, the heart cannot call upon a venous oxygen reserve when faced by increased demands, and is largely dependent upon the ability of the coronary arteries to increase their diameter.

Drugs may affect myocardial blood supply directly, by their action on the coronary arteries, or indirectly, by influencing factors such as blood pressure and myocardial contractility. Nitrates, such as glyceryl trinitrate (nitroglycerin or trinitrin) are potent coronary vasodilators in the normal person, but in the subject with coronary artery disease their beneficial effect is probably mainly due to the reduction in cardiac work consequent upon venodilatation. The beta-adrenergic blocking drugs, such as propranolol are effective antianginal agents which also operate through a reduction in cardiac work. In this instance the drugs antagonize the effects of the sympathetic nervous system and catecholamines, which cause a rise in myocardial oxygen requirement which is disproportionately great in relation to the increase in cardiac work which they produce. Secondary to this reduction in myocardial oxygen requirement, the coronary arteries constrict.

Coronary artery disease

Coronary artery disease is the commonest cause of heart disease and the most important single cause of death in the affluent countries of the world. In the overwhelming majority of cases, disease of the coronary arteries is due to atherosclerosis. However, they may also be involved in other disorders:

Congenital abnormalities such as arteriovenous fistulae and anomalous origin from the pulmonary artery.

Coronary embolism associated with thrombosis arising in the left atrium or ventricle or from mitral or aortic valve prostheses, or from infective endocarditis.

Syphilitic aortitis involving the coronary ostia (p. 273).

Occlusion of a coronary artery due to dissecting aneurysm (p. 254).

Polyarteritis (p. 279) and other connective tissue diseases.

Coronary artery spasm which may affect both diseased and otherwise normal vessels. Typically, it gives rise to episodes of angina at rest accompanied by ST segment elevation (Prinzmetal's variant angina). Transient heart-block and ventricular arrhythmias may occur.

Spasm usually responds well to nitrates or calcium antagonists.

The remainder of this chapter is concerned with coronary artery disease of atherosclerotic origin.

Definitions

Atherosclerosis. This has been defined (by a WHO study group) as 'a variable combination of changes of the intima of arteries (as distinguished from arterioles) consisting of a focal accumulation of lipids, complex carbohydrates, blood and blood products, fibrous tissue and calcium deposits, and associated with medial changes'. It is synonymous with *atheroma* but not with *arteriosclerosis*, which is a less specific term used to describe hardening of arteries and arterioles.

Coronary artery disease. This term is used to describe coronary arteries which are affected by a pathological process. Coronary artery disease usually exists for many years before a disorder of myocardial function develops. It is, therefore, not synonymous with ischaemic heart disease.

Ischaemic heart disease. This term is used to describe cardiac disease resulting from myocardial ischaemia. Although myocardial ischaemia also occurs in such conditions as aortic stenosis, ischaemic heart disease is generally applied only to cases of atherosclerotic origin.

Coronary heart disease and *atherosclerotic heart disease.* These are used synonymously with ischaemic heart disease.

Coronary thrombosis. This is used to describe the occlusion of a coronary artery by thrombus. This may or may not lead to myocardial infarction.

Coronary occlusion. This is used to describe occlusion of the coronary artery by any cause. Again, this may or may not cause myocardial infarction.

Myocardial infarction. This is used to indicate necrosis of a portion of heart muscle as a result of inadequate blood supply.

Clinical manifestations of ischaemic heart disease

Coronary atherosclerosis may lead to a variety of syndromes which can affect the same patient at different times. These are: angina pectoris, acute myocardial infarction, unstable angina, cardiac failure, arrhythmias and sudden death.

Pathology of coronary atherosclerosis and its complications

The characteristic lesion is the plaque, whose major components are lipid, much of it extracellular, and arterial smooth muscle cells and their products, such as fibrous proteins and complex carbohydrates. Advanced plaques have a necrotic centre consisting of cholesterol crystals and esters, cell debris and calcium, covered by a fibrous cap composed of smooth muscle cells, fibrin and lipid. These deposits are focal and are most commonly located at the bends and bifurcations of arteries. Atrophy of the media is a secondary phenomenon.

The atheromatous plaque, which is produced by this process, may itself narrow the lumen of the artery. At least as important is the liability of the fibrous cap to fracture, allowing the necrotic core to ulcerate and trigger off platelet aggregation and fibrin deposition. The occlusion of a coronary artery by plaque rupture or thrombosis usually causes myocardial infarction.

When patients who have experienced *angina pectoris* come to necropsy, there is usually found to be widespread but patchy coronary atherosclerosis and myocardial fibrosis. There is commonly evidence of old coronary occlusion and myocardial infarction. The basic pathological cause for the angina is the coronary arterial narrowing which has reduced the lumen of at least one of the three main coronary arteries by 75%. In most cases, two or all three of these arteries are affected.

Sudden death is often attributed to coronary artery disease when widespread coronary atherosclerosis is present, but recent coronary occlusion or myocardial infarction can be demonstrated in only a minority of cases. In many instances, it is probable that acute myocardial ischaemia has provoked fatal ventricular fibrillation.

The essential pathological feature of *acute myocardial infarction* is myocardial necrosis. This is usually, but not always, the consequence of total occlusion of a coronary artery. If death occurs soon after the onset of acute myocardial infarction there are sometimes no gross or microscopic changes in the myocardium, although enzyme-staining reactions and electron microscopy may reveal evidence of damage. Later, the infarcted area appears pale and is surrounded by a reddish area due to hyperaemia. Microscopically, the muscle cells lose their nuclei and, subsequently, necrotic changes take place in adjacent connective tissue and blood vessel walls. Leucocytic infiltration occurs at the edges of the infarction. The removal of necrotic muscle fibres starts about the third day and continues for about 2 weeks. At the same time granulation tissue containing blood vessels and fibroblasts invades the necrotic area. Finally, the infarcted area is replaced by fibrous scar tissue over a period lasting between 2 and 8 weeks. If the infarction reaches the endocardial surface, a mural thrombus may develop. If it impinges on the pericardium, pericarditis occurs.

The location and size of a myocardial infarction depend upon the artery that is occluded and the collateral blood supply. In some cases the infarct extends from endocardium to epicardium (transmural infarction); in others, only subendocardial territory is involved. If the left anterior descending artery is occluded, the infarction affects the anterior wall of the left ventricle and may involve the septum. If the left circumflex artery is occluded, the infarction affects the lateral or posterior walls of the left ventricle. If the right coronary artery is occluded, the infarction chiefly affects the inferior (diaphragmatic) surface of the left ventricle, but also the septum and the right ventricle. Coronary occlusion may not lead to myocardial infarction if the area supplied by the occluded vessel has a collateral supply from adjacent arteries.

Of patients surviving myocardial infarction, 10 to 20 % develop an aneurysmal dilatation of the infarcted area of the left ventricle. This may be of no haemodynamic importance, but in some cases the paradoxical movement impairs left ventricular function and leads to cardiac failure in the weeks or months following the acute event.

Incidence and prevalence of ischaemic heart disease

The incidence of ischaemic heart disease increases with age. It is relatively uncommon under the age of 40; the frequency rises rapidly after this age in males, but less so in females. Under the age of 45, ischaemic heart disease is more than ten times as common in males as in females; between 45 and 60 it is at least twice as common in males; in the older age groups the incidence is approximately equal in the two sexes. The number of deaths attributed to ischaemic heart disease has increased considerably in the last 40 years. This is partly due to the ageing population and partly to improved diagnosis. However, there can be no doubt that there has been a real increase in its incidence in early middle age. It appears that the annual death rate from this cause is falling in a number of countries including the United States, Australia and New Zealand, but not in some others such as the United Kingdom.

Aetiological factors in ischaemic heart disease

Coronary atherosclerosis is a necessary precursor of ischaemic heart disease but it may require a further pathological process, such as thrombosis, to produce clinical manifestations. There is some evidence that the incidence of coronary atherosclerosis has not changed greatly over a period of many years, but that myocardial infarction and sudden death have increased strikingly.

Pathogenesis of coronary atherosclerosis.   There are two main theories as to the pathogenesis of atherosclerosis — the lipid-infiltration (or 'insudation') theory and the thrombogenic theory.

The lipid-infiltration theory proposes that the principal factor in the development of atherosclerosis is accumulation of plasma constituents, notably lipids by passage through the arterial wall. This concept is supported by the strong relationship between serum cholesterol levels and the development of atheroma. It seems that the presence of low density lipoproteins stimulates the proliferation of smooth muscle cells, which are the cells mainly involved in atherogenesis. The alternative hypothesis is that the process starts with the formation of thrombi, at a defect in the arterial intima. These are subsequently endothelialized and absorbed as a fibrous lesion into the intima. Even if this latter explanation of the origin of atheroma is incorrect, it is probable that the development of mural thrombi and their incorporation into the arterial wall is a factor of importance in the progression of atherosclerosis. Indeed platelets liberate a peptide that causes smooth muscle cells to proliferate.

In addition to the mechanisms mentioned, injury to the endothelium, as may result from hypertension and cigarette smoking, is probably an important factor.

Lipid disorders.   There is much circumstantial evidence to incriminate lipid abnormalities in the genesis of atheroma:

1. Deposition of lipid in the arterial wall occurs at an early, if not at the initial, stage of the process.

2. Atheroma can be induced in animals by cholesterol feeding and other means of raising plasma cholesterol levels. However, the lesions

Table 8. Hyperlipoproteinaemias

Types	Chylo-microns	Chole-sterol	Triglyce-rides	Clinical aspects
I	+ + +	↑	↑	Rare. Familial. Childhood hepato-splenomegaly Xanthomata. No definite association with coronary disease.
IIa	—	↑	—	Often familial. Tendinous and tuberous xanthomata associated with early atherosclerosis.
IIb	—	↑	↑	
III	—	↑		Orange and yellow palmar creases. Xanthomata. Peripheral and coronary artery disease.
IV	— — —		↑	Familial or dietary. Also oral contraceptives. Probable association with atherosclerosis.
V	+ +	↑	↑	Rare. Abdominal pain. Pancreatitis. Not definitely associated with atherosclerosis.

differ from those in the human in not being associated with thrombosis.

3. There is a high incidence of ischaemic (atherosclerotic) heart disease in individuals with elevated plasma lipid levels, particularly if they have familial hyperlipoproteinaemia.

4. There is increasing epidemiological evidence that high levels of high density lipoproteins (HDL) are protective against ischaemic heart disease in contrast to the adverse effects of high levels of low density lipoproteins.

Hyperlipoproteinaemias are subdivided into several types, based on whether cholesterol, triglycerides or chylomicrons are increased (see Table 8). Only Types II and III are clearly associated with coronary atherosclerosis, although a relationship to Type IV seems probable.

Certain other types of disorder which disturb lipid metabolism are associated with a high incidence of coronary disease. These include myxoedema and diabetes mellitus. Women who have had bilateral öophorectomy are liable to develop hypercholesterolaemia and premature coronary disease.

Even when these specific disease processes are excluded, there is a strong relationship between hyperlipidaemia and the risk of developing coronary disease at a relatively early age. Thus, in countries such as the United States and the United Kingdom, in which the average plasma cholesterol level of the community is relatively high, there is a much higher incidence of coronary artery disease than in those countries in which hypercholesterolaemia is rare. In long-term studies of whole populations, it has been shown that the higher the level of plasma cholesterol, the greater is the individual's risk of developing coronary artery disease. The cause of the high cholesterol levels is not yet fully established, although it seems likely that it is related in part to dietary factors. A high content of saturated fat (mainly of animal origin) in the diet is particularly suspect.

Diagnosis and treatment of coronary atherosclerosis. Coronary atherosclerosis cannot be diagnosed on clinical grounds until ischaemic heart disease produces manifest symptoms and signs. It is possible to demonstrate coronary artery disease radiologically either by visualizing coronary artery calcification or by coronary angiography, but the latter investigation is seldom justifiable in asymptomatic patients.

An increased liability to atherosclerosis can be suspected in individuals with a strong family history of coronary disease and in those exhibiting the signs of hypercholesterolaemia such as xanthomatous deposits and a presenile corneal arcus.

Coronary atherosclerosis is a slowly advancing process, which starts in youth. By the time symptoms develop, fibrosis and calcification have occurred which limit the benefit to be expected from lowering plasma lipids. There is no convincing proof of the benefit of lowering lipid levels either in hyperlipidaemic individuals without evidence of coronary disease or in patients with clinical disease; indeed as a long-term trial with clofibrate suggested, there may be a risk of promoting other, mainly gastrointestinal disorders. Nonetheless, it seems reasonable to treat patients who have hyperlipidaemia with appropriate therapy. This should start with weight reduction. In Type II hyperlipidaemia a low cholesterol diet is desirable; in Type IV carbohydrates and alcohol intake must be reduced. If dietary modifications fail, either cholestyramine (16 to 32 g per day) or clofibrate (2 g per day) may be tried.

Predisposing factors in ischaemic heart disease

The aetiology of ischaemic heart disease is still largely obscure, but a number of predisposing factors have been suggested from clinical and epidemiological studies. The characteristics which have been associated with the highest risk of ischaemic heart disease are hyperlipidaemia, hypertension, obesity, a strong family history and cigarette consumption.

Hyperlipidaemia (see p. 131). High serum cholesterol and triglyceride levels are common in the younger patients with ischaemic heart disease, but not particularly so in the older victims.

Hypertension. The higher the blood pressure, whether systolic or diastolic, the greater is the risk of developing ischaemic heart disease. Hypertension may contribute to its development in two ways: by accelerating the development of arterial disease and by increasing the work load on the left ventricle.

Obesity. Though common in patients with ischaemic heart disease, it cannot necessarily be implicated as a causal factor.

Family history. Coronary artery disease often occurs in several members of the same family and there can be little doubt that hereditary factors are involved. To some extent, at least, the familial incidence is due to the inheritance of hyperlipidaemia or hypertension.

Cigarette smoking. Heavy consumption of cigarettes is associated with a high incidence of myocardial infarction and sudden death, but less convincingly with angina pectoris.

Physical activity. There is some evidence that physical exercise has some protective effect — perhaps by encouraging the enlargement of the coronary arteries and their anastomoses.

Mental stress. This factor is difficult to evaluate, but claims have been made that ischaemic heart disease is commoner in individuals with excessive drive and impatience.

Diabetes. Ischaemic heart disease appears to develop more frequently and at an earlier age in those with diabetes than in other individuals.

Factors precipitating acute myocardial infarction

Physical exertion. There is much conflicting evidence on the role of excessive physical exertion in promoting the development of acute myocardial infarction. In general, it can be said that in the vast majority of cases no such provoking factor can be found but in a few, circumstantial evidence suggests that severe physical strain has precipitated myocardial infarction or sudden death.

Surgical operations and haemorrhage. Acute myocardial infarction is a not uncommon complication of major surgery and of acute blood loss, such as that from a gastric or duodenal ulcer. It is probable that the precipitating factor in both cases is hypotension leading to a critical reduction in coronary blood flow.

Angina pectoris

Definition

As originally described by Heberden, angina pectoris was a symptom complex; there was no implied association with the heart. Today, the term is still used to describe a symptom, but one which is the consequence of myocardial ischaemia.

Anginal pain has four major characteristics: its location, its character, its relation to exercise and its duration.

The location of angina pectoris

Angina pectoris is most often felt behind the middle or upper third of the sternum. Even when the discomfort may be more obvious in another area, the sternal region is usually involved to a greater or lesser extent. Angina may also be felt in the lower sternal or xiphisternal region, over both sides of the chest, more commonly the left, in the neck and lower jaw and in both arms, again particularly the left. It may affect only the upper arm, but often reaches the elbow, the wrist or the fingers. In some patients the elbow region escapes and the patient is aware of discomfort in the upper arm and a tingling feeling in the fingers. Rarely, it may radiate through to the left scapular region. It is very unusual for the pain to be located predominantly under the left nipple and virtually never is it confined to this area.

The character of angina pectoris

Angina pectoris is most frequently likened to a pressing feeling, a tight band, or a heavy weight. Many patients deny actual pain and refer only to a sense of discomfort. It is not usually severe but can cause much anxiety and distress. It is not stabbing in quality, but the terms 'sharp' (perhaps meaning rather intense) and 'burning' are sometimes used. The sensation appreciated in the neck and arms is often of a different type. In the neck, it is frequently described as 'choking', in the jaw it is often a dull ache or 'like toothache'. The feeling in the arms is usually one of numbness, heaviness or tingling.

The relationship of angina pectoris to exercise and other provoking factors

Angina pectoris is usually provoked by exertion, nearly always that of walking, particularly up hill. The amount of exercise required to produce angina varies from time to time in any individual, but it is more readily provoked after a heavy meal or in cold weather. Emotion is also an important provoking factor; angina often develops during sexual intercourse and may be induced by anger and irritation.

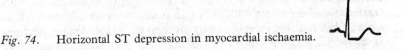

Fig. 74. Horizontal ST depression in myocardial ischaemia.

Some patients experience nocturnal angina, which wakes them up. In some cases this may be due to dreams, but it is probable that increased coronary artery tone, which is maximal in the early morning, is usually responsible.

Angina pectoris may be provoked by several different types of tachycardia, particularly paroxysmal tachycardia associated with very rapid ventricular rates. Anaemia also contributes to its development, although it is unusual for it to do so in the absence of coronary atherosclerosis.

The duration of the attack

Most attacks last 1 to 3 minutes. Their duration is seldom less than 30 seconds or more than 15 minutes, although a vague sensation of discomfort may persist after the pain has stopped.

Other symptoms and signs in angina pectoris

Some patients complain of breathlessness accompanying the anginal pain. Other symptoms include flatulence, feelings of faintness, and acute anxiety. Tachycardia and a rise in blood pressure may be noted during an attack but there are usually no abnormal signs.

The electrocardiogram

In between attacks of angina pectoris, the ECG is usually normal. There may, however, be evidence of old myocardial infarction, or non-specific changes such as flattening or inversion of T waves in the leads in which these are normally upright, or signs of a conduction defect. If the patient is seen during an attack there are usually well-marked abnormalities which take the form of a horizontal or downward sloping depression of the ST segment (Fig. 74). Similar changes may be provoked by an exercise test (see below).

Diagnosis

In the majority of patients, a confident diagnosis can be made from the history. There is usually no problem in determining the location of the pain and the factors that provoke it, but patients often find it difficult to find the words to describe the sensation and estimates of the duration of the attack are often inaccurate. Most weight must therefore be placed on the first two elements. If the pain is located in the left sub-mammary region, or if it lasts for only a few seconds, it is almost certainly not of ischaemic origin. Angina is seldom associated with tenderness of the chest wall, although it may occasionally be so. It is usually, but not always, relieved by glyceryl trinitrate. Angina pectoris is unlikely if walking is not a provoking factor, but some patients take so little exercise that the symptom arises only on emotion or at night.

Physical examination and investigations other than electro-cardiography are of comparatively little value. However, because angina pectoris is often associated with hypertension, with diabetes and with aortic valve disease, the characteristic findings of these conditions may be observed.

The most certain evidence of angina pectoris is the presence of characteristic ST segment changes during an attack. As spontaneous attacks are seldom witnessed, it may be necessary to carry out an exercise test. The patient may be made to exercise on steps, a bicycle ergometer or a treadmill, preferable until the chest discomfort is provoked. Standard and chest lead ECGs should be obtained during exercise and during the first 10 minutes of rest. A positive exercise test is one which shows horizontal downward sloping ST depression of 1 mm or more (Fig. 74). Interpretation is often difficult and many patients with undoubted angina do not have a positive ECG exercise test. Furthermore, a 'positive' test may be seen in those with normal hearts. ST segments which slope upwards from the J point should not be regarded as evidence of ischaemia as they are often seen in normal individuals with tachycardia (see Fig. 18).

Unfortunately, even after careful history-taking and ECG examination, one may remain uncertain as to whether or not a patient has angina pectoris. Radionuclide studies with thallium-201 may be helpful, but in some cases it is necessary to resort to coronary arteriography to establish the presence of coronary arterial disease. The use of this expensive and potentially hazardous procedure is seldom justified for diagnostic purposes alone, but it is essential in patients being considered for coronary artery surgery. It involves the introduction of specially designed catheters into the brachial or femoral arteries. The left and right coronary arteries are entered and radio-opaque medium is injected. Ciné-angiographic records are obtained in various positions to ensure a good visualization of all the major vessels. Left ventriculography is also undertaken to assess myocardial function.

Deaths from coronary angiography may result from coronary occlusion and dissection. Ventricular fibrillation may occur also, but is usually corrected without difficulty. The mortality of this investigation is between 0.1 and 0.5%.

Differential diagnosis

Although the diagnosis of angina can usually be established on the basis of the history and ECG, there are a number of other conditions which have to be considered in the differential diagnosis. Perhaps the most common difficulty arises with musculoskeletal pains in the chest wall. Frequently no cause is found for such pains which are often associated with tenderness and usually located on one side of the chest rather than centrally. These pains are most likely to be provoked by such actions as lifting and pulling, which produce tension of the muscles attached to the ribs. Amongst identifiable musculoskeletal conditions may be included Tietze's syndrome (in which there is an inflammation of one or more costochondral junctions), a slipping rib cartilage, fractured ribs, or metastatic lesions in ribs. In these conditions, unlike angina, there is tenderness and the symptoms may be aggravated by inspiration. The pain of cervical spondylosis is sometimes most severe in the upper chest region and accompanied by discomfort in the shoulders and arms.

Stabbing pains under the left breast and persistent aches in the same region are common and are most unlikely to be due to ischaemic heart disease. It is often not possible to establish their cause, but these symptoms are very common in those with anxiety neurosis.

Disorders of the gastrointestinal tract may be difficult to differentiate from angina pectoris. Oesophageal reflux, often associated with hiatus hernia, gives rise to a central chest pain, but this seldom radiates to the arms, is of a more burning or bursting character, and is more readily provoked by stooping or lying flat, although it may be produced by exercise. The pain of peptic ulcer is usually situated in the epigastric region, and is associated with tenderness. It is related to food rather than to exertion and is usually relieved by alkalis or milk and not by glyceryl trinitrate. Cholecystitis and cholelithiasis may give rise to pain in the lower sternal region, but there is usually tenderness either in the epigastrium or in the right subcostal area; there is frequently associated nausea, and the pain is not related to exertion. It is important to recognize that these gastrointestinal conditions, particularly hiatus hernia and cholecystitis, are common in patients with ischaemic heart disease, and the presence of one of these disorders does not preclude the coexistence of angina pectoris.

Prognosis

Most patients who develop angina pectoris live a normal or nearly normal life for many years. Symptoms are liable to vary from time to time, becoming worse in winter and improving the subsequent summer. They may disappear altogether for months or years.

It is difficult to give an accurate prognosis for any individual, but the outlook is relatively unfavourable if there is associated hypertension, advanced age, cardiac failure or preceding myocardial infarction.

Coronary angiographic studies have shown that the prognosis is good if disease is confined to one artery. By contrast, severe narrowing of the left main coronary artery and diffuse lesions of all three arteries are associated with a high risk of early death.

Most patients live for 5 years and about one-third live for 10 years or more. The risk of sudden death or acute myocardial infarction is always present; before such events occur, there is frequently an exacerbation of the angina.

Treatment

The general management of the patient with angina pectoris is of paramount importance. The anxiety that the diagnosis arouses may cause incapacity, and it is important to emphasize the relatively good prognosis. The patient should be advised to avoid intense cold, walking into a wind or unnecessarily up hill, and taking large meals. He should be told to think about his daily programme in advance so that, for example, he does not have to hurry for a bus or train. Physical exercise should be encouraged provided it does not induce discomfort, but sudden strenuous effort should be avoided. There is no convincing evidence that low fat diets are of any value in the treatment of ischaemic heart disease, but a reduction in saturated fats with some substitution by polyunsaturated fats seems a reasonably policy, especially for the younger patient. Obesity must be corrected. Cigarette smoking should be discouraged because it may provoke angina and increase the risk of acute myocardial infarction.

Nitrates. The most helpful drug in the management of angina pectoris is nitroglycerin (glyceryl trinitrate or trinitrin). It is effective in preventing attacks and stops them within a minute or so. It should be given sublingually in a dose of 0.2 to 0.5 mg. Large doses may produce a bursting sensation in the head even more distressing than angina. Many patients are afraid of becoming drug dependent and must be reassured that the tablets may be taken as necessary, and that the drug is not addictive. They should be encouraged to use them prophylactically if they anticipate an attack. Long-acting nitrates, such as isosorbide dinitrate 10 to 30 mg three to four times a day, are effective in preventing anginal attacks but commonly induce headache. The tendency to headache diminishes with confirmed use.

Beta-adrenoceptor blocking drugs. These are now given routinely to all but the mildest case, unless there are contraindications to their use. They block the action of catecholamines in increasing heart rate, blood pressure and cardiac contractility and thereby limit the myocardial oxygen needs on exercise or psychological stress. Unfortunately, they can exacerbate cardiac failure and may cause bronchospasm in those with obstructive airways disease. When given to patients free of heart failure or a history of asthma or bronchitis, beta-blocking drugs seldom give rise to serious side-effects but minor ones are quite common. These include fatigue, unpleasant dreams and nausea.

In general, the choice of a particular beta-blocker is not of importance, but it is preferable to use a cardioselective drug for patients with suspected obstructive airways disease or insulin-dependent diabetes (see p. 76). Compliance is more likely to be achieved if one uses a preparation which need be given only once or twice a day, such as atenolol, sotalol or nadolol or the long-acting formulations of propranolol and metoprolol. A lower dosage of a beta-blocker may be effective when it is combined with a long-acting nitrate or calcium antagonist.

Calcium antagonists. Calcium has an essential role in both the electrical and mechanical functions of the heart. It is also involved in the contraction of coronary and peripheral arteries. As described on p. 28, the entry of calcium ions into the cell is an important component in the generation of the action potential, being partially responsible for depolarization and for the plateau phase. The slow calcium current is largely responsible for depolarization of the atrioventricular node. Calcium in the cell blocks the action of troponin, which itself inhibits the actin myosin reaction. In the resting phase, calcium is bound to a number of structures within the cell including the nucleus, mitochondria, sarcolemma, the T system and the sarcoplasmic reticulum. The small quantity of calcium that enters the cell during depolarization is not sufficient by itself to initiate contraction but appears to stimulate the release of the ion from the sarcoplasmic reticulum and this in turn inhibits troponin and stimulates the actin-myosin contraction. The process is reversed during relaxation. The rate of development of tension in the myocardium and the total tension developed depends on the rate at which calcium becomes available and the amount which becomes available, respectively.

The two main calcium antagonists currently available are verapamil (Cordilox, Isoptin) and nifedipine (Adalat). They differ in that verapamil has a potent electrophysiological effect, depressing the action potential in the atrioventricular node specifically. It tends to lead to bradycardia and is an effective treatment for supraventricular tachycardias involving the atrioventricular node. Its use in angina pectoris is probably due to a combination of peripheral and coronary vasodilatation and a reduction of the tachycardia which occurs on exertion. It has been found effective both in exercise-induced angina and coronary spasm.

Nifedipine has little effect on the atrioventricular node; it exerts its main pharmacological effect on the peripheral and coronary arteries.

The peripheral vasodilatation it induces leads to a reflex tachycardia and may also lead to hypotension. Although effective in exercise-induced angina, it may aggravate it because of tachycardia. It has been found particularly helpful in the management of coronary artery spasm but when used in exercise-induced angina is better combined with a beta-blocking drug. It is also being used in the management of hypertension in association with other antihypertensive drugs. Many patients suffer from side-effects with nifedipine but they are seldom serious. Some 20 to 30% have peripheral oedema as a result of vasodilatation. Others complain of headaches, gastrointestinal disturbances, flushing, dizziness and syncope.

Some other antianginal drugs such as perhexiline (Pexid) and prenylamine (Synadrin) have some calcium-blocking properties but these probably do not explain their activity. Perhexiline in a dosage of 100 to 200 mg daily is an effective antianginal agent but may produce dizziness, malaise and, in long-term use, peripheral neuropathy and liver enzyme disturbances. It should be given only under careful supervision. The same is true of prenylamine which can produce prolongation of the QT interval and ventricular tachycardia with syncope.

Coronary artery bypass surgery. Operations to bypass narrowed segments of coronary arteries by using a saphenous vein graft are usually effective in relieving angina. In this procedure, one end of the graft is attached to the aorta and the other to an affected artery beyond the most distal area of obstruction as demonstrated by coronary arteriography. Grafts may, as necessary, be inserted into all three major arteries and their larger branches. The operation should not be undertaken on patients whose left ventricle functions so poorly that there is little prospect of benefit as the mortality is high. In properly selected cases, angina is abolished in more than 50% and greatly improved in a further 30 to 40%. Most grafts remain patent for at least 5 years but after this time there is a tendency for symptoms to recur because of the progression of the disease. In most centres, the mortality of the operation is less than 2%. As well as relieving angina, evidence is accruing that coronary artery bypass surgery improves prognosis in patients with severe disease of the left main coronary artery or of the three major vessels.

Surgery is indicated if angina has not responded to full medical treatment but should also be considered as a measure to improve prognosis, particularly in younger patients with advanced coronary lesions even in the absence of severe symptoms.

Coronary artery saphenous vein bypass is indicated for patients with chronic angina whose lives are severely restricted in spite of full medical treatment. The effect of the procedure on prognosis is as yet unknown except that it appears to prolong the life of those with left main coronary artery disease.

Percutaneous transluminal coronary angioplasty. Specially designed catheters permit the insertion of a balloon into a coronary artery which, when inflated, can dilate a narrowed segment. How it does so is not yet certain but cracking and subsequent fibrosis of atheromatous plaques seems to be one mechanism. Although effective in improving coronary blood flow, its value is limited by the fact that the lesion must be relatively proximal, concentric and uncalcified. The best results have been achieved in single vessel disease causing severe symptoms, but this is rather rare. The scope of this technique, however, may increase in the future, particularly if patients are investigated at an earlier stage of the disease process.

Myocardial infarction

The major presenting symptom is chest discomfort. This is predominantly in the sternal region, but may radiate to both sides of the chest, to the jaw, to the shoulders and to one or both arms. It is usually described as tight, pressing, heavy or constricting. Sometimes the patient may deny 'pain' and describe a discomfort, not amounting to pain, in the centre of the chest. Although it can be brief, the pain usually lasts for more than half an hour and may continue for several hours. Unlike the pain of angina, it is seldom associated with exertion and it is not relieved by rest or glyceryl trinitrate. The pain may be maximal at the onset, but often increases in intensity for a period of minutes or hours and then remains constant until it gradually recedes. Frequently, the patient gives a history of the recent onset of angina or the exacerbation of pre-existing angina in the preceding days or weeks.

In some patients, pain is overshadowed by other symptoms, such as breathlessness or syncope. Occasionally, the pain is obscured because the infarction develops during anaesthesia or at the time of a cerebrovascular accident. Rarely, infarction may be truly pain-free.

Once the pain has been controlled, the patient may remain free of symptoms and make an uninterrupted recovery. However, in a substantial proportion of cases, there develop one or more of a number of complications, of which the most important are arrhythmias, cardiogenic shock and left ventricular failure. These complications, which will be considered in detail later, are the common causes of death and are responsible for many of the abnormal physical signs which may be observed.

Physical signs

During the earliest stages of the attack, the patient is obviously distressed, and may be sweaty and cold. The general appearance improves when the pain is controlled and often, within a few hours, the patient looks well.

The pulse may be normal in volume and rate, but in severe attacks it is small and fast. Arrhythmias or bradycardia are also common.

The blood pressure usually falls progressively over a period of hours and days, reaching its minimum some time during the first week, subsequently increasing slowly over the next two or three weeks. There may be, however, a sharp fall in blood pressure at the onset of the infarction, which may progress to the severe hypotension of cardiogenic shock, or may resolve. Transient hypertension, perhaps resulting from intense pain, is sometimes observed.

The jugular venous pressure is usually normal or slightly elevated early in the course of acute myocardial infarction; it is seldom markedly elevated due to right-sided heart failure.

The apex beat, which is often difficult to feel, may be displaced outwards. Between the apex and the left sternal edge a systolic pulsation may be detectable, due to a protrusion of the infarcted anterior wall of the heart.

The first and second heart sounds are often soft. A fourth (or atrial) sound can be heard in most cases; a third heart sound is common when there is heart failure or shock.

A soft pansystolic murmur at the apex is not uncommon and is caused by mitral regurgitation either as a result of papillary muscle malfunction or secondary to dilatation of the left ventricle. Rarely, a loud systolic murmur may develop at the left sternal edge, due to a rupture of the ventricular septum, or at the apex, due to rupture of a papillary muscle. A transient pericardial rub occurs in perhaps 20% of patients, usually on the second or third day.

Pulmonary crepitations are common but of little importance unless they are widespread and numerous because of pulmonary oedema.

Most of the abnormal physical signs described disappear within a few days of the onset of infarction, except in the most severely affected patients.

A fever, seldom exceeding $101°F$ ($38°C$), usually commences within the first 24 hours and subsides in under a week. There is often a slight leucocytosis and an increase in the erythrocyte sedimentation rate. The pyrexia, leucocytosis and raised ESR represent a reaction to myocardial necrosis.

Early complications

Disturbances of rate, rhythm and conduction

These occur in 95% of patients with acute myocardial infarction. In

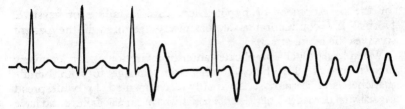

Fig. 75. Ventricular ectopic beat interrupting the T wave of a preceding beat. The second R-on-T beat initiates ventricular fibrillation.

about half of these, they are severe enough to be of clinical importance.

Sinus tachycardia is common and is an index of severity. Sinus bradycardia frequently occurs at the onset of infarction, being sometimes part of the vasovagal syndrome. It is particularly associated with inferior myocardial infarction, but may be provoked by morphine and digitalis. It is usually benign, but can cause hypotension or encourage the development of ectopic rhythms.

The atrial tachycardias, including atrial fibrillation, which occur in about 15% of patients, may precipitate cardiac failure or shock. Atrial arrhythmias are usually transient and seldom last for more than a few days.

Ventricular ectopic beats are almost invariable; they are usually of no consequence, but those of the R-on-T variety (Fig. 75) may be precursors of ventricular fibrillation.

Ventricular tachycardia is dangerous both because it can cause shock and cardiac failure and because it may progress to ventricular fibrillation.

Ventricular fibrillation is the most important single cause of death in acute myocardial infarction and occurs in 8 to 10% of hospitalized patients. In about half of these cases, there has been no preceding shock or cardiac failure and the ventricular fibrillation is 'primary'. In the remainder, it can be regarded as being secondary to these complications.

Heart block occurs in about 5% of patients with acute myocardial infarction. It is particularly common when the inferior surface of the heart is affected because the right coronary artery supplies both this aspect of the myocardium and the junctional tissues. First degree block (prolonged PR interval) is of little significance except as a precursor of more advanced block. Second degree block, usually of the Wenckebach type, is potentially dangerous because bradycardia may be poorly tolerated and because of the risk of progression to complete heart block and ventricular asystole. In spite of the risk, most patients tolerate these conduction defects well but need to be observed closely for the development of hypotension, cardiac failure or asystole. Normal AV conduction is almost always restored if the patient survives the acute attack.

When heart block complicates anterior infarction, it carries a very high mortality. The block results from damage to both bundle branches and is almost invariably accompanied by widespread myocardial damage. The patients usually have cardiac failure and have a bad prognosis even if their heart block is successfully treated.

Cardiogenic shock

As mentioned, the patient at the onset of infarction is often pale, distressed and hypotensive. This situation, which is often transient, may be attributed to pain and should not be described as cardiogenic shock. This term should be restricted to those patients who have the clinical picture of hypotension, with cold cyanosed extremities, sweating, and mental torpor, which lasts at least half an hour, or who deteriorate rapidly until the blood pressure can no longer be recorded. There is a low cardiac output and a peripheral resistance insufficient to compensate for this, together with oliguria, hypoxia, and acidosis. Arrhythmias and cardiac failure are frequently associated and the mortality is 80 to 90% irrespective of treatment. Shock is largely the result of severe myocardial damage with more than 40% of the ventricular wall being infarcted. Occasionally, the shock picture is accounted for by arrhythmias such as ventricular tachycardia or complete heart block, in which case correction of the arrhythmia may result in recovery. In a few patients, particularly those who have been receiving diuretics, hypovolaemia may be a factor. Rarely, a surgically correctable disorder, such as a ruptured papillary muscle or a ventricular septal defect may be responsible.

Left ventricular failure

This is seldom present at the onset, but develops within 48 hours in perhaps two-thirds of patients with acute myocardial infarction. It can be suspected from tachycardia, a third heart sound, widespread pulmonary crepitations and pulmonary venous congestion or oedema on the chest radiograph. Catheterization using a Swan-Ganz or similar catheter, will show a pulmonary wedge pressure in excess of 20 mmHg.

Right ventricular failure

A slight elevation of the jugular venous pressure is common in the first days after acute infarction. Infarction of the right ventricle, which is almost always associated with inferior wall infarction, may cause a high venous pressure and, rarely, the shock syndrome, even in the presence of good left ventricular function. The classical features of failure of the right side of the heart — peripheral oedema and hepatomegaly — are rare and take several days to develop even in the patient with severe myocardial damage.

Pulmonary embolism and infarction

Twenty or more years ago, pulmonary embolism caused death in about 3% of all patients admitted to hospital with acute myocardial infarction. It has become relatively rare presumably because patients are now mobilized as soon as possible. It is usually preceded by deep vein thrombosis in the legs, but this may not be clinically evident. Pulmonary embolism should be suspected when there is the sudden development of hypotension or right heart failure some days after the onset of myocardial infarction, and also when there is a pleural type of chest pain with or without haemoptysis.

Systemic arterial embolism

Embolism may occur from mural thrombi situated in the left ventricle or left atrium. Hemiplegia is the most common result, but there may be occlusion of any artery.

Cerebrovascular accidents

Cerebrovascular accidents may precede, accompany or follow acute myocardial infarction. As mentioned, cerebral embolism is one cause, but cerebral infarction may develop as a result of the fall in blood flow in those with cerebral vascular disease.

Cardiac rupture

Rupture through the wall of the left ventricle is responsible for about 10% of all deaths and particularly affects the elderly and the hypertensive. It is most likely to occur during the first few days and usually causes sudden death. Occasionally, the picture may be that of cardiac tamponade.

Rupture through the interventricular septum occurs in about one in every 200 patients with acute myocardial infarction. This produces the sudden onset of severe heart failure, accompanied by a systolic thrill and murmur at the left sternal edge. The patient deteriorates rapidly over a period of a few days; survival for more than a few weeks is unusual.

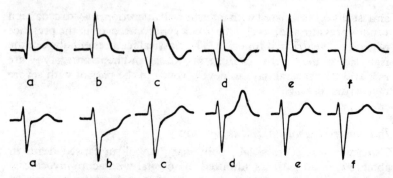

Fig. 76.   a, b, c, d, e and f, showing the progression of changes recorded by an electrode facing the area of infarction (upper series) and from an electrode placed distant from the infarction (lower series). Note the early development of ST elevation and broad Q wave in the record obtained from the electrode facing the infarction. Subsequently the ST segment becomes iso-electric and the T wave inverted. Finally, the T wave becomes upright, but the pathological Q wave persists. In the lower series, so-called 'reciprocal' ST depression can be seen in b and c.

Papillary muscle rupture and malfunction

When a papillary muscle ruptures, a loud apical pansystolic murmur appears in association with the sudden development of left ventricular failure. Death usually occurs within a few hours or days. Partial rupture may produce the features of mitral regurgitation with or without left-sided heart failure.

The electrocardiogram

The ECG is virtually always transiently or permanently abnormal after acute myocardial infarction. Because the ECG diagnosis of infarction depends upon the observation of a sequence of changes with time, serial records are vital.

The characteristic abnormalities are: the appearance of abnormally large Q waves, the development of ST segment elevation and the development of T wave inversion (Fig. 76). Although the precise mechanisms responsible for these ECG changes are not yet determined, it is probable that the Q wave changes are the result of muscle death, that the ST abnormalities are due to muscle injury, and that the T wave abnormalities are due to ischaemia.

Dead tissue, which is unpolarized, takes no part in electrical activation, but can transmit changes in the electrical potential in other

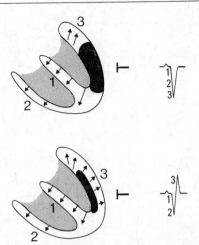

Fig. 77.   (A) The appearances recorded from an electrode over the left
ventricle in extensive left ventricular transmural infarction. The
initial vector is directed, as usual, away from the left ventricle due
to depolarization of the septum, and is followed by that of
depolarization of the right ventricle and non-infarcted areas of the
left ventricle in a direction away from the infarction. A totally
negative deflection (QS) is obtained. (B) The appearances obtained
from an electrode placed over the left ventricle when the infarction
is less extensive. The initial vector is, as usual, directed from left to
right across the septum, and provides the first component of the Q
wave. Subsequently, the right ventricle and the non-infarcted
areas of the endocardium of the left ventricle are depolarized,
continuing the Q wave. Finally, depolarization reaches the
epicardium superficial to the infarcted area, producing a terminal
R wave.

tissues. In Fig. 77 can be seen the effect of infarcted tissue on
depolarization of the heart. With the electrode situated facing the left
ventricle, depolarization commences, as usual, from the left side of the
septum to the right (vector 1). Subsequently depolarization spreads to
affect the right ventricle and those parts of the left ventricle away from
the infarct. Vector 2 is therefore directed away from the electrode and
produces a deepening of the Q wave. Finally, the muscle around the
area of the infarct may become activated and produce a terminal R
wave (vector 3). If infarction involves the full thickness of the muscle, a
QS wave may be produced.

In the injured zone, the cells remain polarized, but the
transmembrane potential is less than normal, because of loss of cellular
potassium. Repolarization of the injured tissue occurs more quickly
than normal and a voltage gradient develops between the normal and
injured tissue. This is reflected in ST elevation over the area of injury.

(a)

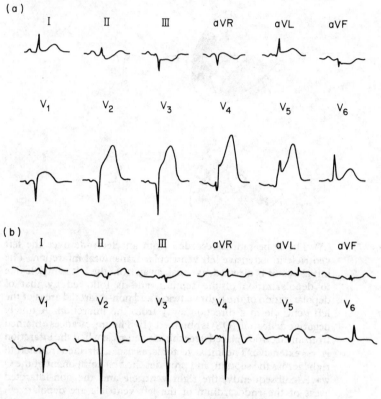

Fig. 78.   Anterior myocardial infarction. (A) Recent infarction with ST elevation in aVL and V1 to V5; reciprocal ST depression in III and aVF. Large Q waves in V1 to V3. (B) One day later ST elevation in I, II, aVL, Q waves V1–V4. ST segments lower with change in shape V1–V5; T waves are inverted in I, aVL and V2 to V6.

The T wave abnormalities are believed to be due to changes in the direction of repolarization in ischaemic tissue.

Q waves may take several hours to develop after the onset of infarction. They usually persist indefinitely because the scar tissue which replaces the infarcted muscle is similarly uninvolved in electrical activation. Normally, Q waves in leads facing the left ventricle do not exceed 2 mm in depth or 0.03 sec in width. Q waves and QS waves are normal in aVR, and are commonly found in V1 and V2. Deep Q waves are often also seen normally in lead III. The Q wave in lead III should only be considered definitely abnormal if it exceeds 0.03 sec in duration, and if it is accompanied by Q waves in either lead II or aVF. The 'normal' Q wave in lead III usually diminishes or

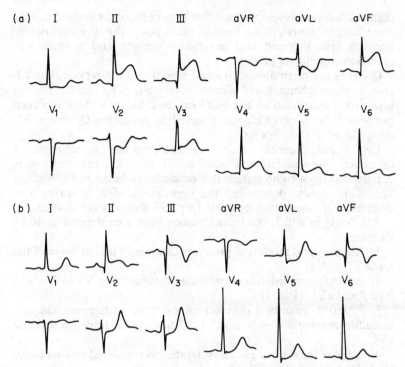

Fig. 79. Inferior myocardial infarction. (A) Recent infarction with ST elevation in II, III and aVF; reciprocal ST depression in I, aVL, V1 and V2. (B) Q waves have become more prominent in II, III and aVF. ST elevation less; T waves inverting.

disappears on deep inspiration, whereas the 'pathological' Q wave persists.

ST segment elevation often commences within minutes of the onset of myocardial infarction but may be delayed for many hours. In the earliest stage, the elevated ST segment may retain the normal upward concavity, but before long it becomes convex and 'coves' downwards to the T wave. ST elevation is confined to those leads facing the infarct. In leads distant from the infarct, so-called 'reciprocal' ST depression is often seen; in fact, this probably represents acute ischaemia in the subjacent territory. The ST segment usually returns to the isoelectric line within 48–72 hours. Persistent elevation suggests a ventricular aneurysm.

T wave inversion occurs slightly later than ST elevation during the course of myocardial infarction; there is a stage in the evolution of the ECG appearances in which the ST segment is returning towards the isoelectric line whilst the T wave is becoming inverted. Later, the ST segment becomes isoelectric and the T wave becomes symmetrically, often deeply, inverted. As healing takes place, the T wave usually becomes less inverted and eventually upright and normal, but inversion sometimes persists.

Q waves are often absent in small myocardial infarctions, but ST and T wave changes are almost invariable. The recognition of myocardial infarction on the ECG can be difficult if there has been previous infarction which has resulted in persistent Q waves, ST elevation or T wave inversion.

Left bundle branch block may also obscure the changes of infarction, because in this conduction disorder the septum is depolarized from right-to-left; this produces an initial R wave in left ventricular leads, preventing the appearance of a Q wave. The diagnosis can sometimes be made from ST and T wave changes.

The leads in which the infarct patterns are seen depend upon its location.

1. Anteroseptal infarction produces changes in one or more of the leads V1 to V4.

2. Anterolateral infarction produces changes from V4 to V6, and lead I and aVL (Fig. 78).

3. Anterior infarction is indicated by more widespread changes including most of the leads from V1 to V6, as well as leads I and II and aVL.

4. Inferior (or diaphragmatic) infarction is registered by changes in leads II, III and aVF (Fig. 79).

5. Strictly posterior myocardial infarction does not produce Q waves in the standard 12 leads. However, the loss of electrical activity from the posterior part of the left ventricle, leads to a tall R in V1, because the forces depolarizing the right ventricle are unopposed.

Further leads may be required for infarcts in unusual sites, V7 and V8 being helpful in lateral infarcts, and leads recorded in the second or third intercostal spaces in high anterior and lateral infarcts.

The location of the infarct is of comparatively little prognostic importance, apart from associations with certain complications. Thus, sinus bradycardia and atrioventricular block are relatively more common with inferior infarction, because the right coronary artery usually supplies the sinus node, atrioventricular node and bundle of His as well as the inferior aspect of the heart.

Serum enzymes (Fig. 80)

Certain enzymes, present in high concentration in cardiac tissue, are released by necrosis of the myocardium. Their activity in the serum, therefore, rises. As there is no enzyme that is exclusive to cardiac muscle it is desirable to estimate the levels of at least two enzymes to ensure that any changes are indeed due to cardiac damage.

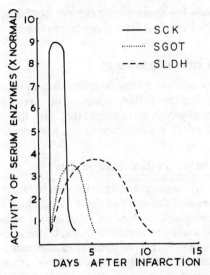

Fig. 80.. Changes in serum enzyme activity following myocardial infarction. Serum creatine phosphokinase (SCK) increases earlier and to a relatively greater extent than SGOT and SLDH (see text).

Serum creatine phosphokinase (SCK)

Creatine phosphokinase, which occurs in heart, skeletal muscle and brain, rises within 6 hours of the onset of infarction, reaching a peak in 18 to 24 hours. It may become normal after 72 hours. Apart from myocardial infarction, abnormally high levels occur in muscle diseases, in cerebrovascular damage, after muscular exercise and with intramuscular injections.

The MB isoenzyme of CK is virtually specific for cardiac muscle but at present estimations are not available in all laboratories.

Serum glutamic oxalo-acetic transaminase (SGOT)

This enzyme, also called aspartate transaminase (ASAT), is found particularly in the heart, skeletal muscle, brain, liver and kidney. After infarction, the SGOT rises in about 12 hours and reaches its peak in 24 to 36 hours, returning to normal from the third to the fifth day.

Serum lactate dehydrogenase (SLDH)

These enzymes are found in the heart, but also in red cells. They rise relatively late after infarction, reach their peak 24 to 48 hours afterwards, and may remain abnormal from 1 to 3 weeks. Unfortunately, even slight haemolysis raises their level. Isoenzymes are more specific.

Diagnostic levels for these enzymes have not been quoted as they vary considerably from one laboratory to another.

Radionuclide investigations

Perfusion defects can be demonstrated using thallium-201 in most patients within the first few hours, but may disappear later; technetium pyrophosphate concentrates in the infarcted area producing a 'hot spot', several hours after the onset.

Diagnosis of myocardial infarction

In the majority of cases, the diagnosis can be suspected from the character, location and duration of chest pain. The persistence of the pain beyond 15 minutes, its lack of relationship to exercise and the failure of glyceryl trinitrate to relieve it usually serve to differentiate it from angina pectoris. The development of abnormal physical signs, and more particularly, the appearance of arrhythmias, shock and failure also suggest that infarction has occurred. Fever, leucocytosis and raised ESR indicate necrosis rather than ischaemia. The definitive diagnosis depends upon the recognition of typical ECG changes, supported by abnormal serum enzyme levels. Infarction is virtually certain if Q waves appear during the course of the illness, or if sequential ST and T wave changes are accompanied by transient but significant elevations of serum enzyme levels. Difficulties in diagnosis arise when the ECG or enzyme level changes are equivocal, or if serial ECG records or enzyme estimations are not made at appropriate times.

It is exceedingly difficult to differentiate some cases of acute myocardial infarction from unstable angina ('acute coronary insufficiency'). This is an ill-defined syndrome, in which there are attacks of ischaemic cardiac pain which are more prolonged and less related to exertion than are those of typical effort-induced angina pectoris, but in which the ECG changes do not indicate infarction, although persisting ST depression may suggest continuing ischaemia. By definition, enzyme changes are absent, and there is no fever, leucocytosis or rise in ESR.

The differentiation of myocardial infarction from massive pulmonary embolism may be difficult, but the chest pain of myocardial infarction is usually more severe and the breathlessness less marked. In pulmonary embolism, the ECG may be normal, or there may be characteristic abnormalities (see p. 261) and although there may be changes in SLDH and SGOT, SCK is usually not raised. In cases of doubt, pulmonary angiography or radio-isotope scanning of the chest may be helpful. Pulmonary infarction can be recognized by the location and pleural character of the pain and the radiographic appearances.

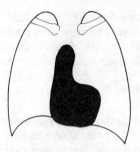

Fig. 81. Rounded protrusion on the left border of the heart in ventricular aneurysym.

Acute pericarditis may produce symptoms and signs very similar to those of an acute myocardial infarction (see p. 164). In many cases, the pericarditis is preceded by an upper respiratory infection and cough. The chest pain is more aching or stabbing in character, and is made worse by deep inspiration, movement or lying flat. Pyrexia often precedes the pain, whereas the temperature rise of myocardial infarction usually takes at least 12 hours to develop. Although pericarditis may produce ST elevation and T wave inversion, the ST elevation is concave upwards and is widespread rather than focal. Abnormal Q waves do not occur.

Dissecting aneurysm can cause severe central chest pain similar to that of acute myocardial infarction (see p. 254). The pain has usually a tearing quality, and tends to move into the upper dorsal spinal region and into the abdomen. The ECG does not show the changes of myocardial infarction. In cases of doubt, the arterial pulses should be repeatedly checked, and a chest radiograph obtained to determine whether there is mediastinal widening.

Late complications in acute myocardial infarction

The major risks of infarction occur during the first few days, but complications can arise over a period of several weeks. These include a further infarction, the recurrence of serious arrhythmias and sudden death. Amongst other complications are ventricular aneurysm formation, the post-myocardial infarction syndrome, and the shoulder–hand syndrome.

Ventricular aneurysm formation occurs in 10 to 20% of patients. Although the prognosis in those affected is reasonably good, the area of paradoxically moving non-contractile myocardium leads to extra work for the remaining heart muscle. In a few cases this contributes to cardiac failure, and there is also a risk of embolism from mural thrombi. The presence of an aneurysm is suggested by a systolic pulsation of the anterior chest wall lasting more than 3 weeks after the infarction. Other evidence includes persistent QS waves and ST elevation in the affected leads, an abnormal rounded protrusion from the left ventricular wall on the chest radiograph (Fig. 81), and paradoxical movement on fluoroscopy. These features are not always present. The aneurysm may be demonstrated by echocardiography and radionuclide studies, but it is best visualized by left ventriculography.

The post-myocardial infarction syndrome ('Dressler's') is characterized by pericardial pain, accompanied by pericardial rub, fever, pleurisy and a leucocytosis. It may occur at any time in the weeks or months after an infarction, and has been attributed to an immune reaction to necrotic cardiac muscle.

The shoulder–hand syndrome occurs in a small percentage of patients with acute myocardial infarction some weeks or months after infarction, particularly if the patient has been immobilized for long. There is limitation of movement of the shoulder joint, associated with tenderness and pain, and there may also be swelling of the hands and fingers with nodules on the palms. It is probable that prolonged disuse at the time of the acute illness is a factor in its production.

Prognosis

In about one-quarter of all episodes of acute myocardial infarction, death occurs suddenly within minutes of the onset. Such cases, of course, are seldom seen by a physician. The remainder of this discussion is concerned with the prognosis of those who survive this immediate period.

The overall mortality, excluding the very early deaths, is approximately 20 to 40%. The risk of death depends upon many factors, including the age of the patient, the previous history of coronary disease and the presence of other diseases, as well as the extent of the infarction.

The mortality of the acute attack rises sharply with age. Death occurs in about 10 to 20% in those under 50 years of age, 20% in those under 60, near 30% in those over 60, and 40 to 50% in the elderly. Mortality is higher in women than in men, but this is largely accounted for by the fact that infarction occurs relatively uncommonly in the younger female. The mortality is higher in those experiencing their second or later infarction than in those having their first, particularly when there has been preceding cardiac failure.

The risk of dying is highest in the first few hours and decreases rapidly thereafter. Some 60% or more of all deaths within 4 weeks occur within the first 2 days. During this time, prognosis is difficult because dangerous arrhythmias may develop unpredictably. At the end of 48 hours, the assessment of the prognosis for the rest of the 4 week period is reasonably accurate if the blood pressure, the signs of cardiac failure and the occurrence of serious arrhythmias are taken into account. Cardiogenic shock carries a mortality of 80 to 90%. Persistent tachycardia, continuing gallop rhythm and the development of right-sided heart failure are unfavourable features. Ventricular tachycardia, bundle branch block and atrial fibrillation are associated with a high mortality. Death may occur unexpectedly, late in the course of acute myocardial infarction, from further myocardial infarction, rupture, and pulmonary embolism.

The ECG provides little information of prognostic value, except that, in general, patients with Q waves do worse than those without. High serum enzyme levels, indicating extensive necrosis, are unfavourable.

In those patients who have survived acute myocardial infarction, the outlook is better than is often appreciated. The prognosis is best in those who are free of hypertension, angina and cardiac failure. Overall, between 80 and 90% of patients survive at least one year, approximately 75% survive 5 years, 50% 10 years and 25% 20 years. The risk of further infarction and sudden death persists but diminishes as time elapses.

Many patients can go back to work within 2 months; nearly all should have returned within 3 months. Failure to do so should call for a careful reappraisal of physical, psychological and social factors.

Treatment

Usually, the most urgent measure is the relief of pain. When this is severe, opiates such as intravenous morphine sulphate (10 to 15 mg) or diamorphine (5 to 10 mg) are required and may have to be repeated. Unfortunately, these drugs may produce bradycardia, hypotension and respiratory depression, and it is advisable to combine them with atropine 0.5 mg, if there is bradycardia, or a drug such as perchlorperazine if there is not. There seems no advantage in giving pethidine (meperidine hydrochloride, demerol) as this is a less potent analgesic, seems no less likely to produce hypotension and can increase the ventricular rate undesirably. The inhalation of nitrous oxide 50% and oxygen 50% is useful if other analgesic measures are unavailable or have failed.

General management

In recent years, it has become usual to admit all those with suspected myocardial infarction to hospital. The main purpose of this is to ensure that intensive care is available in the first few unpredictable hours. There is, however, a case for leaving at home those patients whose circumstances are good if the clinical state is satisfactory several hours after the onset, particularly if they are elderly or live a long distance from the nearest coronary care unit.

The patient must be confined to bed immediately, but the degree of restriction depends upon the severity of the infarction. If this has been mild and there is no evidence of cardiogenic shock or cardiac failure, the patient should be allowed to feed himself, use a commode and gently exercise his legs from the outset. Within 2 to 3 days it may be possible for him to sit out of bed, although still observing rest in a comfortable armchair. The mildest cases may be permitted to walk a few steps shortly after this and may be ready for discharge from hospital after 5 to 10 days, at which time they should be able to walk up a few stairs. The patient with a small infarction should have returned to reasonably normal activity within a period of 1 to 2 months and can then resume light work. If, however, during the first days there is evidence of a severe infarction, or if there have been dangerous arrhythmias, the patient requires strict bed rest which may have to be continued until the complication has been brought satisfactorily under control. When there is hypotension, the patient should be lain flat; the legs may be elevated to augment the venous return. The subsequent progress of patients with more severe infarction is necessarily slow, but in most cases discharge from hospital is possible in 3 to 4 weeks.

The programme of rest and rehabilitation depends upon the severity of the cardiac disability. Increase in activity should be gradual but progressive. One of the greatest dangers is the development of an unwarranted anxiety. This can be prevented by encouragement and explanation from the onset of the illness, and the patient must understand that he has a good chance of recovery, and of return to near normal activity. At every stage an optimistic attitude should prevail, and it should be apparent that the physician expects his patient to recover. Intensive care units may either enhance or reduce anxiety. If they are properly run, the patient should initially be reassured by the constant observation and the excellence of the medical and nursing care. Subsequently, when the most acute stage is over, he should be encouraged because close supervision is no longer necessary. Finally, on discharge from hospital it should be made clear that the patient is expected to return to work within 4 to 8 weeks.

Patients usually have little appetite initially; those who are overweight should be given a low calorie diet.

Anticoagulant therapy

Controversy continues as to the value of anticoagulants. There is no evidence that they influence morbidity or mortality in the acute attack except in so far as they reduce the incidence of deep vein thrombosis, and pulmonary and systemic emboli. With early ambulation, pulmonary embolism is relatively uncommon and there are many physicians who feel that the dangers of anticoagulant therapy are unjustified except for those who are confined to bed for a long time. If anticoagulant therapy is to be given, warfarin is perhaps the drug of choice as being the least toxic of the oral preparations. It may be administered initially in a dosage of 20 mg and the daily dose subsequently adjusted depending upon the prothrombin concentration, which should be maintained at 10 to 20% of the normal level (or the patient's prothrombin time should be 2 to 2.5 times the control value). In the United Kingdom, the British Corrected Ratio (BCR) is used; the recommended therapeutic range is 1.7 to 3.0.

There is some evidence that anticoagulant therapy prevents further myocardial infarction in patients under 55 years of age when continued over a period of 1 to 2 years. Long-term treatment should be undertaken only if the patient is known to be cooperative, if the doctor is prepared to supervise the patient and his anticoagulant control carefully, and if a reliable laboratory is available.

Fibrinolytic therapy remains experimental in the management of acute myocardial infarction. Promising results have been reported with the use of streptokinase injected through a cardiac catheter directly into an artery recently occluded by thrombus.

Management of rhythm and conduction disorders

Ventricular fibrillation is best treated by immediate dc shock of 200 joules, without prior closed-chest cardiac massage or artificial ventilation. If this is given quickly enough, sinus rhythm, blood pressure and consciousness are nearly always restored. If a defibrillator is not immediately available, external resuscitation must be initiated and continued until the apparatus arrives. Under these circumstances, acidosis develops quickly and should be corrected by administering 50 to 75 mmol of sodium bicarbonate intravenously. The necessity for further doses should be judged from the arterial pH. The prognosis of patients with ventricular fibrillation depends upon their condition prior to the onset of this arrhythmia. If free of shock or cardiac failure, and if dc shock is immediately available, 90% have a chance of being alive 1 month later. If either of these complications has been present, the chances are approximately 25%.

Ventricular fibrillation is frequently preceded by other ventricular arrhythmias, notably ventricular tachycardia and ventricular ectopic beats of the R-on-T variety. When these arrhythmias appear, lignocaine should be given (p. 75). An alternative drug is procainamide, which may be given intravenously under electrocardiographic and blood pressure control at 50 mg per minute until the arrhythmia is suppressed. Other anti-arrhythmic drugs including disopyramide and mexiletine may also be of value.

Atrial flutter and fibrillation, should be treated with digitalis glycosides if the ventricular rate is high. Digoxin or ouabain may be given in a dosage of 0.5 mg intravenously (if digitalis has not been administered during the preceding week). Subsequently, digoxin may be given orally. If the heart rate is not brought under control quickly, sinus rhythm should be restored by synchronized dc shock. Supraventricular tachycardias may be treated similarly, if carotid sinus pressure is ineffective.

Asystole responds poorly to therapy, but an attempt should be made to restore electrical activity by a blow on the chest, closed-chest cardiac resuscitation or electrical pacemaking. First-degree heart block requires no treatment but should be closely observed for progression. Bradycardia due to more advanced block is common during the early hours and can often be corrected by atropine. If the bradycardia is persistent, especially if associated with hypotension, an endocardial electrode should be placed in the right ventricle and attached to an external pacemaker. If pacemaking facilities are not available, a slow intravenous infusion of isoprenaline may be given (1 to 5 mg in 500 ml 5% laevulose) taking care to avoid sinus tachycardia and ventricular arrhythmias.

Sinus bradycardia is usually relatively harmless, but if it is producing hypotension or is associated with ventricular ectopic activity, atropine in a dosage of 0.6 mg should be given intravenously, and repeated if necessary, taking care not to induce tachycardia.

Management of shock and cardiac failure

The prompt correction of arrhythmias is important in the prevention of cardiogenic shock and failure; there is little evidence that any form of treatment for *cardiogenic shock* is effective once it is established. Sometimes benefit seems to accrue from small doses of drugs which increase cardiac contractility, such as dopamine and dobutamine, but the effect is usually short-lived. Hypovolaemia may be a factor if the patient has been receiving diuretics, antihypertensives or pressor drugs, or is recovering from cardiac arrest. Infusion of dextrose or dextran may then be beneficial, but carries the risk of provoking pulmonary oedema, and it is advisable to monitor intravascular pressures using a Swan–Ganz catheter. Intra-aortic balloon pumping (see p. 293) will improve the circulatory state in most cases, but is of little long-term value unless there is a lesion which can be subsequently corrected surgically.

Mild degrees of *cardiac failure* are common in acute myocardial infarction and do not necessarily require treatment. However, if there is dyspnoea, oedema on the chest radiograph, or gallop rhythm, the conventional treatment for cardiac failure is indicated. Treatment may be started with frusemide; digitalis may be of value in patients with cardiomegaly or atrial arrhythmias. Arrhythmias are important precipitating factors and their immediate control is essential. Oxygen therapy should be given. If the response to these measures is poor, vasodilator drugs such as isosorbide dinitrate, prazosin and hydralazine should be considered, but their use requires careful monitoring.

Limitation of infarct size

Because it has become apparent that the eventual size of infarction may be affected by a variety of influences during the first hours after the onset of symptoms, there is now great interest in the use of various forms of treatment in this context. As yet, no conclusive evidence in favour of any specific form of therapy has been forthcoming, but suggestive evidence from both animal experiments and human observations indicates that beta-blocking drugs, hyaluronidase and some vasodilators may be beneficial, as many attempts to reperfuse the ischaemic territory by lysing thrombosis with streptokinase. All these approaches must at present be regarded as experimental.

Rehabilitation and secondary prevention after myocardial infarction

Although many patients make an initially satisfactory recovery following myocardial infarction, the longer term outcome in terms of return to normal activities, including work, and freedom from recurrences is often disappointing.

Failure to return to normal activities may be due to physical factors, but is often the result of anxiety or inadequate instruction and rehabilitation. It is helpful if one or two weeks after the infarction in the milder case, a limited exercise tolerance test is carried out in which the patient exercises until a heart rate of 120 or 130 is achieved. If such a heart rate can be attained without cardiac symptoms or ST depression on the ECG, the outlook is very good and the patient can be encouraged to return quickly to a near-normal life. For example, after a month has elapsed, the individual should be walking out of doors and up hills and stairs, be able to return to car driving and sexual activity, and should go back to work, provided this is not physically strenuous shortly thereafter. Patients whose exercise tolerance is less good require slower convalescence and more careful observation. If angina pectoris or dyspnoea are major symptoms, careful attention to drug therapy and consideration for surgery is necessary.

Recently, it has become clear that the long-term effect of beta-adrenoceptor blocking drugs after myocardial infarction reduces mortality in the succeeding year. Whether these drugs should be given to all patients after infarction, in the absence of contraindications, has yet to be settled, but certainly they are indicated for any patient with angina or hypertension after infarction. There is no evidence that any particular beta-blocker is superior to any other in this context.

The stopping of smoking and the control of hypertension and diabetes are all important in the survivor of myocardial infarction.

Antiarrhythmic drugs have been used in an attempt to prevent sudden death, but the results are rather disappointing. Drugs, such as mexiletine, disopyramide and amiodarone, are, however, indicated for patients with recurrent serious ventricular arrhythmias.

Intensive care

For the first few days after the onset of acute myocardial infarction, the risk of sudden and unexpected death is high. This is largely due to arrhythmias, which can be treated or prevented by appropriate therapy. Because of the close observation required at this time, and the need to have appropriate equipment and skills immediately available, intensive care units have achieved popularity in the management of acute myocardial infarction.

Intensive care of patients with myocardial infarction has three essential components: the concentration of patients at maximal risk in special areas, their care by nurses and doctors with specialized training, and the availability of apparatus for monitoring and resuscitation. At its simplest, intensive care can be instituted in the best supervised part of a general medical ward or in a specifically allocated area of a general intensive care unit. Alternatively, patients can be accommodated in a purpose-built Coronary Care Unit, with individual rooms separated from each other by opaque and soundproof partitions but with good visibility from a central monitoring area. The unit requires bedside ECG monitors for each patient, with alarm systems relayed to a central monitoring station, at which ECGs can be viewed on an oscilloscope. Additional equipment includes defibrillators, pacemakers, manometers for the measurement of intracardiac pressures and apparatus for artificial ventilation.

Doctors and nurses caring for patients with acute myocardial infarction require training in the techniques of external cardiac resuscitation, including defibrillation. They should also be able to recognize and treat arrhythmias, manage the haemodynamic disorders and utilize pacemaking apparatus.

The effectiveness of Coronary Care Units is difficult to establish, but it has now been shown that by detecting and treating arrhythmias quickly and by the early management of cardiac failure it is possible to reduce the hospital mortality of myocardial infarction by at least one-third.

Because of the risk of sudden death in the first few hours, ambulance teams equipped with intensive care facilities have been developed which can go to the patient at home, correct any complications and transfer the patient to hospital under ideal circumstances. As with other forms of intensive care, specially trained staff are required.

Surgical treatment

Surgery has little part to play in the acute phase of myocardial infarction except for the few patients who develop a ventricular septal defect; these require early repair. Other surgically treatable complications include ventricular aneurysm and papillary muscle rupture; operation is preferably delayed for six weeks. If patients develop these lesions at a time when corrective surgery would be inappropriate, an intra-aortic balloon pump may be invaluable in supporting the circulation for one or two weeks.

Unstable angina

Ischaemic chest pain may start for the first time or pre-existing angina may worsen in the weeks prior to the development of acute myocardial infarction. The attacks of pain are often prolonged and occur at rest. Such patients may exhibit ST depression or elevation or T wave changes during the episodes.

Many names have been given to this syndrome, amongst which are acute coronary insufficiency, prodromal symptoms and preinfarction angina. Although the majority of patients with acute myocardial infarction have experienced such symptoms immediately prior to their attack, only about one-fifth of those presenting with these clinical features proceed to infarction or sudden death. The term 'unstable angina' is perhaps the most suitable description.

Patients with unstable angina should be treated with bed rest and nitrates. If they do not respond to this promptly, beta-blocking drugs and calcium antagonists should be used. For the few patients in whom the attacks persist, consideration should be given to prompt coronary artery by-pass surgery, perhaps preceded by intra-aortic balloon pumping (which usually abolishes the pain).

Cardiac failure

In a small proportion of patients with ischaemic heart disease, the initial manifestation is cardiac failure, which may be either left-sided or right-sided. The clinical picture is that of a cardiomyopathy. If the ECG does not provide evidence of coronary disease, coronary angiography may be necessary to establish the diagnosis.

Sudden death

Death often occurs suddenly in patients with coronary atherosclerosis. In about 50% of cases, the subject is known to have suffered from angina pectoris, or to have had a previous myocardial infarction. In a proportion of the remainder, it is possible to obtain a history from relatives that an attack of pain had preceded the fatal event, but in quite a substantial number death occurs without any warning whatsoever.

When sudden death occurs under circumstances in which the patient is observed, ventricular fibrillation is nearly always its cause.

Occasionally ventricular asystole is responsible; in the elderly, ventricular rupture is not uncommon.

Prompt defibrillation is frequently effective in restoring life in those who appear to die suddenly. As most cases occur outside hospital, success depends upon there being someone trained in cardiopulmonary resuscitation at hand and the ready availability of personnel equipped with the necessary apparatus.

Further reading

AHA Committee Report (1980) Risk factors and coronary disease. *Circulation* **62**, 449A.

PANTRIDGE, J. F., ADGEY, A. A. L., GEDDES, J. S. and WEBB, S. W. (1975) *The Acute Coronary Attack*. London: Pitman Medical.

RAHIMTOOLA, S. H. (1982) Coronary bypass surgery for chronic angina. *Circulation,* **65**, 225.

REEVES, T. J. (1982) Medical management of the patient with angina pectoris: An overview of the problem. *Circulation,* **65**, *Suppl.* **II**, 3.

WHO Expert Committee (1982) *Prevention of coronary heart disease*. Geneva: WHO.

9

Diseases of the Pericardium, Myocardium and Endocardium

The pericardium

Pericardial disease, which may be acute or chronic, is usually associated with a generalized disorder or with pulmonary disease.

Pathology

Pericarditis may be fibrinous, purulent or constrictive. In acute fibrinous pericarditis, the serous pericardium is inflamed and covered with an adherent layer of fibrin. There may be an accompanying effusion. In purulent pericarditis, there is usually a thick fibrinous exudate, containing polymorphonuclear cells and organisms. In pericardial constriction, the pericardium is a dense mass of fibrous tissue which is often heavily calcified. Sometimes a mixed picture of effusion and constriction is seen ('effusive-constrictive pericarditis').

Acute pericarditis

Aetiology
1. Infective; viral, pyogenic or tuberculous
2. Connective tissue disorders: rheumatic fever (p. 178), rheumatoid arthritis (p. 279), systemic lupus erythematosus (p. 279), polyarteritis (p. 279)
3. Allergic and autoimmune reactions, including the postcardiotomy (p. 197) and post-myocardial infarction syndromes (p. 153)
4. Neoplastic invasion, particularly from carcinoma of the lung
5. Metabolic: uraemia and gout
6. Myocardial infarction
7. Trauma
8. Idiopathic
9. After cardiac surgery

'Idiopathic' pericarditis is common but is probably, in most instances, due either to a viral infection or to allergy or autoimmunity. The viruses most frequently isolated have been of the Coxsackie B

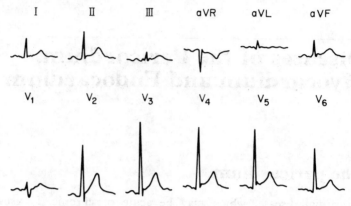

Fig. 82.   ECG appearances in acute pericarditis. Notice widespread ST
elevation, with preservation of the normal upward concavity of the
ST segment.

group, but influenza, measles, mumps and chickenpox have also been
identified. Purulent pericarditis usually results from the spread of
infection from adjacent lung.

Tuberculous pericarditis is preceded by infection in contiguous
mediastinal lymph nodes.

Clinical features and diagnosis

Chest pain is the commonest symptom but is not invariable. Its
distribution simulates that of acute myocardial infarction, being
central and sometimes radiating to the shoulder and upper arm. The
pain may be most severe in the xiphisternal or epigastric regions. It is
often sharp and severe, but may be aching or oppressive. Unlike
ischaemic cardiac pain, it is accentuated by inspiration, by movement
and by lying flat.

The most definitive sign of pericarditis is a pericardial rub, although
this is not always present. A to-and-fro scratchy or grating noise may
be heard in systole, mid-diastole and presystole, or in only one of these
phases. It is often localized to a small area but varies in position from
time to time. It is usually accentuated if the patient leans forward, with
the breath held in expiration, but is sometimes heard better towards
the end of inspiration. Although the rub may disappear with the
development of the pericardial effusion, it does not necessarily do so.
Other signs may include those of pericardial effusion and,
occasionally, of pericardial tamponade.

In the early stages, the ECG usually shows widespread ST elevation
with the ST segment concave upwards (Fig. 82). After a few days the
ST segment returns to the isoelectric line and the T wave becomes
inverted. The ECG may simulate that of myocardial infarction, but Q

waves are not seen and the ST segment elevation is of different configuration.

The chest radiograph is not helpful unless there is a large pericardial effusion.

Acute pericarditis is most likely to be confused with acute myocardial infarction, spontaneous pneumothorax and pleurisy. In differentiating it from acute myocardial infarction, the following points are of importance: (1) the character of the pain, the absence of pre-existing angina, and the history of an upper respiratory infection or of pyrexia preceding the onset of chest pain, (2) the absence of Q waves and of the characteristic infarction type of ST elevation on the ECG, and (3) the absence of serum enzyme changes. In spontaneous pneumothorax, the diagnosis can usually be made without difficulty by the detection of hyper-resonance and absent breath sounds over the affected lung or by the radiological demonstration of air in the pleural space. Pleurisy can be distinguished by the location and character of the pain, the presence of a pleural rub and, sometimes, by the clinical and radiological evidence of pleural effusion. Pleurisy and pericarditis commonly coexist.

Aetiological diagnosis

Viral pericarditis should be suspected if there is a history of an upper respiratory infection and fever preceding the chest pain, and can be confirmed by the demonstration of changing titres of viral antibodies in the blood, or the culture of viruses from the stools. Tuberculous pericarditis may be difficult to diagnose, because there is often no evidence of either pulmonary or miliary infection. Usually, however, there is a history of malaise and weight loss for some weeks prior to the pericarditis. Tuberculosis is unlikely if tuberculin skin tests are negative. If necessary the diagnosis may be confirmed by pericardial aspiration or biopsy. In pericarditis due to straphylococci, streptococci or pneumococci, there is usually infection in the lung or elsewhere in the body. In rheumatic fever, there is accompanying evidence of the rheumatic process as well of myocarditis and endocarditis. In pericarditis due to hypersensitivity or autoimmunity, there is no preceding respiratory infection but there is often a history of similar episodes in the past.

Treatment

This consists of the symptomatic relief of pain by salicylates or indomethacin, the removal of fluid when this is causing pericardial tamponade, and the treatment of the underlying cause when this is possible. No specific therapy is usually necessary for viral or allergic pericarditis, although corticosteroids may be used to abbreviate their course if this is protracted. Tuberculous pericarditis requires

Fig. 83.   Radiographic appearances in pericardial effusion.

prolonged treatment with antituberculous drugs and corticosteroids. Pericardial resection may be necessary even during the acute phase if pericardial constriction develops. Bacterial pericarditis should be treated with the appropriate antibiotics; surgical removal of pericardial pus may be necessary.

Pericardial effusion

Pericardial effusion may result from transudation (in cardiac failure), exudation of serous fluid or pus (in pericarditis) or blood (from trauma or malignant disease). It is also a feature of myxoedema. The hydropericardium of cardiac failure causes few if any symptoms, although it may cause compression of the lungs and reduce the vital capacity. Pericardial effusion due to other causes may produce pain and pericardial tamponade.

Large effusions may be detected by percussion. With the patient lying flat, increased dullness may be noted in the second left interspace, as well as in the fourth and fifth right interspaces, and to the left of the apex beat.

Auscultation may reveal pericardial friction and heart sounds which are often, but not always, soft.

The chest radiograph is valuable in diagnosis, particularly if several films are taken over a period of days — a sudden increase in the cardiothoracic ratio being very suggestive of pericardial effusion. When there is a considerable effusion, the cardiac silhouette is enlarged and the normal demarcation between the chambers is obliterated (Fig. 83). The heart shadow takes on a pear or waterbottle shape, and on fluoroscopy little pulsation can be observed. Similar abnormalities may be seen in some cases of cardiac failure, particularly when the right atrium is much enlarged, but the presence of a very large heart shadow in the absence of pulmonary vascular congestion makes the diagnosis of pericardial effusion likely. Pericardial effusion produces low-voltage ECG complexes which may vary considerably in amplitude from cycle to cycle, sometimes alternating in height ('electrical alternans').

Echocardiography has proved to be a useful diagnostic method.

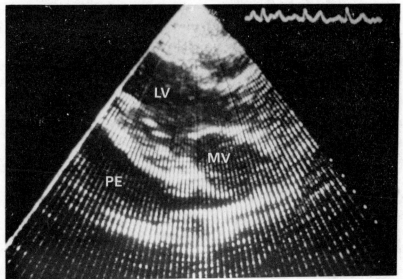

Fig. 84.   Realtime echocardiogram in the long axis parasternal view of a
patient with a large pericardial effusion. An echo-free space is seen
behind the posterior left ventricular wall. No anterior effusion is
seen. LV = left ventricle. MV = mitral valve. PE = pericardial
effusion.

High frequency sound waves normally produce a single 'echo' when
reflected from the posterior wall of the heart. When fluid separates the
contracting and relaxing posterior wall of the heart from the stationary
posterior pericardium, an echo-free space is produced (Fig. 84).
Similarly, the anterior wall of the heart is separated from the chest
wall.

The diagnosis may be most certainly established by pericardial
aspiration, but this is best avoided because of its potential danger.
Fortunately, echocardiography can establish the diagnosis in most
cases.

Pericardial tamponade

The normal pericardium does not impede ventricular distension
during diastole. An accumulation of pericardial fluid, or pericardial
fibrosis or calcification may prevent adequate filling. This may develop
acutely, as when the pericardium fills with fluid, or slowly, as in
chronic pericardial constriction.

The inability of the ventricles to fill during diastole leads to raised
diastolic pressures in right and left ventricles, an increase in systemic
and pulmonary venous pressures, and a fall in cardiac output and in

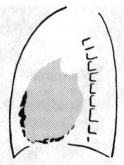

Fig. 85.　Calcification of the pericardium, outlining the ventricles, in the lateral view.

systemic blood pressure. There is a compensatory sinus tachycardia and the pulse is small and often of the paradoxical type. If the cardiac compression is acute and severe, it may be rapidly fatal.

Treatment by the aspiration of pericardial fluid is urgent.

Pericardial constriction ('constrictive pericarditis')

Constriction of the heart by a fibrosed or calcified pericardium is relatively uncommon and seems to be getting rarer. In most patients, no identifiable cause can be found, although in some communities a tuberculous infection is responsible for the majority of cases. Constriction can also be a late complication of other types of infection, neoplastic invasion and intrapericardial haemorrhage.

Adequate filling of the ventricles during diastole is prevented by thick, fibrous and, often, calcified pericardium. Although extension of the disease process may affect the superficial areas of the myocardium, the rest of the heart is usually normal.

The inability of the ventricles to distend during diastole leads to an increase in diastolic pressure and to a consequent rise in pressure in the left and right atria and in both pulmonary and systemic veins. The stroke volume is low and there is a compensatory tachycardia.

The onset may be subacute or chronic. Symptoms resemble those of right-sided cardiac failure. The presenting complaint is often that of abdominal swelling due to ascites, but dyspnoea and ankle swelling are also common.

The pulse is of small volume and often exhibits paradox. Sinus tachycardia is usually present, but atrial fibrillation develops in the advanced case. The neck veins are grossly engorged and show two characteristic features: a rapid 'y' descent and an increase in pressure on inspiration. The first and second heart sounds are soft, and there is nearly always an early diastolic sound heard best at the lower end of the

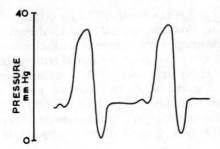

Fig. 86. Characteristic right ventricular pressure pulse in pericardial constriction. Note early diastolic dip, followed by a plateau.

sternum. This is an unusually early third heart sound associated with rapid but abbreviated ventricular filling.

The liver is enlarged and often tender, although it may be difficult to feel because of gross ascites. In contrast with the severity of the ascites, peripheral oedema is comparatively slight.

One of the most characteristic features of pericardial constriction is the shell-like rim of calcified pericardium, which is particularly well seen in lateral radiographs of the heart (Fig. 85). However, calcification is not invariable, nor does its presence necessarily imply constriction. The heart is usually small or normal in size, but is occasionally large. Reduced cardiac pulsation is observed on fluoroscopy. The ECG is not diagnostic, but usually shows low-voltage QRS complexes associated with flattened or slightly inverted T waves. If atrial fibrillation is not present, the P waves are often broad and bifid.

Cardiac catheterization reveals raised left ventricular diastolic, left atrial, pulmonary arterial, right ventricular diastolic and right atrial pressures. In the right ventricular pressure pulse, there is an early diastolic dip followed by a plateau (Fig. 86). This appearance is not specific to pericardial constriction and may be seen in cardiomyopathy.

Pericardial constriction is suggested by a small and paradoxical pulse, a high venous pressure, a quiet heart with an early third heart sound and pericardial calcification, although not all these features are necessarily present. An important clue to the diagnosis is the combination of advanced right-sided failure with a normal-sized heart.

Pericardial constriction is most likely to be confused with cirrhosis of the liver, but the characteristic arterial and venous pulses in pericardial constriction should permit differentiation. In other forms of right-sided heart failure, cardiac valve lesions or pulmonary disease are usually evident. Differentiation of pericardial constriction from cardiomyopathy may be difficult or impossible without thoracotomy if there is no pericardial calcification and no evidence of concomitant disease elsewhere. However, in most cases of cardiomyopathy, even of the so-called constrictive type, there is cardiac enlargement.

The other effective treatment is surgical removal of the thickened pericardium. However, pericardial constriction sometimes supervenes during the acute or subacute phase of tuberculous pericarditis, and preliminary treatment should then be undertaken with antituberculous drugs and corticosteroids. Indeed, this therapy may prevent the development of what appears to be inevitable constriction.

The medical treatment of the failure associated with pericardial constriction is seldom successful, although some improvement may follow the use of diuretics. Digoxin is of value when atrial fibrillation supervenes.

Progress following pericardiectomy is usually satisfactory but may not be so if there has been extensive myocardial involvement or severe liver damage.

Pericardial paracentesis

Fluid may have to be removed from the pericardium either for diagnostic purposes or to relieve tamponade. It is a potentially dangerous procedure and should be undertaken only if essential. The patient should be sitting nearly upright, with his back supported. The needle may be inserted in the angle between the left costal margin and the xiphisternum and advanced sharply upwards. If the aspiration is being carried out for diagnostic purposes only, a 20-gauge needle attached to a plastic 3-way tap and a 10 ml syringe may be used, but for aspiration of larger quantities or of blood or pus, an 18- or 16-gauge needle some 10 cm long should be used. The site of insertion should be anaesthetized with 2% lignocaine. The ECG should be monitored during the procedure. If possible, this should be done using the needle as an electrode; a sterile insulated wire with a clip at each end is attached both to the needle and to the V lead terminal. If the atrium is entered, a large P wave is seen. ST segment elevation is observed if the needle is in contact with a ventricle. The needle should be advanced slowly while gentle suction is applied. A sudden 'give' will usually be felt when the pericardial space is entered. If blood is withdrawn, it should be observed for clotting to determine whether the specimen has been obtained from a cardiac chamber. Fluid from a haemo-pericardium will not clot.

Myocardial disease

The myocardium is involved in most types of heart disease. The terms *myocarditis* and *cardiomyopathy* are reserved for those relatively uncommon types of myocardial disease which cannot be attributed to coronary atherosclerosis, congenital or valvar heart disease, thyrotoxicosis or hypertension.

Myocarditis is used to describe inflammatory disorders of the myocardium due to infection and toxins. Cardiomyopathy is used for those diseases of the myocardium which cannot be described as myocarditis.

Myocarditis

Myocarditis usually forms part of a generalized infection such as diphtheria, Chagas' disease, trichinosis, toxoplasmosis, and viral infections, particularly Coxsackie B, influenza, and poliomyelitis (see also Chapter 16). Occasionally, septicaemia may lead to focal suppurative lesions. Myocarditis is an important component of acute rheumatic fever (see Chapter 10).

Mild forms of myocarditis also occur in a large number of infectious diseases causing only sinus tachycardia and non-specific ECG changes. They may also give rise to arrhythmias such as atrial fibrillation or supraventricular tachycardia without producing other overt cardiac effects.

In severe cases, tachycardia may be considerable, or, particularly in diphtheria, there may be a bradycardia due to heart block. The symptoms and signs of left and right cardiac failure may develop, with dyspnoea, gallop rhythm, cardiac enlargement and murmurs due to dilatation of the ventricles. There is a risk of acute circulatory failure (shock) and of sudden death. Minor ECG abnormalities are common, but such changes may occur in infections even in the absence of myocarditis. Occasionally, there is ST elevation or depression, or inversion of T waves, or disturbances of conduction and rhythm.

The diagnosis depends upon recognizing the significance of a disproportionate tachycardia and cardiac enlargement complicating a generalized disease.

There is no specific treatment. Rest and the usual therapy for cardiac failure are required, but digitalis is usually ineffective.

Cardiomyopathy

Aetiologically, cardiomyopathies fall into two groups: those in which the heart disease is the major or only abnormal feature, and those in which the myocardial disease is a complication of a generalized disorder.

In a substantial proportion of cases in the first group, no cause for the cardiomyopathy can be found. In some, there is a family history of heart disease and sudden death; in others, excessive intake of alcohol appears to be responsible (see p. 278). There is an increased liability to heart muscle disorders in the weeks before and after childbirth (peripartal cardiomyopathy, see p. 284).

Endomyocardial fibrosis. This is a relatively common form of cardiomyopathy seen in a number of areas of Africa. At necropsy the endocardium and inner part of the myocardium are replaced by dense fibrous tissue. The rigid endocardium prevents adequate filling and death occurs from cardiac failure or from thrombo-embolism.

Endocardial fibro-elastosis. This is a disorder almost confined to infants. In this condition, the endocardium of the left ventricle and left atrium is replaced by elastic tissue and collagen. The mitral valve is often involved and there is usually associated congenital heart disease.

Cardiomyopathy may be secondary to connective tissue disorders (systemic lupus erythematosus, scleroderma and polyarteritis), to amyloidosis, sarcoidosis, neuromuscular diseases (Friedreich's ataxia, progressive muscular dystrophy and myotonia atrophica) to haemochromatosis, and to glycogen storage disease.

Clinical features

There are three main clinical patterns: dilated, hypertrophic, and restructive. The latter two types are rare.

Dilated (congestive) cardiomyopathy is the commonest form. The major physiological defect is the decreased contractile force of the left ventricle, with slow and inadequate systolic emptying. The ventricle dilates and the pressure rises in the left atrium. Subsequently, pulmonary hypertension and right ventricular failure occur.

Patients usually present with dyspnoea and oedema whose onset may be abrupt or insidious. Tachycardia is common as are ventricular ectopic beats and atrial fibrillation. The venous pressure is raised and there may be systolic venous pulsation from tricuspid regurgitation. Cardiac enlargement affects both left and right ventricles. Third and fourth heart sounds are common. There may be the pansystolic murmurs of mitral or tricuspid regurgitation.

The ECG frequently demonstrates arrhythmias, as well as abnormalities of the ST segment and T waves. The chest radiograph confirms cardiac enlargement affecting all chambers. Echocardiography reveals a dilated, poorly contracting ventricle. Cardiac catheterization and angiocardiography are of little value in diagnosis as they demonstrate only evidence of ventricular failure and, occasionally, tricuspid and mitral regurgitation.

The diagnosis requires the exclusion of coronary artery disease, thyrotoxicosis, hypertension, rheumatic heart disease and congenital heart disease as aetiological factors: it is supported by evidence of one of those generalized disorders which is associated with cardiomyopathy.

In *hypertrophic cardiomyopathy*, there is massive hypertrophy of the ventricles. The rigid non-complaint chambers impede diastolic filling. The ventricular septum is often the site of the most conspicuous hypertrophy, which may obstruct the left ventricular outflow tract (obstructive cardiomyopathy or idiopathic hypertrophic subaortic stenosis). The obstruction increases as systole progresses, and the more vigorously the ventricle contracts the more severe is the obstruction.

Hypertrophic cardiomyopathy is sometimes a familial condition and one may obtain a history of heart disease or sudden death in relatives.

The symptoms are often those which occur in aortic stenosis, including dyspnoea, angina and syncope. Arrhythmias are common and there is a high risk of sudden death. The pulse has a steep upstroke due to the rapid ejection of blood by the hypertrophied ventricle during early systole. The venous pulse may show a large 'a' wave, and there may be evidence of both left and right ventricular hypertrophy. Left ventricular outflow obstruction causes the systolic murmur and thrill of subaortic stenosis, maximal at the lower left sternal edge or apex. The pansystolic murmur of mitral regurgitation is frequent; less often there may be the signs of tricuspid regurgitation or of pulmonary stenosis. A fourth heart sound is usual. Both the 'a' wave and fourth heart sound are due to forceful atrial contraction against the non-complaint hypertrophied ventricle.

The ECG shows left ventricular hypertrophy and, sometimes, conduction defects. The echocardiogram is of great value. The two most characteristic features are asymmetrical hypertrophy of the septum (ASH) and systolic anterior movement of the mitral valve (SAM); when both are present, hypertrophic obstructive cardiomyopathy is highly probable. The chest radiograph may show left ventricular hypertrophy. On cardiac catheterization, a systolic pressure difference can be demonstrated between the body and the outflow tract of the left ventricle if there is obstruction. This difference is increased by drugs such as isoprenaline, which increase myocardial contractility, and may be abolished by drugs such as propranolol, which decrease myocardial contractility. Angiocardiography demonstrates a small left ventricular cavity with narrowing of the outflow tract and, often, mitral regurgitation. Obstructive cardiomyopathy has usually to be differentiated from other types of aortic stenosis. In valvar aortic stenosis, the pulse is usually small and flat, and there is either an early systolic click or calcification of the aortic valve. In congenital subaortic stenosis, the pulse is small and flat and there is frequently aortic regurgitation, which is not a feature of obstructive cardiomyopathy.

Restrictive cardiomyopathy.   This resembles constrictive pericarditis because the rigid myocardium impedes filling. The main causes are amyloidosis, polyarteritis, leukaemic infiltration and haemochromatosis. The clinical differentiation from pericardial constriction may be impossible but helpful clues are the absence of pericardial calcification and the presence of cardiac enlargement.

Treatment

In general, the treatment of cardiomyopathies is disappointing. Dilated cardiomyopathy should be treated with bed rest, digitalis, diuretics and vasodilators; a transient improvement in symptoms and signs is often achieved. Sooner or later, the response to treatment fails and the patient develops progressive cardiac failure or dies suddenly.

A transient improvement in hypertrophic cardiomyopathy may be achieved by the administration of propranolol. Surgical resection of a wedge of the hypertrophied septum may succeed in abolishing the obstruction, at least temporarily, but the long-term prognosis is still poor.

The other forms of cardiomyopathy respond poorly to treatment.

Endocardial disease

Endocarditis is an inflammation of the inner lining of the heart, affecting predominantly the valve structures. It may be infective or non-infective. The non-infective processes, which include rheumatic fever and systemic lupus erythematosus, are considered in more detail elsewhere.

Infective endocarditis

Infective endocarditis may be due to bacteria, fungi, Coxiella or Chlamydia and may be acute or subacute. The commonest variety is bacterial in origin and subacute in its course. Infective subacute endocarditis seldom affects a previously normal heart. The process is most frequently superimposed upon pre-existing mitral or aortic valve disease, a ventricular septal defect or persistent ductus arteriosus. Prosthetic valves may also become infected. Acute endocarditis (almost always *Staph. aureus*) may occur on previously normal hearts.

Infective endocarditis used predominantly to affect the young female with rheumatic heart disease. It is now seen quite as frequently in the elderly male with calcific aortic disease.

Pathology

Streptococcus viridans.   This is an oral commensal of several varieties, and an organism most frequently responsible for endocarditis. Other organisms include *Streptococcus faecalis*, *Staphylococcus aureus*, fungi, *Coxiella burneti*, and *Chlamydia psittaci* (psittacosis).

The infection leads to the formation of friable vegetations which have necrotic tissue, platelets, fibrin, white cells and red cells in their base, with superficial layers of fibrin and micro-organisms. Ulceration may lead to erosion or perforation of the valve cusps or of a sinus of Valsalva. The location of the endocarditis depends upon the underlying lesion. In aortic regurgitation, endocarditis affects the ventricular surface of the valve; in mitral regurgitation it involves the atrial surface of the mitral valve. In a ventricular septal defect, the vegetations may form around the defect itself but are often located either on the tricuspid valve or where the jet impinges on the right ventricular wall.

Embolization from the vegetations is frequent and is responsible for many of the clinical features of the disease. Large emboli may cause occlusion of the cerebral, renal or splenic arteries. Micro-emboli affect nearly all parts of the body and, in particular, lead to skin lesions and a glomerulonephritis. Pulmonary emboli develop when the right side of the heart is involved, as it is when there is a ventricular septal defect or persistent ductus arteriosus.

Several of the manifestations of the disease, including arthritis and glomerulitis, are thought to be due to immune complex deposition.

Clinical features

A history of dental treatment or infection is present in some patients, and in a small proportion there has been preceding urethral, pelvic or cardiac surgery.

The onset is often insidious with malaise and feverishness being the earliest complaints. The symptoms often mimic those of influenza. If left untreated, there develops a characteristic clinical picture which was common in the days before antibiotic therapy. The complete syndrome of fever, anaemia, petechiae in the skin, clubbing, splenomegaly, a cardiac murmur and microscopic haematuria is seldom seen nowadays.

Fever is usually present but is variable. Petechiae may develop in any part of the body, but should be looked for particularly in the conjunctivae, in the ocular fundi and under the nails (splinter haemorrhages). They may have pale centres and tend to occur in crops. Other superficial lesions include tender, palpable nodules in the tips of the fingers and toes (Osler's nodes). Clubbing of the fingers takes 1 to 2 months to develop.

In nearly all patients there are signs of organic heart disease, but the infection sometimes obscures them. The cardiac signs may become more obvious either because of the anaemia or because of further damage to valves. Murmurs may, therefore, appear or disappear during the course of the disease. Heart failure is not common in the earlier stages, but frequently complicates the recovery process.

Most patients with infective endocarditis are anaemic, but the anaemia is not of a specific type. The spleen is often enlarged and occasionally tender. Proteinuria and microscopic haematuria are usual.

Neurological complications are common and are due to embolic occlusion of cerebral vessels or to mycotic aneurysms. Coma, convulsions and hemiplegia may occur and meningitis, encephalitis and subarachnoid haemorrhage may be mimicked.

Diagnosis

The diagnosis should be suspected in all patients with valve disorders or congenital heart disease in whom unexplained pyrexia develops. Confirmation of the diagnosis depends on obtaining a positive blood culture, which is possible in some 90% of cases. At least six specimens of blood should be obtained over a period of 1 or 2 days. The blood should be incubated aerobically and anaerobically, and special cultures should be set up for fungi. If the patient has received penicillin previously, penicillinase should be incorporated in the culture medium. Complement fixation tests must be undertaken for the diagnosis of Coxiella and Chlamydial infection.

Prognosis

Recovery from infective endocarditis is rare unless effective and prolonged antibiotic therapy is given. Death, which may be due to heart failure, emboli or renal failure, often does not occur until several months after the onset. Even if the infection is cured, damage to the valves may be so serious as to lead to intractable heart failure.

Treatment

It is important that the responsible organism should be identified without delay, so that the appropriate antibiotics can be given. However, the start of therapy should not be postponed beyond 2 to 3 days in spite of negative blood cultures. Bactericidal agents should be employed, because bacteriostatic drugs produce only temporary suppression of the infection.

When the organism is penicillin-sensitive, a penicillin (penicillin G or ampicillin) is given. Administration is usually intravenous, at least for the first two weeks and adequate dosage (e.g. penicillin G, 8 million units/day), preferably confirmed by laboratory testing, is essential. Change to oral therapy may be possible later, given a good response. In penicillin-resistant infection (*Streptococcus faecalis*) a combination of a penicillin (penicillin G or ampicillin) and an aminoglycoside (streptomycin, or increasingly, gentamicin) will be necessary. Infections due to penicillin-sensitive Staphylococci will respond to penicillin, but the more common penicillin-resistant strains demand large doses of penicillinase-resistant drugs, e.g. flucloxacillin 2G IV every 4 hours. Blood culture-negative endocarditis should be treated as for *S. faecalis* infections; infection with Coxiella and Chlamydia having first been excluded. A minimum of 4 weeks therapy is thought necessary in all cases. Antibiotic therapy is constantly changing as new drugs become available and as organisms become resistant to those in current use.

The temperature usually falls to normal within 3 days of the start of effective antibiotic therapy. The recurrence of pyrexia suggests the emergence of resistance organisms, superinfection by another organism or, perhaps most commonly, the development of a reaction to the antibiotic. Further blood cultures should be obtained and a change of antibiotic considered.

Surgery may be necessary for the correction of congenital heart disease or for the replacement of damaged valves, but should, if possible, be deferred until the infection is under control.

Prophylaxis

Because of the importance of *Streptococcus viridans* infections, dental manipulations and extractions should be undertaken in patients with valvar and congenital heart disease only with appropriate antibiotic cover. Penicillin, given intramuscularly just prior to the dental procedure and continued orally for a further 3 days is commonly used. A more recent suggestion is amoxycillin 3G orally prior to the event, and repeated once only. Prophylaxis during genital and urinary operations (against *S. faecalis*) requires the addition of an aminoglycoside, e.g. gentamicin, to the penicillin.

Further reading

FOWLER, N. O. (1981) Pericardial diseases. Key references *Circulation*. **63**, 1429.

GOODWIN, J. F. (1982) The frontiers of cardiomyopathy. *Brit. Heart J.*, **48**, 1.

HIRSCHMANN, J. V. (1978) Pericardial constriction. *Am. Heart J.*, **96**, 110

KRIKORIAN, J. G. and HANCOCK, E. W. (1978) Pericardiocentesis. *Amer. J. Med.* **65**, 808.

PERLOFF, J. K. (1981) The Cardiomyopathies: Dilated and Restrictive. Key references *Circulation*, **63**, 1189.

RAHIMTOOLA, S. H. (1978) *Infection Endocarditis*. New York: Grune and Stratton.

SHABETAI, R. (1978). The pericardium: an essay on some recent developments. *Am. J. Cardiol.*, **42**, 1036.

10

Rheumatic Heart Disease

Rheumatic fever and its sequel, chronic rheumatic heart disease, is a major cardiac cause of disability and death.

Rheumatic fever

Acute rheumatic fever is a disease which follows infection by group A haemolytic streptococci and produces manifestations in many tissues and organs. Arthritis is often the most conspicuous feature, but cardiac involvement is of much greater importance. The duration of rheumatic activity is very variable; it may cease in 2 weeks or persist for many months. Recurrences are common. Death is rare in the acute phase but chronic rheumatic heart disease is responsible for a considerable morbidity and mortality.

Aetiology
Rheumatic fever seems to occur only after a group A streptococcal infection. It is a complication of less than 1% of episodes of streptococcal pharyngitis, developing some 10 to 20 days after the onset of the sore throat. No history of sore throat, however, can be obtained in some 30–50% of cases.

It is still far from clear how the infection leads to rheumatic fever. It seems probable that rheumatic fever is a result of a hyperimmune reaction either to bacterial allergy or to autoimmunity.

Over the last 50 years, rheumatic fever has been becoming progressively less frequent and less severe in many countries, including the United Kingdom, the United States and Scandinavia. However, in Asia and South America, there seems to have been little or no reduction in its incidence and severity. The decline of rheumatic fever in Western countries cannot be solely the result of the use of antibiotics for it preceded their discovery. It may be attributed both to a change in the virulence of streptococci and to improving social conditions, for poverty is associated with a relatively high risk of the disease. Overcrowding is an important factor, probably because it encourages cross-infection.

Rheumatic fever most commonly occurs between the ages of 5 and 15, with the peak about the age of 8. It is rare under the age of 4 and becomes progressively less common after the age of 15, although occasional cases are seen even after the age of 30. Rheumatic fever affects males and females equally often, but females are more susceptible to chorea. Rheumatic fever or its sequelae are often seen in more than one member of the same family. Although this may in part be due to the sharing of unfavourable social circumstances, there is good evidence of a genetic predisposition to the disease.

Pathology

Microscopic evidence of acute rheumatic fever is widespread, but particularly affects tissues lined by endothelium such as blood vessels, the endocardium, the pericardium and synovial membranes. The earliest lesion is one of swelling in and around collagen fibres, accompanied by oedema and lymphocytic infiltration. Later, and more specifically, granulomatous Aschoff nodules appear. These are formed by collections of round cells, fibroblasts and multinucleated giant cells, and are usually surrounded by an area of polymorphonuclear cells, lymphocytes and plasma cells. The Aschoff nodules occur throughout the heart and are common in the interstitial tissue close to small blood vessels situated beneath the endocardium of the left ventricle.

Macroscopically, the lesions of rheumatic fever are most obvious in relation to the heart valves and the pericardium. The valve cusps become thickened by oedema and by the infiltration of capillaries. Grey or yellow warty vegetations ('verrucae') form along the lines of closure. These are particularly common on the mitral and aortic valve cusps, and seldom affect the tricuspid or pulmonary valves. When the pericardium is involved, it becomes thickened and may contain a fibrinous straw-coloured effusion.

Chronic rheumatic heart disease is a sequel to acute rheumatic carditis, and many of its features are the result of fibrosis occurring during the healing of the acute lesion. Its pathology will be discussed in more detail later in this chapter.

Clinical features

In most cases, some 2 to 3 weeks after the onset of acute pharyngitis, the child begins to feel unwell, loses his appetite and complains of pains in the limbs. Fever is present, but it is not usually high. The major clinical features are carditis, polyarthritis, subcutaneous nodules, erythema marginatum and chorea.

Carditis occurs in about half of the first attacks of rheumatic fever. *Endocarditis*, with valvar involvement, is suggested by the appearance of cardiac .murmurs; of all patients who develop carditis, three-quarters have murmurs in the first week. An apical pansystolic murmur indicates either mitral valve damage or functional mitral regurgitation associated with myocarditis. Rheumatic involvement of the mitral valve is also strongly suggested by the appearance of a low-pitched and short mid-diastolic apical murmur (Carey Coombs). This murmur is usually transient, but may persist for months or years until the characteristic features of mitral stenosis develop. However, the presence of a short mid-diastolic murmur at the apex in rheumatic fever can not be taken as evidence of mitral stenosis or of its subsequent development. Midsystolic murmurs in the aortic or pulmonary area are less certain evidence of cardiac involvement, as they are common in febrile children without heart disease and usually disappear as recovery takes place. The diastolic murmur of aortic regurgitation is not uncommon, and usually persists after the acute rheumatic process has subsided.

Myocarditis. This is an important and common feature of acute rheumatic fever, but is difficult to diagnose with confidence. It is suggested by a tachycardia which is greater than would be expected from the height of the fever or which persists after the temperature falls, and by cardiac enlargement. More diagnostic is the appearance of left-sided or right-sided heart failure when this cannot be attributed to valve damage. The symptoms include dyspnoea, orthopnoea, and oedema. Gallop rhythm is common but does not necessarily imply myocarditis, as it may occur in any child with fever and tachycardia.

When clinical evidence of *pericarditis* is present, the carditis is usually severe and involves the myocardium and endocardium as well (pancarditis). Retrosternal pain and pericardial friction occur and there may be a pericardial effusion.

When rheumatic activity has subsided, there are often residual signs of valve damage. Because of this, abnormal cardiac signs cannot be taken as evidence of continuing active carditis.

Polyarthritis. This is common but its severity is variable. Characteristically, the joints become swollen, painful and hot, but in the younger child there may be only vague aches. The arthritis usually affects one joint after another, giving the impression of 'flitting', but it may involve several joints simultaneously. The knees, ankles, shoulders, wrists and elbows are most commonly involved, but the smaller joints of the hand and feet may be affected, particularly in the older patient. The inflammation in each joint usually develops within a few hours and may take up to a week to subside. Salicylates and corticosteroids produce a dramatic relief of symptoms and signs and are of some diagnostic value in this respect. Even in the absence of treatment, the polyarthritis usually disappears within 3 weeks and leaves no residual abnormality.

Subcutaneous nodules. These seldom give rise to symptoms but are of diagnostic importance. They are firm painless structures which are attached to tendon sheaths, joint capsules and fascia, and the skin is movable over them. They occur mainly over the extensor surfaces of the wrists, elbows, knuckles, knees and tendo Achilles and also over the scalp. They usually last about a week.

Erythema marginatum. This consists of lesions which develop rapidly from small macules or papules into large circles with pink, slightly raised, sharply circumscribed edges and pale centres. As these circles intersect, a pattern of segments develops. These appear and disappear within a period of hours. Erythema marginatum affects the trunk and limbs, but never involves the face. It is neither painful nor itchy; recurrences may ensue after all other features of rheumatic fever have disappeared.

Chorea (St. Vitus' dance). This is a neurological manifestation of the acute rheumatic process. It often occurs without the other features, but cardiac involvement is common. It can affect children of both sexes, but after puberty, it is confined to females. The onset is usually insidious with the development of an apparent clumsiness in an otherwise healthy child. Jerky and non-repetitive movements occur and muscle tone is reduced. When the arms are extended the wrist is flexed and the fingers hyperextended, giving rise to a 'dinner fork' configuration. Chorea must be differentiated from tics, which are also jerky but are repetitive, and from athetosis, in which the movements may not be repetitive but are of a more writhing character.

Laboratory investigations

In most cases there is a moderate leucocytosis of 12 000 to 15 000 white blood cells per mm^3 and an increased erythrocyte sedimentation rate (ESR). These features suggest rheumatic activity, but they are not reliable indices when steroids are given as the leucocytosis may persist and the ESR fall as a result of the therapy itself. However, a persistently raised ESR suggests, but does not prove, continuing activity.

In only about one-quarter of patients can a group A streptococcus be grown from the throat. The presence of a high antistreptolysin 'O' (ASO) titre provides good evidence of recent infection, particularly if it rises and falls.

A number of electrocardiographic abnormalities occur in acute rheumatic fever. Amongst these are a prolonged PR interval and, more rarely, more advanced degrees of atrioventricular block. Non-specific T wave changes are common and the ST and T wave changes characteristic of pericarditis may be seen.

The diagnosis of rheumatic fever

There is no certain way of establishing the presence of rheumatic fever, but the combination of certain clinical features and laboratory findings is highly suggestive. It may be diagnosed with some confidence if evidence of a recent streptococcal infection is present together with two or more of the following: carditis, polyarthritis, chorea, erythema marginatum and subcutaneous nodules. The diagnosis is also likely to be correct if evidence of streptococcal infection is combined with *one* of the clinical features mentioned together with two or more of the following: previous evidence of rheumatic fever or rheumatic heart disease, arthralgia, fever, raised ESR or white cell count, or prolonged PR interval. (Revised Jones' Criteria, American Heart Association, 1965.)

Differential diagnosis

The diagnosis of rheumatic fever is often difficult because the classical picture is seldom present. Furthermore, although the criteria described are valuable, they depend upon accurate observation and the correct timing and performance of laboratory tests. A history of sore throat may be misleading, as this is often due to organisms other than streptococci. Likewise, polyarthritis may be wrongly diagnosed when only the vague limb pains so common in childhood have occurred. Cardiac signs can also be deceptive, as functional systolic murmurs often come and go in the child with pyrexia from any cause. Another problem is posed by the patient with chronic rheumatic heart disease who develops a sore throat. Nevertheless, if the above-mentioned criteria are adhered to, the correct diagnosis will usually be made.

Diseases which are particularly important to differentiate from rheumatic fever are bacterial arthritis, rheumatoid arthritis and subacute infective endocarditis. In most cases of acute septic arthritis, the disease process is confined to a single joint and the inflammation is liable to extend into adjacent soft tissue. The diagnosis can be confirmed by bacteriological examination of fluid from the joint. Staphylococcal and meningococcal septicaemias can be diagnosed from blood cultures. Rheumatoid arthritis tends to involve smaller joints than rheumatic fever, but observation over a long period may be necessary in order to be certain of the diagnosis. Subacute infective endocarditis may be difficult to differentiate from rheumatic fever if blood cultures are negative, but a polyarthritis is rare, and some of the characteristic features such as microscopic haematuria and anaemia, which are seldom found in rheumatic fever, are usually present.

Course and prognosis

The course of rheumatic fever is variable and unpredictable. In some apparently severely ill patients, complete recovery takes place within a few days, whereas in others the disease drags on for months. In either case, the liability to recurrences of rheumatic activity following further streptococcal infection remains and it is common for the victim of one attack to experience one or more further episodes over the succeeding years.

The first attack is seldom fatal, but recurrences may lead to increasing cardiac damage and heart failure. By contrast, if the patient has escaped cardiac damage in the first attack, it is unlikely to develop subsequently. It has been estimated that more than two-thirds of patients who have experienced rheumatic fever eventually develop chronic rheumatic valve disease.

It is rare for the young child with rheumatic fever to escape cardiac damage. The risk of developing valve disease after an acute episode diminishes with age and it is not unusual for those first affected in adult life to have no sequelae. There can be no doubt that many cases of rheumatic fever escape diagnosis because about half of the patients with proven chronic rheumatic heart disease give no history of an acute episode.

Treatment

During the acute phase of the disease the subject wants and needs bed rest. When the temperature, pulse rate and ESR have returned to normal and the evidence of acute arthritis and carditis has disappeared, the patient may be gradually mobilized and rehabilitated. Active carditis requires complete rest, and this may have to be continued for several weeks. Subsequent increases in activity must depend upon the individual response, and a full resumption of normal physical activity usually has to be delayed to 6 months from the time when the last signs of active carditis have resolved.

Both salicylates and corticosteroids have a dramatic effect on the fever and polyarthritis of rheumatic fever. Although controversy continues as to the relative merits of the two forms of drug therapy, it is now common practice to use salicylates for rheumatic fever without carditis, and to add or substitute corticosteroids if there is undoubted evidence of cardiac involvement. However, it does not seem that any drug prevents the development of chronic valve damage. It is important not to give large doses of salicylates which can lead to salicylate intoxication; it is particularly undesirable to administer large doses of sodium salicylate as this may precipitate cardiac failure. For children, 50 mg of acetylsalicylic acid per kg body-weight may be given daily, and the dose subsequently adjusted to control symptoms. Salicylates should be continued until signs of rheumatic activity have ceased. There is great variation in the dosage of corticosteroids necessary to control activity. An initial dose of 40 mg of prednisone daily may be given and subsequently reduced to 20 mg daily, continued for 6 weeks and gradually withdrawn. Some patients have a rebound of rheumatic activity subsequently, and it is best to try to control this with salicylates.

The manifestations of cardiac failure are often suppressed by corticosteroids but diuretics and digitalis should be administered if necessary.

Prevention of rheumatic fever

Rheumatic fever may be prevented by the prophylaxis and treatment of acute streptococcal infections.

Acute streptococcal infections are probably most effectively treated by a single injection of 0.6 to 1.2 mega-units of benzathine penicillin, but this is painful. Alternatively, phenoxymethyl penicillin may be given for 10 days.

All patients who have experienced acute rheumatic fever should receive long-term prophylactic therapy. For this purpose, benzathine penicillin may be injected monthly in a dosage of 0.6 to 1.2 mega-units, or oral therapy given as 125 mg penicillin V twice daily or sulphadiazine 0.5 g twice daily. It is not known how long prophylaxis should be continued, but it is common practice to recommended this up to the age of 25.

The healing of rheumatic carditis and the development of chronic rheumatic heart disease

Chronic rheumatic heart disease is the result of damage produced by recurrent attacks of acute rheumatic carditis and the subsequent healing process. These changes are largely confined to the valve structures, although in some instances myocardial damage may also be severe. Rheumatic pericarditis heals without residual effects. It is difficult to know to what extent the chronic lesions are the result of continuing and smouldering rheumatic activity. It is unusual for adult patients with chronic rheumatic heart disease to exhibit clinical evidence of acute rheumatic infection, but laboratory investigations may reveal evidence of repeated subclinical streptococcal infections, and biopsy of myocardial muscle in the adult frequently shows Aschoff bodies.

Because valve damage predominates in patients with chronic rheumatic heart disease, this condition will be considered in detail under the individual valve lesions. It is important to recognize that myocardial damage co-exists and that correction of a valve abnormality will not necessarily restore normal cardiac function.

The pathological processes that cause valve deformity include thickening and distortion of the cusps at the time of rheumatic fever, and contracture of the valve structures, fusion of the commissures, shortening of the chordae tendineae and, finally, calcification during the phase of healing. The nature of the valve lesion depends upon the relative importance of these factors in the individual case. Stenosis occurs if fusion of the cusps predominates; regurgitation is produced by shortening of the chordae tendineae and contracture of the valve leaflets.

The valve deformities may take many years to develop and, in particular, narrowing is not critical until the affected orifice is reduced to less than a quarter of its normal size. Regurgitation may be important from the time of the attack of acute rheumatic fever but its appearance, also, is likely to be delayed. Therefore, although the signs of mitral and aortic regurgitation may be present in childhood or early adult life, symptoms due to these lesions seldom develop until the third or fourth decade. The same is true for mitral stenosis; in aortic stenosis symptoms are often postponed even longer.

Further reading

Committee Report. (1965) Jones' criteria (revised) for guidance in the diagnosis of rheumatic fever. *Circulation,* **32,** 664.
DISCIASO, G. and TARANTA, A. (1980) Rheumatic fever in children. *Amer. Heart J.* **99,** 63–65.

11

Disorders of the Cardiac Valves

Mitral valve disease

The normal mitral valve (Fig. 87) consists of the valve ring, two unequal cusps (leaflets), chordae tendineae and papillary muscles. The larger antero-medial (or aortic) cusp is interposed, when open, between the mitral and aortic orifices, and forms part of the outflow tract of the left ventricle (Fig. 88). The papillary muscles arise from the ventricular wall opposite the commissures and are attached to the cusps on either side of the commissures by the chordae tendineae (Fig. 89). The chordae are collagenous strands, which, when tensed by the contracting papillary muscles, prevent the cusps from prolapsing into the left atrium during ventricular systole.

Chronic mitral valve disease is usually due to rheumatic endocarditis. Most commonly, this takes the form of mitral stenosis with little or no mitral regurgitation. Combined stenosis and regurgitation also occurs frequently. Pure mitral regurgitation of rheumatic origin is

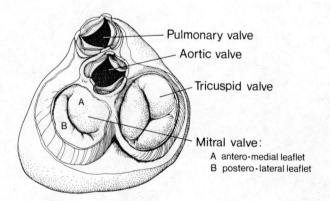

Fig. 87.   Appearances of the heart valves, with the atria and great vessels removed. The heart is viewed from behind, with the left ventricle and mitral valve on the left.

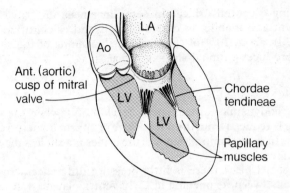

Fig. 88.   Diagrammatic representation of relationships of left atrium (LA), left ventricle (LV) and aorta (AO). Note that the aortic cusp of the mitral valve separates the mitral valve orifice from the out-flow tract of the left ventricle.

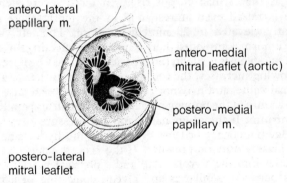

Fig. 89.   Open mitral valve viewed from the left atrium. Note that the papillary muscles arise opposite the commissures and are attached to the cusps on either side of the commissures by the chordae tendineae.

relatively rare. This lesion may also be due to ruptured or defective chordae tendineae, papillary muscles or valve cusps, or to dilatation of the valve ring following left ventricular enlargement from a variety of causes.

Mitral stenosis

Pathology

Mitral stenosis is usually the result of recurrent rheumatic inflammation followed by healing. The leaflets adhere at their commissures, leaving a central orifice. In some instances the valve cusps remain pliant and mobile; in others fibrosis and calcification make them rigid. In about 10 % of cases severe shortening of the chordae tendineae produces a funnel-shaped orifice.

Pathophysiology

Serious haemodynamic consequences develop only when the mitral valve orifice is reduced from the normal size of approximately 5 cm² to about 1 cm². In several mitral stenosis, the orifice is a slit less than 1 cm long and 0.5 cm across.

In the normal heart there is little pressure difference across the mitral valve between its opening in early ventricular diastole and its closure. In mitral stenosis, a pressure difference develops which depends upon the area of the mitral valve orifice and the volume of blood flowing through it (Fig. 90).

When the stenosis is relatively mild, the mean pressure in the left atrium may be normal at rest (i.e. less than 12 mmHg) but increases on exercise as the cardiac output rises. In more severe stenosis, the pressure is raised even at rest, and in the most severe grades is persistently elevated to 25 mmHg or more. The left ventricular pressure is normal, provided there is no disease affecting this chamber.

When the stenosis is slight, the cardiac output may be normal, but as the narrowing increases, the cardiac output diminishes to about half the normal value, and may not rise in response to exercise.

The pressure in the pulmonary veins and capillaries parallels that in the left atrium. If the pulmonary capillary pressure rises rapidly to 30 mmHg, pulmonary oedema develops as the hydrostatic pressure exceeds plasma osmotic pressure. If the process takes place slowly, fluid exudes into the alveolar wall and a physical barrier eventually develops between capillaries and alveoli consisting of a thickened capillary basement membrane, increased collagen and oedema. These changes increase the tissue tension of the alveolar wall and limit the exudation of fluid. As a consequence, patients with mitral stenosis can sometimes tolerate high pulmonary capillary pressures without developing severe pulmonary oedema. Because of the increased fluid in the interstitial tissues, the lymphatics become engorged.

As the pulmonary capillary pressure increases, there is a concomitant rise in pulmonary arterial pressure. Thus, as left atrial and pulmonary capillary pressure increases from about 10 to 30 mmHg, the pulmonary mean arterial pressure rises from 20 to 40 mmHg. However, in many cases of severe mitral stenosis, pulmonary arterial hypertension is much more severe than can be accounted for by this passive rise. This disproportionate elevation of pulmonary arterial pressure does not occur until there is a persistently high left atrial pressure. It is largely due to an increase in tone in the pulmonary

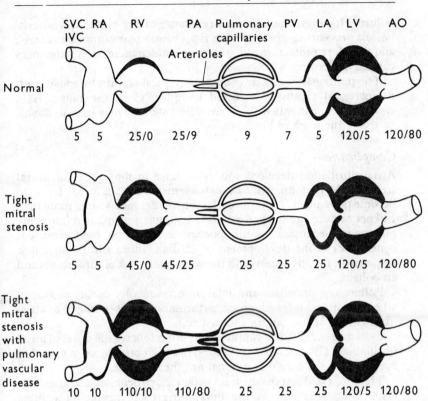

	SVC RA	RV	PA	Pulmonary capillaries	PV	LA LV	AO

Normal

5   5   25/0   25/9   9   7   5   120/5   120/80

Tight mitral stenosis

5   5   45/0   45/25   25   25   25 120/5   120/80

Tight mitral stenosis with pulmonary vascular disease

10 10   110/10   110/80   25   25   25 120/5   120/80

Giant 'a' wave

Fig. 90.   The haemodynamic effects of mitral stenosis. In the normal heart, the pressure in the left atrium is similar to that of the left ventricle during ventricular diastole. With the development of mitral stenosis, the pressure in the left atrium rises, and this rise is transmitted to the pulmonary veins, capillaries and arteries. When pulmonary vascular disease develops, there is a narrowing of the pulmonary arterioles which leads to a disproportionate rise in the pulmonary arterial and right ventricular systolic pressures. With right ventricular failure both the right ventricular end-diastolic pressure and the mean right atrial pressure may rise to 10 mmHg. If sinus rhythm persists, there may be giant 'a' wave in the right atrium as the hypertrophied right ventricle impedes filling.

arterioles and small pulmonary arteries, which is largely reversible when the mitral valve disease is corrected. Sometimes pulmonary arterial hypertrophy and secondary atheroma develop; these changes may be irreversible. Severe pulmonary arterial hypertension is disadvantageous in that it leads to right ventricular hypertrophy and failure. However, the increased resistance of the pulmonary arterial vessels prevents an abrupt rise in right ventricular output on exercise and therefore protects the lungs from a sudden increase in pulmonary capillary pressure.

The pulmonary vascular congestion typical of mitral stenosis leads to increased rigidity (decreased compliance) in the lungs. As a consequence, patients with severe mitral stenosis may have to double or treble the work of breathing.

Complications

Atrial fibrillation develops sooner or later in most cases of mitral stenosis. At first this may be paroxysmal, but it is usual for it to become permanent. At its onset the ventricular rate is often more than 140 per minute and the patient may be rapidly precipitated into acute pulmonary oedema. It is an important complication, both because it contributes to the development of cardiac failure and because it is responsible for atrial stasis and the consequent risk of thrombosis and embolism.

Pulmonary embolism and infarction frequently occur, especially when the disease is far advanced, as thrombosis is encouraged by atrial fibrillation, cardiac failure and bed rest.

Systemic embolism is common and often follows the onset of atrial fibrillation. The embolism is cerebral in a high proportion of cases but may involve the mesenteric, renal or other arteries.

The congested respiratory tract makes the patient liable to attacks of acute bronchitis and to the development of chronic bronchitis. Infective endocarditis is a rare complication of pure mitral stenosis.

Symptoms

The patient with mitral stenosis, who is often symptom-free for many years, eventually develops features of left-sided cardiac failure and, later, those of right-sided failure. Various factors, such as pregnancy and the onset of atrial fibrillation, may suddenly precipitate the patient from one of these stages into the next.

The major symptom of mitral stenosis is shortness of breath. This occurs at first only on strenuous exercise, but as time passes less and less exertion is required to evoke it. Eventually, orthopnoea develops and the patient is liable to attacks of paroxysmal dyspnoea and acute pulmonary oedema. Acute pulmonary oedema is less likely to occur after advanced pulmonary arterial hypertension has developed.

Haemoptysis occurs in some 10 to 20% of patients with mitral stenosis but is seldom severe. In some cases, the sputum is frothy and pink due to acute pulmonary oedema, but frankly bloody sputum may be expectorated by a patient who is almost free of breathlessness. This is probably due to the rupture of dilated pulmonary or bronchial veins.

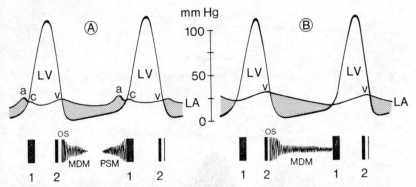

Fig. 91.   (A) The pressure pulses in left ventricle and left atrium and the phonocardiographic appearances in mitral stenosis. A pressure difference is present throughout diastole (shaded area), and is accentuated by atrial contraction. Mid-diastolic and presystolic murmurs result. (B) Atrial fibrillation has developed with loss of the 'a' wave.

Another important cause of haemopytsis is pulmonary infarction.

Patients may also complain of palpitation, cough and angina pectoris. Severe breathlessness and orthopnoea have usually been present for years before right-sided heart failure develops. The earliest symptom of this is oedema of the legs, but abdominal discomfort due to engorgement of the liver or to ascites also occurs. Breathlessness may then become less noticeable.

Physical signs

Patients with long-standing mitral stenosis often have a characteristic facies — a dusky malar discoloration. This may be attributed to peripheral cyanosis associated with a low cardiac output and vasoconstriction.

The arterial pulse is usually normal in volume but may be small, and is often irregular due to atrial fibrillation. In the earlier stages, the venous pressure is normal, but rises with the onset of right-sided heart failure. When there is severe pulmonary hypertension, there may be a large venous 'a' wave due to forceful right atrial contraction against the hypertrophied noncompliant right ventricle.

The apex beat is usually in the normal place but may be deviated to the left by right ventricular hypertrophy. It often has a tapping quality, which is associated with the characteristic loud first heart sound. In more advanced cases, right ventricular hypertrophy produces a heaving impulse to the left of the lower sternum. Mid-diastolic and presystolic thrills may be present at, or internal to, the apex beat.

There are four cardinal auscultatory features of mitral stenosis: a

Fig. 92.   Broad and notched P wave in mitral stenosis (P mitrale).

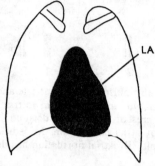

Fig. 93.   The bulge produced by the left atrial appendage is seen on the left border of the heart between the positions of the pulmonary artery and left ventricle.

loud first sound, an opening snap, a mid-diastolic murmur and a presystolic murmur (Fig. 91). The first sound is accentuated and the opening snap loud when the cusps are mobile; these signs may disappear with the development of rigidity and calcification of the valves (see p. 98). A mid-diastolic murmur is usually present, and its length, but not its intensity, gives an indication of the severity of the lesion. The presystolic murmur is often a relatively early sign but easily heard if the patient is exercised and then turned into the left lateral position.

The second sound splits normally, but the pulmonary component is often accentuated because of pulmonary hypertension. An apical third heart sound is impossible in significant mitral stenosis because the rapid filling of the left ventricle necessary for its production cannot occur.

The ECG

If sinus rhythm is present, there is usually P mitrale (Fig. 92). Atrial fibrillation is common; other atrial and ventricular arrhythmias occur occasionally. Evidence of right ventricular hypertrophy develops in cases with severe pulmonary hypertension.

Radiological appearances

The most characteristic radiological feature of mitral stenosis is the selective enlargement of the left atrium, which, in the postero-anterior view, produces a bulge below the pulmonary artery on the left border of the heart, and a rounded dense shadow within or outside the middle part of the right border of the heart (Fig. 93). Left atrial enlargement can be confirmed by observing the displacement of the barium-filled oesophagus in the lateral view. Other radiological features may include calcification of the mitral valve, a normal or small left ventricle, and a normal or small aorta. The upper pulmonary veins are usually prominent. When the pulmonary capillary pressure is high, horizontal septal lines (Kerley's B lines) appear in the costophrenic angles, and the radiological features of pulmonary oedema may be seen. Haemosiderosis may produce mottling of the lungs. Pulmonary artery, right ventricular and, occasionally, right atrial enlargement may also be present when there is pulmonary arterial hypertension.

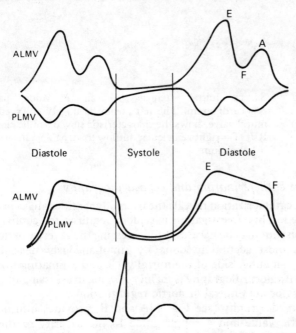

Fig. 94A. Schematic echocardiogram of mitral valve movement. Top tracing, normal valve; middle tracing, mitral stenosis; lower tracing, ECG. ALMV: anterior leaflet of mitral valve. PLMV: posterior leaflet of mitral valve. The major abnormalities in mitral stenosis are: (1) The reduced EF slope. Because of the narrowed orifice, blood flow from left atrium and left ventricle is abnormally slow and the anterior leaflet is held open longer. (2) Posterior leaflet is tethered to the anterior leaflet and moves fowards with it, rather than moving away from it as in the normal valve.

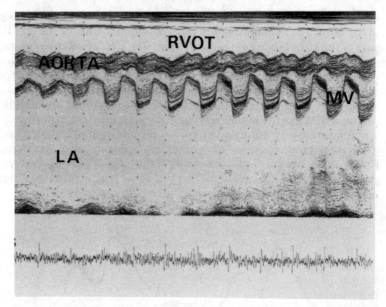

Fig. 94B. Severe mitral stenosis — an M-Mode parasternal echocardiogram. The left atrium is hugely enlarged and the mitral valve shows the characteristic slow diastolic closure rate. RVOT = right ventricular outflow tract. MV = mitral valve. LA = left atrium.

Cardiac catheterization and echocardiography

Cardiac catheterization reveals the haemodynamic changes previously described. This investigation is seldom required for confirming the diagnosis, but may be necessary for assessing the severity of the lesion. This is most accurately done by simultaneously measuring the pressure on either side of the mitral valve and estimating the cardiac output. Angiocardiography is mainly of value in assessing the severity of any associated mitral or aortic regurgitation.

Echocardiography (see Fig. 94A and B) provides information of diagnostic value and a rough guide to the severity of the lesion. Calcification of the valve produces multiple strong echoes.

Combined valve disease

Mitral stenosis is frequently complicated by disease of the other cardiac valves. The combination of rheumatic aortic regurgitation with mitral stenosis is a common one; in most cases the aortic regurgitation is the less important defect. The severity of the aortic regurgitation can be judged with reasonable assurance by the pulse volume, and by the diastolic pressure, which in severe cases is usually less than 60 mmHg. The combination of severe mitral stenosis and aortic stenosis is unusual but important, because one may mask the presence of the other.

Severe tricuspid stenosis complicates about 3% of cases of mitral stenosis and often obscures its signs.

Tricuspid regurgitation is common in advanced mitral stenosis because of dilatation of the tricuspid valve ring secondary to right ventricular enlargement. The associated pansystolic murmur may be heard not only at the left sternal edge but as far out as the apex. This may lead to the erroneous diagnosis of mitral regurgitation. Systolic venous pulsation in the neck, the increase in the murmur on inspiration, and the lack of transmission of the murmur to the axilla serve to identify its tricuspid origin.

Diagnosis

The presence of mitral stenosis can often be suspected from a history of rheumatic fever combined with progressive dyspnoea, a small and irregular pulse, and a mitral facies. In the milder case, these features may be absent, and palpation and auscultation first reveal the diagnosis. A high proportion of patients have a tapping apex beat, right ventricular heave, loud first sound, opening snap, and mid-diastolic and presystolic murmurs. The experienced auscultator is usually first struck by the loud first sound and the opening snap rather than by the diastolic murmurs, which may be audible only if they are specifically sought with the patient lying in the left lateral position. The diagnosis is supported by P mitrale in the ECG, by the demonstration of left atrial enlargement in the radiograph and by the characteristic echocardiographic and catheterization features.

Probably the commonest cause for the mistaken diagnosis of mitral stenosis is the misinterpretation of normal splitting of the first sound for a presystolic murmur (a presystolic murmur is seldom the only auscultatory abnormality in mitral stenosis). A third heart sound may be wrongly interpreted as being an opening snap or a mid-diastolic murmur, and differentiation may be impossible without a phonocardiogram. One should hesitate to diagnose mitral stenosis on the basis of either a presystolic murmur or a short 'mid-diastolic murmur' alone without collateral evidence.

When an apical pansystolic murmur complicates the physical signs in mitral stenosis, it may be difficult to establish whether there is a significant degree of mitral regurgitation. This is unlikely if there is a loud first sound and an opening snap, or if there is evidence of advanced pulmonary hypertension. Important mitral regurgitation is probable if the systolic murmur is loud and radiates to the axilla, or if there is left ventricular hypertrophy, a soft first heart sound or a third sound rather than an opening snap.

Mitral stenosis may be simulated by the mid-diastolic murmurs

encountered in conditions leading to high flow through the mitral
valve, such as ventricular septal defect and persistent ductus
arteriosus, and by the Austin Flint murmur associated with severe
aortic regurgitation as well as by the mid-diastolic murmur of left atrial
myxoma. The possibility that a mid-diastolic murmur is not due to
mitral stenosis should be considered particularly if there is neither a
loud first sound nor an opening snap. In left atrial myxoma, the signs
may entirely mimic those of mitral stenosis, but tend to vary from time
to time (see also p. 280). Echocardiography is particularly valuable in
differentiating the mid-diastolic murmur of mitral stenosis from that
due to other causes.

Course and prognosis

The characteristic physical signs of mitral stenosis, which can develop
within a year of acute rheumatic fever, may precede the development
of symptoms by 10 or 20 years. Breathlessness, which is usually the
first complaint, is most likely to occur for the first time between the
ages of 20 or 30 but may be delayed much longer. In those in whom
complications do not develop, the course is slowly but steadily
downhill over a number of years, and, without treatment, the majority
of patients die by the age of 40. However in Western countries,
patients with signs of mitral valve disease are not infrequently seen in
late middle or old age, whereas in parts of Asia and Africa, severe
rheumatic mitral disease is predominantly found in adolescents and
young adults.

Sooner or later, some complication usually arises which leads to
temporary or permanent deterioration. In young women, pregnancy is
often responsible for the onset or aggravation of breathlessness; in the
patient with severe stenosis, parturition may lead to pulmonary
oedema and death. Rapid deterioration may also occur as a result of
pulmonary infection or infarction and at the onset of atrial fibrillation.
Although these complications are often serious and even fatal, one or
more pregnancies may be well tolerated, and patients may return to
normal activity after infection or infarction has been treated, or atrial
fibrillation controlled.

Once right-sided heart failure has developed, the prognosis without
surgical treatment is poor.

Medical treatment

Surgery is eventually required in most cases, but it is usually necessary
to prepare the patient for it by appropriate medical therapy. Even after
successful surgery, treatment is often needed for the control of
arrhythmias and the prevention of emboli.

Patients with mitral stenosis should be encouraged to live
reasonably normal lives, but to avoid excessive exertion. They should
be advised against being overweight, and discouraged from smoking.

Infections should be promptly treated with appropriate antibiotics, and anticoagulants used if there is evidence of venous thrombosis or of pulmonary or systemic embolism. Careful supervision is required during pregnancy (see p. 282).

Digitalis is required for atrial fibrillation, but is of no value in pure stenosis in sinus rhythm. Cardiac failure is best treated by diuretics. An attempt to restore sinus rhythm should be made after mitral valvotomy in patients with atrial fibrillation, if this is known to be of fairly recent onset.

Surgical treatment

There are two types of surgery available for mitral stenosis: mitral valvotomy and mitral replacement. Mitral valvotomy can be performed as a closed operation (i.e. without direct vision of the valve and without cardiopulmonary bypass) or under the conditions of open heart surgery. When the valve cusps are pliant and mobile, this procedure leads to relief of the stenosis for many years, but re-stenosis of the valve frequently takes place after 5 to 10 years. When the valve is rigid or calcified, valvotomy is seldom successful for more than a few years, if at all. The mortality of closed mitral valvotomy depends upon the severity of the disease and the presence of complications. If the patient is in reasonably good health prior to the operation, and free of severe pulmonary hypertension and mitral regurgitation, the mortality should be less than 5% and, in the most favourable cases, less than 1%. Where there is advanced pulmonary hypertension or right-sided failure, the mortality may rise to 10% or more. In reaching a decision as to whether valvotomy should be undertaken, one must take into account the mortality even in relatively mild cases, the possibility of producing mitral regurgitation, the relatively high incidence of re-stenosis and the risk of causing cerebral embolism. Operation should be avoided in the presence of rheumatic activity. Surgery should also be deferred until cardiac failure has been brought under control or if there has been recent pulmonary or systemic embolism.

Mitral valvotomy is indicated in the following circumstances:

1. Where there are symptoms attributable to pure or almost pure mitral stenosis.

2. Where there are signs indicating severe stenosis, particularly if there is advanced pulmonary arterial hypertension, even in the absence of symptoms. 'Prophylactic' valvotomy should be undertaken in young women with moderate or severe stenosis to avoid operating during pregnancy.

Atrial fibrillation develops shortly after the operation in about one quarter of cases but often resolves spontaneously within 3 weeks. If it fails to do so, correction with dc shock should be undertaken.

The postcardiotomy syndrome which is characterized by pericarditis, pleurisy, pyrexia and malaise, may arise 1 to 8 weeks after surgery. It has been attributed to an autoimmune reaction to heart muscle, or to the presence of blood in the pericardium. Corticosteroids relieve the symptoms but are usually unnecessary.

Successful valvotomy is effective in reducing symptoms, but signs of residual stenosis usually persist. The first heart sound and opening snap remain, but the diastolic murmurs are shortened or abolished.

When there is marked rigidity or severe calcification of the valve cusps, mitral valve replacement must be undertaken. This requires cardiopulmonary bypass, with its increased risks, and involves the complications associated with the use of prosthetic materials (see also Chapter 18).

Because of an operative mortality of about 5%, and the risks of subsequent morbidity, mitral valve replacement should only be undertaken in patients in whom symptoms are severe or whose prognosis is clearly limited to a few years.

Mitral regurgitation

Mitral regurgitation can be caused by a number of different disease processes:

It is frequently the end result of *rheumatic endocarditis* and may predominate over mitral stenosis. The valve cusps are usually rigid and deformed and the chordae tendineae fused and shortened. Calcification is common. In a small proportion of cases, however, the valve cusps are preserved, but the orifice enlarges as a consequence of scarring and dilatation of the mitral valve ring. Regurgitation may develop at the time of rheumatic fever, especially if this is severe, but does not usually produce major haemodynamic effects for several years because the progression of valve damage is slow.

Infective endocarditis may produce destruction or perforation of the cusps, or rupture of chordae tendineae.

Congenital mitral regurgitation occurs with or without other congenital abnormalities (see 'atrial septal defect', p. 219).

Papillary muscle malfunction or rupture may result from myocardial infarction (p. 146).

Tearing of cusps may occur at *mitral valvotomy.*

Left ventricular dilatation from any cause, such as hypertension, coronary artery disease and aortic valve disease may lead to dilatation of the valve ring. The mitral regurgitation so produced leads to further enlargement of the left ventricle, and therefore further dilatation of the valve ring, with the development of a vicious circle.

Spontaneous rupture of chordae tendineae of unknown aetiology may occur.

Mitral valve prolapse (billowing or ballooning of the posterior mitral valve leaflet). This common condition may be associated with rheumatic and ischaemic heart disease and with the Marfan syndrome, but usually there is no other disease process. The usual auscultatory finding is a mid-systolic click and/or a late systolic murmur, but the click and murmur may occur at other times during systole. Most patients are asymptomatic, but chest pain and arrhythmias affect some patients and the ECG may show minor ST abnormalities. Echocardiography, which has demonstrated this abnormality in some 5% of normal young people, characteristically reveals a midsystolic 'buckling' of one or both leaflets into the left atrium. Some cases have a posterior 'hammocking' of the leaflets throughout systole. Although there is a slight risk of infective endocarditis and of serious arrhythmias, the prognosis is usually excellent. Reassurance is an essential part of management; an anxiety state is the commonest complication of this lesion.

Pathophysiology

The severity of mitral regurgitation depends on a number of factors:
1. The size of the mitral valve orifice during ventricular systole. Although this can be of fixed size, as it is when the valve is calcified, it may be variable, depending on the degree of left ventricular dilatation.
2. The pressure relationships between the left ventricle, aorta and left atrium.
3. The left ventricular output.

Any factor which augments left ventricular output or raises aortic impedance increases mitral regurgitation. The degree of mitral regurgitation is limited by the distensibility of the left atrium and pulmonary veins. However, the pressure in the left atrium is much lower than that in the aorta, so that with a large valve orifice, as much blood may regurgitate into the left atrium during systole as is ejected into the aorta. A feature of chronic severe mitral regurgitation is that the left atrium is much larger than is usual in mitral stenosis.

During systole, the pressure in the left atrium may rise to a high 'v' peak, but will not do so if the regurgitated blood is readily accommodated in a voluminous left atrium. When mitral regurgitation develops abruptly, as with papillary muscle malfunction and ruptured chordae tendineae, the left atrium is often small and the 'v' wave tall.

In diastole, there is a large flow from left atrium to left ventricle, consisting of the blood received from the pulmonary circulation combined with that which regurgitated during the preceding systole. At this time the pressure in the left atrium falls rapidly to the ventricular level. Therefore, although there may be a high 'v' wave the mean left atrial pressure is often not greatly raised, and the pulmonary capillary pressure is seldom as high as that encountered in mitral stenosis. Eventually, however, with the development of left ventricular failure, the pulmonary capillary pressure rises and, with it, the pulmonary arterial pressure. Severe pulmonary hypertension and right-sided cardiac failure are unusual unless there is also an appreciable degree of mitral stenosis.

Complications

The complications are similar to those of mitral stenosis. Atrial fibrillation is frequent when mitral regurgitation is of rheumatic origin but less so when other disease processes are responsible. Infective endocarditis is relatively common.

Symptoms

In cases of rheumatic origin, the physical signs precede symptoms by many years. When symptoms do occur, they usually increase slowly. Fatigue, perhaps attributable to the low cardiac output, may be the first complaint, but eventually dyspnoea on exertion, orthopnoea and, rarely, paroxysmal nocturnal dyspnoea develop.

When mitral regurgitation is due to perforation of a cusp, or to rupture of chordae tendineae or papillary muscles, the onset of symptoms is abrupt; the patient may present with acute pulmonary oedema.

Physical signs

The pulse is usually of normal volume; irregularity due to atrial fibrillation is common. The venous pressure is normal except when there is right-sided cardiac failure. The apex beat, which may be displaced downwards and outwards, often has the vigorous thrusting character of left ventricular hypertrophy and dilatation, and there is sometimes a systolic thrill.

The first sound is usually soft and introduces an apical pansystolic murmur which radiates to the axilla. The murmur may be of the same intensity throughout systole, but often increases towards the end of this period. When the regurgitation is due to papillary muscle malfunction or ballooning of a mitral cusp, the murmur may be exclusively in late systole. Rarely, it may radiate to the left sternal edge rather than to the axilla and may be mistaken for aortic stenosis. The intensity of the murmur bears some relation to the severity of the regurgitation, but is not a reliable guide. In most cases there is a third heart sound, followed by a short mid-diastolic murmur due to rapid filling of the left ventricle. An opening snap is unusual in the absence of mitral stenosis.

The ECG

The ECG may be normal but P mitrale is often present if atrial fibrillation has not supervened. Left ventricular hypertrophy occurs in severe mitral regurgitation, but if there is significant stenosis there may be no abnormality or evidence of biventricular hypertrophy.

Radiography and echocardiography

Radiologically, the most conspicuous feature is the marked enlargement of the left atrium, but there may also be evidence of left ventricular enlargement. Calcification of the mitral valve is often visible in rheumatic cases. Evidence of pulmonary vascular dilatation and pulmonary oedema develops when there is left ventricular failure.

When mitral regurgitation is of acute onset due to malfunction or rupture of valve cusps, papillary muscles or chordae tendineae, there may be little left atrial or left ventricular enlargement in spite of high left atrial pressure and pulmonary oedema.

Echocardiography may not reveal any abnormality in mitral regurgitation, but if the reflux is large, there is dilatation of the left atrium and left ventricle. Calcification or thickening of the cusps may be seen. Other possible findings include mitral valve prolapse or a flail valve due to ruptured chordae or papillary muscles.

Cardiac catheterization

The confirmation and quantitation of mitral regurgitation is best made by injecting radio-opaque contrast medium into the left ventricle. Left ventriculography is of particular value in assessing the severity of mitral regurgitation complicating mitral stenosis. The presence of left ventricular failure may be confirmed by finding a high left ventricular end-diastolic pressure. A tall 'v' wave in the left atrial or pulmonary arterial wedge pressure tracing is suggestive of, but not diagnostic of, mitral regurgitation.

Diagnosis

The diagnosis is usually based on the finding of an apical pansystolic murmur radiating to the axilla. The pansystolic murmur of tricuspid regurgitation may reach the apex, but does not radiate further and is usually increased on inspiration. The systolic murmur of aortic stenosis may be heard best at the apex, but is midsystolic and does not radiate to the axilla. The murmur of ventricular septal defect is heard best at the lower left sternal edge.

It may be difficult to differentiate mitral regurgitation from a benign systolic murmur, but benign murmurs are never pansystolic, are seldom of grade 3 or greater intensity and tend to vary with posture and respiration.

Suggestive evidence of mitral regurgitation is provided by left atrial and left ventricular enlargement on the chest radiograph, and by P mitrale and left ventricular hypertrophy on the ECG.

Echocardiography is valuable in prolapse of the mitral cusps and in ruptured chordae and papillary muscles. The definitive diagnosis is made by left ventriculography.

In mitral regurgitation of non-rheumatic origin, the diagnosis may be suggested by the sudden appearance of a loud apical systolic murmur accompanied by left ventricular failure.

Course and prognosis

The course of patients with mitral regurgitation is very variable. Those with mild regurgitation and without cardiomegaly may live a normal life span, although exposed to the risk of infective endocarditis. In rheumatic mitral regurgitation of moderate severity, the course is one of slow deterioration over 10 to 20 years with gradually increasing heart size until left ventricular failure develops. Unless this has been precipitated by a complication that can be corrected, the prognosis is then poor and death is likely to occur within a few years. When mitral regurgitation has been due to ruptured chordae tendineae, papillary muscles or cusps, the prognosis is generally poor, although the regurgitation is occasionally slight and well tolerated.

Medical treatment

Medical treatment does not differ from that for mitral stenosis, except that inotropic drugs, such as digitalis, may be of value even in sinus rhythm. Reduction in afterload, by vasodilator therapy, is helpful, particularly in acute mitral regurgitation.

Surgical treatment

Mitral regurgitation can be successfully treated surgically only under direct vision, with cardiopulmonary bypass. In some instances, it is possible to restore valve function by plicating the ring or ruptured chordae. In the majority of cases, however, it is necessary to insert a mitral valve prosthesis. The problems associated with this are discussed on p. 292.

Because of the risks of open-heart surgery and of prosthetic valves, patients with mitral regurgitation should be considered for surgery only if they are becoming increasingly disabled and it is likely that they will succumb to their disease within a few years. The long-term outlook of mitral valve replacements is, as yet, inadequately known, although there are many patients who have received benefit from such valves for a period of more than ten years.

Aortic valve disease

The normal aortic valve consists of three semi-lunar cusps attached to a fibrous valve ring. Immediately above the insertion of the valve cusps

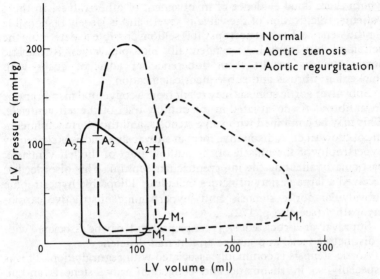

Fig. 95. Relationships between left ventricular volume and pressure in the normal heart, in aortic stenosis and in aortic regurgitation. M_1 = mitral valve closure. A_2 = aortic valve closure. Note high pressure generated in aortic stenosis and large end-diastolic volume (at M_1), with increased stroke volume in aortic regurgitation.

are the sinuses of Valsalva, from two of which the coronary arteries arise. In about 1% of individuals the aortic valve has only two cusps.

The aortic valve and adjacent structures may be involved in congenital, rheumatic, bacterial, syphilitic and atherosclerotic changes. Both stenosis and regurgitation may occur as isolated lesions but are often combined. Calcification of the cusps is an important factor in the development of aortic valve disease and is often responsible for the stenosis that occurs in those with congenitally bicuspid valves.

Aortic stenosis

Aortic stenosis is most commonly the result of disease of the aortic valve cusps, but may also be due to narrowing in the outflow tract of the left ventricle below the cusps (subvalvar) and, very rarely, a constriction in the first part of the aorta (supravalvar stenosis).

Aetiology and pathology

Aortic valve stenosis may be congenital, rheumatic or sclerotic. Most instances of aortic stenosis occur in individuals of late middle age, in whom there is no evidence of involvement of other valves. In these patients, calcification of the valve is severe and is largely responsible for the stenosis. Even at necropsy it is seldom possible to determine the aetiology, but many have congenitally bicuspid valves. Rheumatic aortic stenosis results from adherence of adjacent cusps with thickening, fibrosis and subsequent calcification.

Subvalvar aortic stenosis may result from a congenital membrane or from fibrous tissue situated in the outflow tract of the left ventricle. This may be combined with valve stenosis, and thus form a tunnel in the outflow tract. A distinctive form of subvalvar stenosis is caused by hypertrophy of the muscle of the outflow tract of the left ventricle, particularly affecting the interventricular septum. This disorder has received a large variety of names including 'idiopathic hypertrophic subvalvular aortic stenosis' and 'hypertrophic obstructive cardio-myopathy' (see also p. 172).

Supravalvar aortic stenosis is congenital and may be associated with a distinctive facial appearance and mental deficiency.

Aortic stenosis is commonly associated with regurgitation. This is especially so in rheumatic and congenital valve stenosis and in congenital subvalvar stenosis. It is seldom severe in the calcific stenosis of the elderly and almost unknown in hypertrophic subaortic stenosis. Mitral valve disease usually predominates over aortic stenosis in rheumatic valve disease.

The left ventricle hypertrophies in response to the pressure load imposed upon it. The weight of the heart is often doubled in severe cases. There is usually little ventricular dilatation unless there is associated aortic regurgitation. Coronary artery disease may coexist with aortic stenosis, but commonly the coronary arteries are larger than normal. In aortic valve stenosis, there is a dilatation of the ascending aorta (an effect of the jet of blood which is propelled through the valve); this is not seen in subvalvar stenosis.

Pathophysiology

A minor degree of stenosis has little or no effect upon the function of the heart; only when the area of the valve orifice is reduced to a quarter of the normal are there serious consequences. The left ventricle responds to the pressure load by contracting more forcibly, and the left ventricular systolic pressure increases (see Fig. 95). A systolic pressure difference develops between the left ventricle and aorta (Fig. 96). The magnitude of this difference in pressure depends on the size of the orifice and the flow of blood through it. The obstruction delays emptying of the left ventricle, so that the phase of ejection becomes prolonged. The cardiac output is usually maintained within the normal range but at the expense of a considerable increase in left ventricular work. In consequence, left ventricular hypertrophy

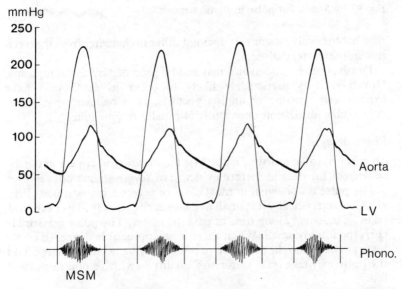

Fig. 96. Simultaneous pressure recordings and phonocardiographic appearances in aortic stenosis. Note the systolic pressure difference between the left ventricle and aorta, and the corresponding mid-systolic murmur MSM.

increases progressively as the valve orifice narrows. Although the hypertrophy is a compensatory phenomenon, it eventually contributes to the burden on the heart. The thickened ventricle is less compliant and is therefore less easily filled during diastole; atrial contraction contributes more and more to the filling process. The hypertrophied muscle increasingly outstrips the ability of the coronary arteries to supply it with blood.

Symptoms

There is a characteristic triad of symptoms: breathlessness, syncope on exertion, and angina pectoris. To this may be added the liability to sudden death.

Breathlessness is the earliest symptom in most cases. Later orthopnoea and paroxysmal nocturnal dyspnoea may occur. Eventually, right-sided heart failure with peripheral oedema may develop.

Syncope is much commoner in aortic stenosis than in other types of valvar heart disease and its relationship to exertion is of diagnostic value. Its mechanism is uncertain, but it is probably due to the inability of the heart to increase its output sufficiently.

Like syncope, anginal pain is much commoner in aortic stenosis

Fig. 97.   Small, flat pulse in aortic stenosis.

than in other valve lesions. It does not differ in character from that seen in coronary artery disease.

Death is often sudden and may not be preceded by any symptoms. However, it is particularly likely to occur in those who have experienced syncope or angina pectoris. It is believed that either ventricular fibrillation or asystole is usually responsible.

Physical signs

An aortic systolic murmur is the first abnormality to appear and may be present for decades before evidence of severe stenosis develops.

The pulse is abnormal in most cases of severe aortic stenosis (Fig. 97). Characteristically it is small in volume, rises slowly to its peak, and takes an unusually long time to pass the finger. The pulse pressure is correspondingly small. When there is an appreciable degree of aortic regurgitation as well, the pulse pressure may be normal or large, and the pulse may take on a 'bisferiens' quality in which a double pulse is felt.

The apex beat may be in the normal position or displaced downwards and to the left. It has a slow heaving quality. A systolic thrill can often be felt in the second right intercostal space, and also in the carotid arteries and along the left edge of the sternum.

There is a midsystolic murmur, which is usually loud and harsh. This may be best heard in the second right interspace, along the left sternal edge, or even at the apex. It is often audible over the carotid arteries. It is accompanied by an early systolic ('ejection') click in those cases in which there is aortic valve stenosis without heavy calcification. This sign is probably due to sudden tension of the valve cusps at the time of opening. Other signs may include a fourth (atrial) heart sound over the left ventricle and reversed splitting of the second heart sound. This latter sign is due to delay in left ventricular emptying and aortic valve closure. The aortic component of the second heart sound may not be audible if there is calcification.

ECG, chest radiograph and echocardiography

The ECG usually shows left ventricular hypertrophy, the extent of which roughly parallels the severity of the stenosis. Other abnormalities which sometimes occur include asymmetrical inversion of T waves and left bundle branch block. The chest radiograph may be normal, but the ascending aorta is usually dilated in aortic valve stenosis. Left ventricular enlargement may be evident. Calcification of the valve when present is best visualized by fluoroscopy. Apex cardiography is of value in demonstrating large 'a' waves which provide an index of severity.

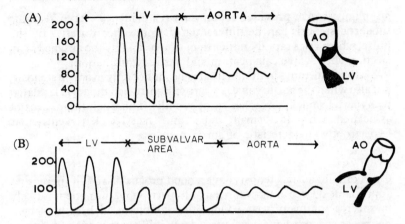

Fig. 98.   (A) Pressure tracing recorded as catheter is withdrawn from left ventricle to aorta in aortic valve stenosis. Note sudden fall in systolic pressure as the catheter tip enters the aorta. (B) Pressure tracing from the left ventricular body (LV), subvalvar area of left ventricle, and aorta, when catheter is withdrawn from left ventricle to aorta in subaortic stenosis. Note the fall in systolic pressure as the catheter is withdrawn past the subvalvar stenotic area, with preservation of the left ventricular diastolic pressure. No further systolic fall is observed as the catheter is withdrawn into the aorta, but the diastolic pressure rises.

Echocardiography may reveal thickening and calcification of the cusps; bicuspid valves are seen to open eccentrically. The supravalvar or subvalvar location of the obstruction may be apparent.

Cardiac catheterization

The systolic pressure difference across the stenosis is measured with catheters in left ventricle and aorta or by the withdrawal of a catheter from left ventricle to aorta (Fig. 98). If the stenosis is severe, the left ventricular systolic pressure exceeds that in the aorta by more than 50 mmHg.

Complications

The most frequent cause of death is cardiac failure, but there is considerable risk of sudden death. Infective endocarditis may occur and, by eroding the cusps, cause severe aortic regurgitation.

Diagnosis and differential diagnosis

The diagnosis is often suggested by the triad of symptoms (dyspnoea, angina, syncope on exertion), or by the finding of the typical murmur associated with a thrill and a small pulse. Calcification of the valve seen on fluoroscopy provides confirmatory evidence. Hypertrophic subaortic stenosis can be differentiated from other varieties by the pulse, which rises rapidly rather than slowly, and by the absence of an ejection click, valve calcification and aortic regurgitation.

Systolic murmurs in the aortic area occur not only in aortic stenosis, but also when the aortic valve is sclerosed, and when the aorta is dilated by hypertension, atherosclerosis or syphilis. These conditions are not associated with the small pulse and massive left ventricular hypertrophy characteristic of aortic stenosis.

Prognosis

Cases of mild aortic stenosis have a good prognosis and, if there is no appreciable degree of left ventricular hypertrophy, the patient is likely to survive for many years. Once the symptoms of breathlessness, angina or syncope have developed, death is likely to occur suddenly at any time, or within 5 years from heart failure.

Treatment

Little or no benefit can be expected from medical treatment. When symptoms have developed, strenuous activity should be avoided and the conventional treatment of heart failure and angina pectoris employed. Surgery is indicated for nearly all patients; this necessitates open-heart techniques. In some cases of non-calcific aortic valve stenosis and in subvalvar stenosis, corrective operations to widen the stenosed orifice may be successful. When there is calcification of the aortic valve, it must be replaced. For this purpose, either prosthetic valves, homograft or heterograft valves can be inserted. Homograft and heterograft valve surgery has the advantage of not requiring subsequent anticoagulant therapy, but the technique is more difficult and the long-term results are still uncertain. The mortality of aortic valve replacement varies greatly from centre to centre, but averages about 5%. This risk must be weighed against the grave prognosis in those with advanced symptoms.

Aortic regurgitation (Synonyms: aortic incompetence, insufficiency)

Aetiology

Aortic regurgitation is most commonly due to rheumatic heart disease. It can also be of congenital origin, in which case it is usually of less importance than the lesions which accompany it, such as aortic and subaortic stenosis and ventricular septal defect. Other causes include hypertension, infective endocarditis, the Marfan syndrome, dissecting aneurysm, syphilitic aortitis, ankylosing spondylitis and Reiter's disease.

Pathology

Aortic regurgitation can result either from damage to the cusps or from dilatation of the aorta and the valve ring. In rheumatic heart disease, the cusps are thickened and shortened and there may be some fusion of commissures. Varying degrees of stenosis and regurgitation occur. Calcification of the valve, which is usually severe in aortic stenosis, is seldom of importance in pure aortic regurgitation.

Syphilitic aortitis leads to aortic regurgitation as a result of dilatation of the aorta and the valve ring; stenosis is not a feature.

Pathophysiology

In aortic regurgitation, a large volume of blood is regurgitated into the left ventricle in each diastole. The left ventricular output may be more than doubled. The increased stroke volume necessary is associated with dilatation of the left ventricle (see Fig. 95). The regurgitant flow is greatest in early diastole when the difference in pressure between the aorta and left ventricle is maximal. The amount of blood that regurgitates is largely determined by the severity of the aortic valve disease but is also influenced by the compliance of the left ventricle and the systemic vascular resistance.

The dilated left ventricle contracts more powerfully in accordance with Starling's law, but there is an increased tension in the myocardium and increased oxygen consumption. The initial dilatation thus leads eventually to hypertrophy.

The diastolic pressure in the aorta is abnormally low, partly due to the leak and partly to peripheral vasodilatation. The left ventricular end-diastolic pressure is normal in the milder case but rises when cardiac failure supervenes.

Clinical features

Rheumatic aortic regurgitation usually develops at the time of acute rheumatic carditis and persists subsequently. Many years elapse between its appearance and the onset of symptoms.

Almost invariably the first complaint is that of dyspnoea on exertion, although fatigue is also frequent. Other minor symptoms include dizziness and an awareness of the vigorous heart action.

The dyspnoea progresses slowly; eventually orthopnoea and paroxysmal dyspnoea may develop. Typical angina pectoris also occurs, but only when the regurgitation is severe. In the advanced case, signs of right-sided failure complicate those of left-sided failure.

The arterial pulse in aortic regurgitation, often called 'collapsing' or 'water-hammer', rises rapidly and falls abruptly. This is most easily appreciated by placing the palm of one's hand on the anterior aspect of the patient's forearm (the arm being held vertically upright) because by this means one may accentuate the backflow of blood during diastole. Sometimes the pulse is of bisferiens type, i.e. is felt to have two equally prominent waves, particularly if the regurgitation is accompanied by stenosis. The cardiac rhythm is usually normal unless there is associated mitral valve disease. The systolic pressure is often abnormally high and the diastolic low. In a severe case the systolic pressure may be 250 to 300 mmHg and the diastolic 30 to 50 mmHg. Vigorous arterial pulsation is often visible in the neck.

If the regurgitation is substantial, the apex beat is displaced outwards and downwards and is overactive and heaving. The essential feature on auscultation is an early diastolic murmur, usually best heard over the midsternal region or at the lower left sternal edge. In some cases, particularly in syphilitic aortitis, it is loudest in the second right intercostal space. There is often an accompanying systolic murmur; this does not necessarily indicate co-existent aortic stenosis but may be due to the increased stroke volume. The early (or 'immediate') diastolic murmur is often difficult to hear, and is frequently overlooked by the inexperienced. It must be specifically sought, with the stethoscope diaphragm placed at the lower left sternal edge, with the patient sitting up, his breath held in expiration.

In some patients with advanced aortic regurgitation, a mid-diastolic murmur may be heard even in the absence of mitral stenosis. This murmur (known as the Austin Flint murmur) has been attributed to the effect of the regurgitant jet on the aortic leaflet of the mitral valve which is interposed between the mitral and aortic valve orifices (see Fig. 86). One should hesitate to diagnose an Austin Flint murmur in rheumatic heart disease because concomitant mitral stenosis is likely, particularly if there is a loud first sound or opening snap.

ECG, chest radiography and echocardiography

The ECG shows increasing evidence of left ventricular hypertrophy as the disease process advances. On the chest radiograph, there is usually left ventricular enlargement, with an elongated heart shadow and dilatation of the ascending aorta. Echocardiography often shows a vibration of the anterior leaflet of the mitral valve, and, if the regurgitation is severe, the mitral valve is seen to close abnormally early.

Cardiac catheterization

Gross aortic regurgitation is so readily recognized clinically and by non-invasive methods that cardiac catheterization is seldom required for diagnostic purposes. This investigation is, however, necessary when the degree of severity is in doubt; it is of particular value in evaluating the significance of an aortic diastolic murmur in a patient needing surgery for concomitant mitral valve disease. The ciné-angiographic demonstration of the regurgitation of contrast medium injected into the aorta provides the best estimate of severity.

Differential diagnosis

The clinical diagnosis of aortic regurgitation is usually not difficult if it is moderate or severe. A large pulse pressure is also observed in other conditions, such as persistent ductus arteriosus, arteriovenous fistulae, pregnancy, anaemia and thyrotoxicosis. The early diastolic murmur may be confused with that of pulmonary regurgitation, but this rare lesion is seldom found in the absence of severe pulmonary hypertension. Angiography provides the most certain method of diagnosis, but echocardiographic demonstration of fluttering of the mitral valve is very suggestive.

In determining the aetiology of aortic regurgitation, it is important to look for other valve lesions and for evidence of disease in other systems. The signs of mitral stenosis or regurgitation suggest a rheumatic origin. Syphilis should be suspected particularly when there is aneurysmal dilatation of the aorta or calcification of the ascending aorta. Congenital aortic regurgitation is usually overshadowed by aortic or subaortic stenosis.

Clinical course and prognosis

Minor degrees of aortic regurgitation are compatible with freedom from symptoms and a normal life span. In the moderate to severe case, symptoms and signs develop slowly, and it is usually not until the fourth or fifth·decade that disability sets in. The severity of aortic regurgitation can be judged, to a large extent, by the pulse pressure and the size of the left ventricle. Increasing dyspnoea and an enlarging heart are signs that the patient is unlikely to survive for more than a few years. Sudden death is unusual in asymptomatic patients but may occur when an advanced stage has been reached.

Treatment

In less severe cases, considerable symptomatic improvement can be obtained by conventional treatment of cardiac failure such as the restriction of activity, and the use of digitalis and diuretics. When symptoms and heart size are increasing in spite of medical measures, surgery should be considered. In good hands the results of aortic valve replacement, either by artificial valves or bioprostheses are reasonably satisfactory, but there is an operative mortality of about 5%. Artificial prostheses necessitate permanent anticoagulant therapy; bioprostheses do not. Successful surgery is accompanied by a diminution in heart size, although not necessarily to normal. Symptoms are relieved, but medical measures may still be required.

Combined aortic stenosis and regurgitation

Aortic stenosis and regurgitation are often combined. When the lesion is congenital, atherosclerotic or calcific, the stenosis is usually the more important. In rheumatic heart disease, all gradations between the two can occur. In deciding which is dominant, the character of the pulse and the pulse pressure are of great value. A collapsing pulse is incompatible with severe stenosis; a small pulse makes major regurgitation unlikely. The murmurs can be deceptive as loud aortic systolic murmurs are not uncommon in aortic regurgitation even when stenosis is slight or absent. Likewise, the intensity of an aortic diastolic murmur is an unreliable guide to the extent of regurgitation.

Tricuspid valve disease

The structure of the tricuspid valve is similar to that of the mitral valve, except for the presence of three cusps. It may be affected by either stenosis or regurgitation. Tricuspid stenosis is nearly always rheumatic in origin and is rarely the dominant cardiac lesion. Some degree of tricuspid stenosis occurs in about 10% of cases of rheumatic heart disease, but is of significance in only about 3%. Organic tricuspid regurgitation, which is uncommon, is usually due to rheumatic heart disease. Functional tricuspid regurgitation is a frequent complication of right ventricular failure whatever the cause.

When tricuspid valve lesions are due to rheumatic heart disease, the pathological appearances are similar to those seen in the mitral valve. The valve cusps are thickened and the chordae may be adherent and shortened. Dilatation of the tricuspid valve ring is a major factor in regurgitation and occurs as a result of either dilatation of the right ventricle or the rheumatic process.

Tricuspid stenosis

The narrowed valve obstructs flow from the right atrium to the right ventricle during ventricular diastole. As a consequence, right atrial pressure rises, cardiac output falls, and the right atrium and venae cavae dilate. Atrial contraction becomes increasingly forceful and produces large 'a' waves in the venous pulse if sinus rhythm is preserved. Hepatic engorgement follows and ascites and peripheral oedema eventually develop.

In most cases of tricuspid stenosis, mitral stenosis is also present and dominates the clinical picture. For this reason, breathlessness is the commonest symptom, but because tricuspid stenosis restricts right ventricular throughput, pulmonary congestion is often less severe than it is in isolated mitral stenosis. The patient with mitral stenosis may become less breathless as tricuspid stenosis progresses, but at the expense of right-sided cardiac failure.

Large flicking venous 'a' waves may be seen even in early cases. When the lesion is more advanced the venous pressure as a whole is elevated. The 'a' wave disappears when atrial fibrillation develops. The flow of blood from the atrium into the ventricle during diastole is slow and the 'y' descent of the venous pulse is therefore prolonged. The liver is enlarged and may exhibit presystolic pulsation corresponding with the large 'a' waves. On auscultation, mid-diastolic and presystolic murmurs may be heard at the lower left sternal edge which are similar in timing to those of mitral stenosis but of a rather more scratchy quality. The murmurs are accentuated by inspiration, because of increased return to the right atrium at this time. It is not uncommon in the patient with tricuspid stenosis for the signs of mitral stenosis to be masked.

On the ECG the only characteristic feature is the presence of the tall P waves of right atrial enlargement. The chest radiograph shows enlargement of the right atrium and superior vena cava; the features of mitral stenosis are also usually present. The lung fields are often relatively clear. Echocardiography may reveal reduced movement or thickening of the cusps.

On cardiac catheterization, a diastolic pressure difference can be demonstrated between right atrium and right ventricle, and there is usually a large 'a' wave in the right atrial pulse.

The prognosis of patients with tricupid stenosis is often relatively good. However, if the lesion is severe, progressive signs of right-sided cardiac failure develop; ascites, jaundice and cachexia are characteristic.

In the majority of patients with tricuspid stenosis, the lesion is insufficiently severe to warrant surgery, which should be undertaken only if the stenosis is responsible for major symptoms. Valvotomy seldom restores normal valve function; replacement by a prosthesis is usually necessary.

Tricuspid regurgitation

As mentioned, functional tricuspid regurgitation is a common complication of right ventricular failure and pulmonary hypertension. Since most patients with this condition have evidence of rheumatic heart disease, it is often difficult to be sure whether or not there is organic tricuspid disease as well. One can, however, deduce that the regurgitation is functional if the signs disappear with the use of digitalis and diuretics or the successful treatment of mitral valve disease.

The features of tricuspid regurgitation are the consequence of a large volume of blood being regurgitated through the valve from the right ventricle. As a result, the forward flow into the pulmonary circuit is reduced and the right ventricle has to cope with a large volume load. When regurgitation is severe, large systolic ('cv') waves develop in the right atrium, which are transmitted to the peripheral veins and liver. There is a high flow of blood through the tricuspid valve during diastole, as both the regurgitated and the forward flow must be transported at this time. Both diastolic and systolic flow through the valve is increased on inspiration as an increased volume of blood is drawn into the heart.

Coexistent mitral valve disease usually dominates the clinical picture and dyspnoea is the major symptom. Tricuspid regurgitation may reduce the effects of the mitral valve disease on the lungs at the expense of producing right-sided heart failure. As the disease progresses, there is an increase in venous pressure, hepatic enlargement, ascites and peripheral oedema. Large systolic waves are present in the jugular veins; systolic pulsation of the liver may be felt. A systolic murmur is heard at the lower left sternal edge; and it is usually increased on inspiration. There may also be a tricuspid diastolic murmur due either to concomitant tricuspid stenosis or to high flow through the orifice during this phase.

There are no specific ECG features of tricuspid regurgitation; the chest radiograph usually shows right atrial enlargement. If the tricuspid regurgitation is secondary to mitral valve disease and pulmonary hypertension, the characteristic radiological features of these lesions will be present.

On cardiac catheterization, the chief feature is the large systolic venous wave of the right atrial pulse. The finding of severe pulmonary hypertension suggests the regurgitation is functional. A near normal pulmonary artery pressure is an indication that the tricuspid disease is organic.

It is often difficult to differentiate mitral regurgitation from tricuspid regurgitation, or to determine whether there is a combination of the two. Mitral regurgitation is suggested by radiation of the murmur to the axilla and by left ventricular enlargement; tricuspid regurgitation by systolic venous pulsation and by inspiratory accentuation of the murmur.

Tricuspid regurgitation is often tolerated for a long time, but sooner or later the features of advanced right-sided cardiac failure become disabling. Severe oedema and ascites develop and are progressively less responsive to treatment.

If the tricuspid regurgitation is functional, there may be striking improvement with digitalis and diuretic therapy. Usually, surgery for associated mitral valve disease is required, and, if succesful, leads to the disappearance of the tricuspid leak. When severe tricuspid regurgitation does not diminish in response to these measures, repair or replacement of the valve by a prosthesis becomes necessary.

Pulmonary valve disease

Pulmonary valve disease is relatively uncommon. Pulmonary valve stenosis is usually of congenital origin and is discussed in Chapter 12. Other causes of pulmonary stenosis include rheumatic heart disease, malignant carcinoid of the small intestine and hypertrophic cardiomyopathy.

Pulmonary regurgitation is usually secondary to pulmonary hypertension, but occasionally occurs as a consequence of infective endocarditis, as a complication of the surgical relief of pulmonary stenosis and as a congenital anomaly. It is nearly always overshadowed by the heart disease to which it is secondary. In most cases, there are signs of pulmonary hypertension, and the only feature which suggests the diagnosis is an early diastolic murmur (the Graham Steell murmur) in the second or third left intercostal spaces which becomes louder on inspiration. It is often difficult to decide whether a murmur in this position is due to pulmonary or aortic regurgitation. Pulmonary regurgitation is unlikely in the absence of signs of pulmonary hypertension and right ventricular hypertrophy. Aortic regurgitation is suggested by a collapsing pulse and the signs of left ventricular hypertrophy, although these signs may be absent if the regurgitation is slight. The diagnosis may be confirmed by demonstrating angiocardiographically a reflux of radio-opaque material from the pulmonary artery. Pulmonary regurgitation produces no serious haemodynamic effects and its prognosis and treatment are those of the associated pulmonary hypertension.

Further reading

BONCHEK, L. I. (1981) Current status of cardiac valve replacement: selection of a prosthesis and indications for operation. *Amer. Heart J.*, **101**, 96.

Editorial (1981) Mitral valve prolapse. *Brit. med. J.*, **282**, 1411.

Key References (1982) National history of valvular heart disease, *Circulation*, **65**, 1283.

RAPAPORT, E. (1975) Natural history of aortic and mitral valve disease. *Amer. J. Cardiol.*, **35**, 221.

12

Congenital Heart Disease

A congenital abnormality of the heart is present in nearly one in every hundred babies born. About half of the affected babies die either from their heart disease or from some associated congenital anomaly during the first year of life if untreated. The prognosis of those who survive this period is reasonably good; from 5 years of age until early adult life, the prevalence of congenital heart disease remains at about three per thousand. The less severe types of lesion then begin to take their toll and it is unusual for patients with most forms of uncorrected congenital heart disease to survive much beyond the age of 40.

Embryology

At an early stage, the heart consists of a simple tube of endocardium surrounded by myocardium and epicardium. As it grows, the tube twists into an S shape and by the fourth week of pregnancy it is divided by constrictions into five segments: (1) the sinus venosus, which receives the systemic veins, (2) the common atrium, (3) the common ventricle, (4) the bulbus cordis, and (5) the truncus arteriosus (Fig. 99). Between the fifth and eighth week, changes of the greatest importance occur; it is at this time that congenital abnormalities are most likely to arise through arrested or faulty development. Septa develop in the atria and in the ventricles to subdivide each of these chambers into two. Simultaneously, the atria are divided from the ventricles by endocardial cushions from which the mitral and tricuspid valves are formed (Fig. 100A). A spiral septum divides the bulbus cordis into the outflow tracts of the left and right ventricles respectively, and the truncus arteriosus into aorta and pulmonary artery (Fig. 100B).

By the end of the eighth week, the heart has largely assumed the features which it retains until birth. The right atrium in the fetal circulation then receives blood from the superior vena cava and from the vitello-umbilical veins which later become the inferior vena cava. A proportion of the venous blood, particularly that from the superior vena cava, flows into the right ventricle, thence into the pulmonary artery and, by way of the ductus arteriosus, into the descending aorta. Only about 5 % of the blood flow traverses the pulmonary circulation.

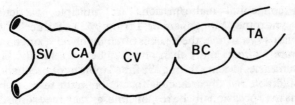

Fig. 99. The heart at the fourth week of pregnancy, divided by constrictions into sinus venous (SV), common atrium (CA), common ventricle (CV), bulbus cordis (BC) and truncus arteriosus (TA).

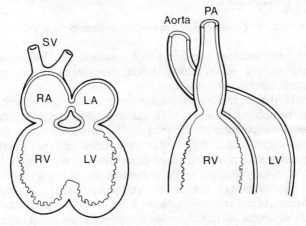

Fig. 100. (A) The heart at 8 weeks. The ventricles and atria are each being divided by septa into two chambers. Endocardial cushions develop from which the mitral and tricuspid valves are formed. (B) The spiral septum divides the bulbus cordis into the outflow tracts of the left and right ventricles, and the truncus arteriosus into aorta and pulmonary arteries.

Most of the highly oxygenated inferior vena caval blood is directed through the foramen ovale in the atrial septum into the left atrium and thence, by the left ventricle, into the ascending aorta. Within a few hours or, at most, days of birth the ductus arteriosus closes, and the relatively high pressure in the left atrium closes the valve of the foramen ovale.

Aetiology

No aetiological factor can be found in most cases of congenital heart disease. In a minority there is evidence of either a genetic abnormality or an environmental factor affecting the mother during the early stages of pregnancy.

When congenital malformations are multiple, particularly in Down's syndrome (Mongolism or Trisomy 21), Turner's syndrome and Marfan's syndrome, the heart is often involved. Congenital heart disease rarely affects more than one member of a family. If rubella (German measles) occurs during the first 3 months of pregnancy, there is a considerable risk of cardiac malformation in the fetus. Other virus infections may occasionally be responsible, as may may some drugs, of which thalidomide is the most notorious.

The varieties of congenital heart disease

The varieties of congenital heart disease can be divided into:

1. *Communications between the left (systemic) and right (pulmonary) circulations*, e.g. atrial septal defect, ventricular septal defect and persistent ductus arteriosus.

The resistance to flow is normally lower on the right side of the heart and in the pulmonary artery than it is on the left side of the heart and in the aorta. Consequently, the intracardiac pressures are relatively low on the right side. When the two sides of the heart are in communication, provided there is no other abnormality, there is a shunt of blood from left to right through the defect and an increased blood flow through the lungs. In ventricular septal defect and persistent ductus arteriosus, the volume load falls predominantly on the left ventricle, which enlarges accordingly. In atrial septal defect, the load falls on the right ventricle.

The greatly increased pulmonary blood flow frequently leads to a moderate elevation of pulmonary arterial pressure. In most cases, the resistance of the pulmonary arteries is normal, but sometimes, for reasons still unknown, changes take place in the arterial walls which cause a high pulmonary vascular resistance. Severe and irreversible pulmonary hypertension may then ensue and, eventually, lead to reversal of the shunt (Eisenmenger syndrome p. 232).

2. *Obstructive lesions*, e.g. coarctation of the aorta, aortic stenosis and pulmonary stenosis.

When these lesions are isolated, they impose a burden on the related ventricle and may eventually cause cardiac failure on this account. They may be combined with abnormal communications, the most important anomaly being that of tetralogy of Fallot, in which there is pulmonary stenosis with a ventricular septal defect.

3. *Displacement of chambers, vessels or valves.* These may be associated with abnormal communications or obstructions. Some

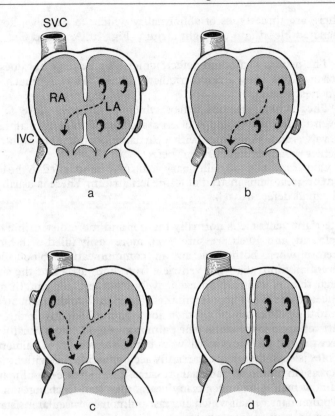

Fig. 101. (A) Atrial septal defect of ostium secundum type. The valve cusps are not affected. (B) Ostium primum defect, associated with abnormalities of the mitral or tricuspid valves. (C) Anomalous drainage of the right pulmonary veins into the right atrium, associated with an atrial septal defect of the secundum type. (D) Unsealed foramen ovale. The valvar construction of the foramen ovale prevents shunting from left to right.

displacement lesions such as dextrocardia and right-sided aorta may be unimportant. Others, such as transposition of the great arteries, are associated with a high mortality.

Abnormal communications

Atrial septal defect ASD

The foramen ovale, which is unsealed in some 25 % of adults, does not normally permit the flow of blood from the left atrium to the right atrium because of its valvar construction (Fig. 101D).

There are three types of abnormality which do permit a flow of oxygenated blood into the right atrium (Fig. 101A, B and C):

1. The ostium secundum defect, which may be large but does not encroach upon the atrioventricular valves. This is much the commonest variety.

2. The ostium primum defect which is situated close to the atrioventricular valves and is often associated with abnormalities of these valves and, sometimes, with a partial or complete atrioventricular defect ('endocardial cushion' defect).

3. One or more of the pulmonary veins may be attached to the right atrium or great veins instead of to the left atrium. There is usually an atrial septal defect as well.

The right ventricle is normally thinner and more distensible than the left and, at a given pressure level, more easily filled with blood. Therefore when both atria are in communication, blood flows preferentially into the right ventricle from both atria and the shunt through the defect is almost exclusively from left to right. In most instances, more blood flows from the left atrium into the right atrium and into the pulmonary circuit than flows from the left atrium through the left ventricle to the aorta. The pulmonary blood flow is usually two or three times the aortic blood flow, but the distensibility of pulmonary arterioles is such that they can readily accommodate this with little or no increase in pulmonary arterial pressure. The increase of pulmonary blood flow maintained over many years, may lead to changes in the small pulmonary vessels which increase pulmonary vascular resistance and cause severe pulmonary hypertension.

Defects of the atrial septum seldom give rise to disabling symptoms before the third decade of life, but breathlessness and fatigue are likely to develop before the age of 40. Symptoms are usually progressive and are exacerbated when atrial arrhythmias develop, as they commonly do.

The arterial pulse is relatively small; the venous pressure is usually normal. The right ventricle is strikingly overactive. Splitting of the second sound is wide, and varies little with respiration. This is due to relatively late closure of the pulmonary valve as a consequence of delayed emptying of the overburdened right ventricle. A systolic murmur in the second left interspace due to high flow across the pulmonary valve is almost invariable. Larger defects have a mid-diastolic murmur at the lower left sternal edge, accentuated by inspiration, and produced by increased flow through the tricuspid valve. In the ostium primum type of defect, in which an abnormal mitral valve may permit regurgitation, there may be left ventricular enlargement and an apical systolic murmur.

The ECG nearly always shows the features of partial right bundle

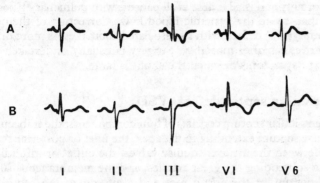

I   I I   I I I   V I   V 6

Fig. 102.   ECG appearances in (A) ostium secundum defect, and (B) ostium primum defect. Note left axis deviation in the latter.

branch block ('rsr' complex). In the common ostium secundum type, there is frequently right axis deviation, whilst in the ostium primum type there is usually left axis deviation. This feature is of importance in differentiating the two types of defect (Fig. 102).

On the chest radiograph, the heart is usually slightly enlarged, and the pulmonary artery and its branches prominent, as are the right atrium and the right ventricle. The aorta is abnormally small and may not be visible. Expansile pulsation of the pulmonary arteries ('hilar dance') may be a striking feature on fluoroscopy.

Echocardiography, in ostium secundum defect, demonstrates 'paradoxical' septal motion. As a result of right ventricular overloading, the septum moves towards the right ventricle in systole instead of its usual movement towards the posterior left ventricular wall at this time.

In ostium primum, abnormalities of the mitral valve are usual.

Two-dimensional echocardiography reliably demonstrates primum and secundum defects and differentiates easily between them.

These clinical features are usually sufficiently characteristic for accurate diagnosis. Confirmation by cardiac catheterization is required when the diagnosis is in doubt or surgical treatment is planned. The oxygen saturation in the right atrium is markedly higher than that in the superior vena cava, and the catheter tip may be advanced through the septal defect into the left atrium and thence to the left ventricle. In the ostium primum defect, injection of radio-opaque contrast medium into the left ventricle often reveals mitral regurgitation. When there are anomalies of the pulmonary veins (Fig. 101C), the anomalous veins may be entered directly from the right atrium or, occasionally, from connections to the superior or inferior venae cavae.

Closure of an ostium secundum defect is relatively easy, carries a low mortality and is advisable in all patients with pulmonary blood flow more than twice the systemic blood flow. Correction of the ostium primum type of defect, with its associated anomalies, is more difficult and carries a higher mortality. Surgery is usually undertaken when there are symptoms or when the shunt is large.

Ventricular septal defect (VSD)

The ventricular septum consists of four components: the trabecular or muscular septum extending to the apex, the inlet or posterior septum lying between the atrioventricular valves, the outlet or infundibular septum subtending the great arteries, and the membraneous septum which lies under the aortic root and abuts on to the other three components. Defects can arise in any one of these three components, but the membranous septum is the most commonly affected.

Defects of the ventricular septum, which may be large in relation to the size of the heart at birth, tend to become smaller or to close in early childhood. If closure is insufficient to prevent a large shunt, the small pulmonary vessels may be damaged by being exposed to the ejectile force and pressure of left ventricular contraction. Irreversible pulmonary hypertension may be produced.

The effect of a ventricular septal defect depends upon its size and upon the resistance to blood flow imposed by the pulmonary arterial vessels. If the defect is small, the jet of blood from the high-pressure left ventricle to the low-pressure right ventricle has little haemodynamic effect. If the defect is large and the resistance of the pulmonary vessels low, a large shunt develops and the pulmonary blood flow becomes more than twice the systemic flow. If, on the other hand, there is a high pulmonary vascular resistance, the pulmonary blood flow is little or no more than the systemic and the pressure in both circuits is similar. If the pulmonary vascular resistance is very high, the shunt reverses.

In the patient with a small defect ('maladie de Roger'), there are no symptoms, but there may be a loud 'tearing' systolic murmur accompanied by a thrill, maximal to the left side of the lower sternum.

A large left-to-right shunt at ventricular level is liable to produce cardiac failure in the second or third month after birth. The special problems associated with this type of abnormality are discussed under the section 'The diagnosis and management of the infant with heart failure and cyanosis' (p. 236). If a large shunt does not produce symptoms during infancy, there is usually little disturbance until late adolescence or early adult life. Breathlessness and fatigue may then develop and cardiac failure subsequently ensue. In the presence of a large left-to-right shunt with pulmonary blood flow greater than twice systemic, the pulse is usually small and the venous pressure normal, unless there is right heart failure. Both left and right ventricles may be hyperdynamic, and there may or may not be a systolic thrill between the apex and the left sternal edge. A pansystolic murmur is heard at this site, usually accompanied by a mid-diastolic murmur at the apex due to high flow through the mitral valve.

In patients with a high pulmonary vascular resistance, breathlessness, fatigue and cyanosis are likely to develop during the second or third decade with progression to effort syncope, recurrent haemoptysis or heart failure. The signs of the ventricular septal defect are then less obvious, although there may still be a systolic murmur between the apex and the left sternal edge. Right ventricular hypertrophy is evident and the pulmonary second sound may be accentuated and followed by the early diastolic murmur of pulmonary regurgitation.

The ECG in small defects is normal. When the left-to-right shunt is large there is usually biventricular hypertrophy, manifested by abnormally deep but narrow Q waves and tall R waves in the left chest leads and an rSr pattern in V1. In cases with a high pulmonary vascular resistance, the ECG pattern of isolated right ventricular hypertrophy develops.

The chest radiograph is normal with a small defect, but with a large left-to-right shunt there is some enlargement of the heart and, more specifically, prominence of the pulmonary vessels, left atrium and both ventricles.

With small defects, the realtime echocardiogram is often normal. With larger defects, there is usually a 'drop-out' of septal echoes, and both left atrium and ventricle may be enlarged.

Correlation of these features usually provides sufficient evidence for accurate clinical diagnosis in spite of the various forms which defects of the ventricular septum may take. Further investigation may be advisable when the diagnosis is not clear-cut and is necessary if surgical treatment is contemplated. Cardiac catheterization usually demonstrates that the oxygen saturation of right ventricular blood is higher than that in the right atrium. However, if the defect is small or if there are equal pressures in the systemic and pulmonary circulations, no shunt of oxygenated blood may be demonstrable. The injection of radio-opaque material into the left ventricle may then be necessary for the angiocardiographic visualization of the defect.

The prognosis of ventricular septal defect depends upon the age of the patient, the size of the defect and the pulmonary vascular changes. Large ventricular septal defects are an important cause of death in the infant; in those who survive, the defect usually becomes smaller or closes. After the first year, a few affected children die, but death is likely to occur in those with major defects between the ages of 20 and 40. Patients with small defects usually live a normal life span, but are exposed to the risk of infective endocarditis.

In deciding upon the appropriate therapy for a patient with

ventricular septal defect, the expected prognosis must be taken into account. In all patients precautions must be taken to avoid infective endocarditis. Because the outlook in small defects is excellent, surgery is not indicated. If there is a large left-to-right shunt, the defect should be closed. When the pulmonary vascular resistance is high, surgery is usually contraindicated as it cannot correct, and may indeed worsen, the pulmonary hypertension.

Persistent ductus arteriosus (Fig. 103)

During fetal life, the ductus arteriosus permits blood to flow from the pulmonary artery into the aorta. Within a few hours or days of birth, it narrows and then closes.

In a few infants, the ductus arteriosus remains open and permits a large flow of blood from the high-pressure aorta to the low-pressure pulmonary artery. This may cause heart failure and death in the first few weeks of life. More commonly the ductus arteriosus undergoes partial closure and the shunt from aorta to pulmonary artery is relatively small. This gives rise to no symptoms during the first few years of life and is usually detected at a routine physical examination. A persistent ductus arteriosus of this kind may eventually become harmful for three reasons. First, it may act as a focus for infective endarteritis. Secondly, the leak of blood from the aorta to the pulmonary artery and the consequent high pulmonary blood flow may lead to cardiac failure in adolescence or adult life. Thirdly, severe pulmonary hypertension may develop.

The patient is usually in good general health. The pulse may be of normal volume if the duct is small, but if it is large, a collapsing pulse may occur due to the diastolic leak from the aorta. Correspondingly, the diastolic blood pressure may be low. The heart may be of normal size, or the left ventricle enlarged. The most characteristic feature of the condition is the 'continuous murmur', situated in the second left intercostal space by the sternal edge and often maximal 5 to 7.5 cm

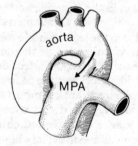

Fig. 103.   Persistent ductus arteriosus. The shunt is from aorta to pulmonary artery because of the low resistance of the pulmonary circuit.

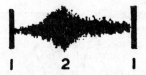

Fig. 104.   The continuous murmur of a persistent ductus arteriosus.

above or to the left of this. This murmur continues from systole into diastole and is maximum about the time of the second sound (Fig. 104). It seldom lasts for the whole of systole and diastole and may occupy only the latter part of systole and the earlier part of diastole. In a few instances, particularly in infants, it may occur as a crescendo in late systole only. The murmur is due to flow of blood from the aorta through the peristent ductus arteriosus into the pulmonary artery in both phases of the cardiac cycle. If the shunt is large, the increased venous return from the lungs causes a mid-diastolic murmur at the apex as it crosses the mitral valve.

The ECG is usually normal but may show the deep Q and tall R waves of left ventricular hypertrophy. The chest radiograph shows enlargement of the left ventricle, aorta and pulmonary artery, and the features of increased pulmonary blood flow. The duct can sometimes be visualized by 2-D echocardiography. Enlargement of the left atrium and left ventricle on the M-mode echo confirm the presence of left ventricular volume overload.

The clinical diagnosis is usually easy because of the characteristic continuous murmur. Special investigation is seldom required even prior to surgical treatment. Care, however, is necessary to avoid confusion with the venous hum which is common in normal children. The hum is usually maximal to the right of the sternum below the right clavicle, diminishes or disappears when the child lies flat and can usually be abolished by compression of the jugular veins on the right side. Continuous murmurs due to other causes are rare and their maximum intensity is usually below and medial to the pulmonary area. When in doubt because of the site or quality of the murmur or the lack of correlation with the electrocardiographic and radiological features, special investigation is necessary. At cardiac catheterization there is a 'step-up' in oxygen saturation in the pulmonary artery. This can be shown to result from a persistent ductus by the passage of the catheter through it into the descending aorta, or by the angiocardiographic delineation of the ductus by the injection of radio-opaque contrast medium into the arch of the aorta.

Surgical treatment of a persistent ductus arteriosus by division and suture carries little risk and is the correct management in almost all patients. Operation should be performed, if possible, before the child starts school.

In symptomatic low birth weight premature infants, the ductus

Fig. 105.   Coarctation of the aorta. The constriction is usually in the
descending aorta just below the left subclavian artery. Beyond
the constriction, there is post-stenotic dilatation.

frequently causes life-threatening cardiac decompensation. Although
immediate surgery is probably still the most successful mode of
treatment, administration of indomethacin, a prostaglandin inhibitor,
can induce duct closure medically. This method is, however, less
certain of success and associated with side effects which may preclude
its use.

Obstructive lesions

Coarctation of the aorta

Coarctation of the aorta is a narrowing of the lumen, usually just
beyond the origin of the left subclavian artery (Fig. 105). It is
characteristically of severe degree and is commonly associated with a
bicuspid aortic valve which may be or may become stenosed or allow
regurgitation. The ductus arteriosus may also persist, commonly when
the coarctation is proximal to the junction of the ductus and aorta.

The systolic pressure in the aorta and its branches proximal to the
coarctation is raised, but this may not be obvious in early childhood;
diastolic hypertension is uncommon before adult life and is seldom
severe at rest. The hypertension may induce irreversible changes in
the arterioles so that the blood pressure may not return to normal even
after the removal of the coarctation.

Only a small volume of blood flows through the narrowed segment;

much of the blood supply of the lower part of the body is by way of collateral vessels which attain great size. The blood pressure in the lower half of the body is lower than that in the upper half and the pulse wave takes longer to arrive.

The hypertension is eventually liable to cause left ventricular failure. Other risks which are less common and are less closely related to the severity of the coarctation or the height of the blood pressure are infection of the coarctation or of a bicuspid aortic valve, rupture or dissection of the ascending aorta, and cerebral haemorrhage. Cystic medial necrosis of the aortic wall, which is present in only a few patients with coarctation, is the deciding factor in rupture. Rupture of an intracranial aneurysm, which occurs in 5 to 10 % of affected individuals, is the usual cause of subarachnoid haemorrhage.

Coarctation may produce no symptoms and is most often suspected during a routine medical examination when a systolic murmur is heard or hypertension detected. However, long segment narrowing in the preductal area of the aorta is associated with heart failure in infancy. In such infants, commonly, the ductus is patent, and pulmonary hypertension is present; a VSD may coexist.

The blood pressure in the upper limbs is raised: that in the legs is normal or low. The femoral arterial pulse is small and delayed in comparison with the radial pulse. In adults, collateral vessels may be seen and felt along the borders of the scapulae and over the posterior chest wall. The left ventricle is occasionally enlarged. A systolic murmur is almost invariably heard over the area of the coarctation at about the level of the fourth intercostal space posteriorly, and tends to be louder than a systolic murmur which is often audible in the second intercostal spaces close to the sternum. A more continuous murmur may be heard over collaterals.

The ECG is usually normal; left ventricular hypertrophy is uncommon before adult years. The chest radiograph is seldom abnormal in childhood, but characteristically shows an abnormal aortic knuckle with an enlarged left subclavian artery and post-stenotic dilatation of the aorta in adults. Another feature is notching of the undersides of the ribs due to the erosion by enlarged intercostal arteries. The left ventricle may also be enlarged.

The diagnosis rarely depends on special investigations, but the severity may be measured by simultaneous intra-aortic pressure tracings above and below the coarctation. The precise anatomy can be outlined by aortography.

The correct treatment is surgical resection of the coarctation and restoration of the aorta by end-to-end anastomosis or, if necessary, by the insertion of a graft. This should be performed electively in early childhood to avoid the development of irreversible hypertension. Even in the absence of symptoms, operation is then much less dangerous than leaving the coarctation untreated.

Aortic stenosis

This condition is considered in Chapter 11.

Hypoplastic left heart

This term is used to describe a number of disorders, such as mitral atresia and aortic atresia, in which the characteristic feature is virtual absence of left ventricular outflow. The diagnosis can usually be established by echocardiogram which reveals a small left ventricle and absent aortic valve. Life can be sustained if there is a large persistent ductus which allows blood to flow from the pulmonary artery to the aorta. Affected infants are intensely cyanosed and usually die within hours of birth. There is, as yet, no treatment.

Pulmonary stenosis

Pulmonary stenosis is almost invariably of congenital origin. Except when it is complicated by a ventricular septal defect (see 'tetralogy of Fallot', p. 230) the stenosis is usually confined to the valve cusps. These may be fused to form a cone-shaped structure with a narrow orifice. Beyond the obstruction the pulmonary artery is dilated; proximal to it the right ventricle is hypertrophied.

The obstruction to right ventricular emptying leads to a high right ventricular systolic pressure and a systolic pressure drop across the pulmonary valve. In the more severe cases, right ventricular failure develops. If the foramen ovale is unsealed, or if there is an atrial septal defect, a right-to-left shunt with central cyanosis may develop as the right atrial pressure rises.

Although pulmonary stenosis may cause cardiac failure in the first few weeks of life, survival into late childhood or adult life is usual. Often the lesion is first detected on routine clinical examination, but some patients present with fatigue, breathlessness or syncope. Frequently, the lesion is so mild that symptoms never occur.

The arterial pulse may be normal or small. The jugular venous pulse is usually normal, but in severe grades it exhibits a large 'a' wave as the right atrium contracts forcibly in the face of the noncompliant hypertrophied right ventricle. On palpation, there is nearly always a systolic thrill in the second left intercostal space; the left parasternal heave of right ventricular hypertrophy can sometimes be felt when the stenosis is severe. The first heart sound is normal, but it is often followed by an early systolic 'ejection' click and a loud midsystolic murmur best heard in the second left intercostal space. The second sound is normal in the mild case, but in the more severe it is split abnormally widely and the second (pulmonary) element is soft.

The electrocardiogram provides useful evidence of the severity of

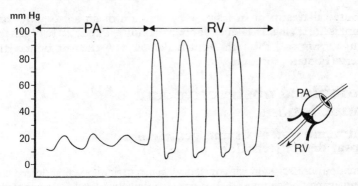

Fig. 106. The pressure pulse obtained as the catheter is withdrawn from pulmonary artery to right ventricle in pulmonary valve stenosis.

the pulmonary valve stenosis for, in general, the greater the degree of right ventricular hypertrophy seen on the ECG, the tighter the stenosis. The chest radiograph shows the post-stenotic dilatation of the pulmonary artery. In severe cases, right ventricular hypertrophy and diminution in the pulmonary vascular markings may be detected.

An accurate diagnosis can usually be made clinically. Cardiac catheterization provides confirmatory evidence; the systolic pressure difference across the pulmonary valve is a valuable index of severity, a drop of more than 50 mmHg suggesting severe stenosis (Fig. 106). Unless the foramen ovale is unsealed or there is an associated atrial septal defect, no intracardiac shunting occurs.

A minor degree of pulmonary stenosis is compatible with a normal life span. When the stenosis is more severe, death is likely to ensue sooner or later from right ventricular failure; surgical treatment should not be delayed too long as irreversible fibrotic changes take place in the hypertrophied right ventricle. Pulmonary valvotomy has a low mortality and should be performed in patients whose symptoms or signs suggest moderate or severe pulmonary stenosis.

Tricuspid atresia

In this relatively uncommon disorder, there is absence of the normal atrioventricular connection on the right side. For life to be sustained in the extra-uterine state, an atrial septal defect and a ventricular septal defect must be present. Frequently there is associated pulmonary stenosis or pulmonary atresia and more rarely transposition of the great arteries. The left ventricle is large and the rudimentary right ventricle which is hypoplastic receives blood by the VSD. Cyanosis in infancy is the rule. The ECG shows left axis deviation and left ventricular hypertrophy. Cross-sectional echocardiography reveals the absent connection and can also demonstrate the VSD and ASD.

Surgical treatment in infancy by creation of an aortopulmonary shunt is life saving. In later childhood a conduit is inserted between the right atrium and the right ventricular outflow tract or pulmonary artery (Fontan procedure).

Combined obstructive and shunt lesions

Pulmonary stenosis and ventricular septal defect (tetralogy of Fallot)

When pulmonary stenosis coexists with a ventricular septal defect, the stenosis may be slight and shunting exclusively from left-to-right. In most cases, however, pulmonary stenosis is severe and the ventricular septal defect large, and there is a right-to-left shunt. These abnormalities are the major features of the 'tetralogy of Fallot', of which the other components are dextroposition of the aorta (with the aortic root overriding the defect) and right ventricular hypertrophy (Fig. 107). The pulmonary stenosis is situated in the infundibulum of the right ventricle and, often, at the pulmonary valve as well. The infundibular stenosis tends to become more severe with advancing age and there is a progressive increase in the proportion of blood shunted from right-to-left.

In the most severe cases, symptoms start soon after birth. More frequently, cyanosis develops in the second half of the first year or not until later in childhood.

With increasing cyanosis, dyspnoea becomes more severe. The child is liable to sudden attacks of intense cyanosis, sometimes associated with syncope, for which spasm of the infundibulum of the right ventricle may be responsible. Children with the tetralogy of

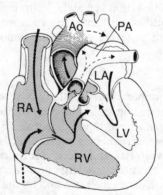

Fig. 107.   Tetralogy of Fallot. Note infundibular pulmonary stenosis and ventricular septal defect, with right-to-left shunt at ventricular level.

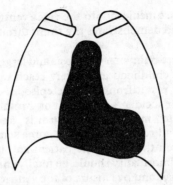

Fig. 108. Radiographic appearances in tetralogy of Fallot. Note prominent and elevated apex.

Fallot are liable to squat after exercise. It is believed that the squatting position, by compressing the abdominal aorta and the femoral arteries, increases the arterial resistance and therefore diminishes the right-to-left shunt at the ventricular level.

The child is often abnormally small and has central cyanosis with finger clubbing. The arterial pulses are small and venous pulses normal. Clinical evidence of right ventricular hypertrophy is slight. There is a loud systolic murmur accompanied by a thrill in the second or third left intercostal space unless the stenosis is so severe that virtually no blood traverses it. The second heart sound is single because the pulmonary valve component is inaudible. The electrocardiogram shows moderate right ventricular hypertrophy. The chest radiograph is characteristic in showing a 'boot-shaped' heart with a concavity on the left border in the place where the pulmonary artery is normally seen, and a prominent and elevated apex (Fig. 108). The pulmonary vascularity is decreased. Echocardiography shows that the aorta is large and overrides the septum, the normal continuity between the anterior aortic wall and septum being lost. Polycythaemia, secondary to the cyanosis, is usual.

The tetralogy of Fallot is the underlying lesion in 70% of children with central cyanosis over the age of 3. This frequency and the characteristic clinical, electrocardiographic and radiological features usually make the diagnosis easy in childhood. In infancy and also later life, a confident diagnosis can less often be reached without further investigation.

On cardiac catheterization, the catheter tip often goes from the right ventricle directly through the ventricular septal defect into the aorta and it may be difficult to enter the pulmonary artery. A systolic pressure drop can be demonstrated between the body and the outflow tract of the right ventricle. Pressures in the right and left ventricles are identical. The oxygen saturation in the aorta is reduced. Injection of radio-opaque contrast medium into the right ventricle delineates the region of stenosis and demonstrates the shunt through the ventricular septal defect.

Patients with severe pulmonary stenosis and large ventricular septal defects often die in childhood and rarely reach middle age without surgery. Death may result from hypoxic episodes during childhood, from cerebrovascular accidents as a result of thrombosis promoted by polycythaemia, from infective endocarditis and from cerebral abscesses. Virtually all require surgery at some stage, but the type of surgery depends upon the age of the patient and the severity of the lesion. Ideally, the abnormality should be totally corrected by relief of the pulmonary stenosis and by closure of the ventricular septal defect. In severely affected infants, some surgeons prefer to perform a palliative procedure. In one type of palliative operation, the pulmonary stenosis alone is relieved (Brock procedure). Another is the creation of a shunt between the aorta and pulmonary circulations, either directly (Waterson operation) or by anastomosing the subclavian artery to the pulmonary artery (Blalock–Taussig procedure). This increases the proportion of blood going through the lungs and thus becoming oxygenated. By one or other of these operations the child can be given several years of comparatively good health before the corrective procedure is performed.

Severe hypoxic attacks should be treated with oxygen and morphine (0.1 mg/kg). The baby should be placed in the knee–chest position. Blood $P\text{CO}_2$ and pH should be estimated and sodium bicarbonate given intravenously as necessary. Propranolol is possibly of value.

High pulmonary vascular resistance with right-to-left shunt through a septal defect or ductus arteriosus (Eisenmenger's syndrome)

Eisenmenger originally described a patient with a ventricular septal defect with central cyanosis in the absence of pulmonary stenosis. It is now known that the reason for the right-to-left shunt in such cases is the presence of a severe pulmonary vascular disease. Because the clinical pictures of pulmonary hypertension with right-to-left shunt are so similar, irrespective of whether the shunt is at atrial, ventricular or aorto-pulmonary level, the term Eisenmenger's syndrome is employed to describe all three lesions.

The cause of the pulmonary vascular disease responsible for the pulmonary hypertension is unknown. Factors which may be involved include:

1. Lack of regression of the fetal type of pulmonary vasculature (see p. 262).
2. Prolonged exposure to high pulmonary blood flow.

3. Prolonged exposure to high pulmonary blood pressure.

4. Genetic predisposition.

Although irreversible pulmonary arterial changes may develop during early childhood, they more commonly occur during adolescence. Dyspnoea and fatigue, which are usually the first symptoms, are liable to develop in late childhood, adolescence or early adult life. Other complaints include syncope, angina pectoris, oedema and haemoptysis.

On examination the patient is usually cyanosed. When the shunt is through a ductus arteriosus, the venous blood is directed into the descending aorta and only the lower limbs become cyanosed ('differential cyanosis').

The arterial pulse is usually small, due to a low stroke volume; a large 'a' wave may be present in the venous pulse, due to forceful atrial contraction in the face of right ventricular hypertrophy. On palpation, one can detect right ventricular hypertrophy and the shock of pulmonary valve closure. On auscultation, the signs are mainly those of pulmonary hypertension: a loud second heart sound, a right ventricular fourth heart sound, a pulmonary early systolic ('ejection') click and, occasionally, the early diastolic murmur of pulmonary regurgitation and the pansystolic murmur of functional tricuspid regurgitation. In atrial septal defect, the second sound remains split on expiration (because only the right ventricle is overburdened). In ventricular septal defect, there is a single second sound, because the pressure in both ventricles is identical. In persistent ductus arteriosus, there is normal splitting of the second heart sound.

The ECG shows right atrial and right ventricular hypertrophy. On the chest radiograph there are large main pulmonary arteries but small peripheral arteries, together with right ventricular and right atrial enlargement. Two-dimensional echocardiography can reliably demonstrate the ventricular or atrial septal defects in these patients.

The diagnosis is suggested by the combination of central cyanosis and pulmonary hypertension in an adolescent or young adult. Eisenmenger's syndrome differs from the tetralogy of Fallot, (the commonest cardiac cause of central cyanosis in this age group), in there being no pulmonary systolic thrill or loud murmur, in the greater severity of right ventricular hypertrophy, and in the large pulmonary arteries on the chest radiograph. The diagnosis can be confirmed by demonstrating by cardiac catheterization that the pulmonary artery pressure equals the systemic pressure, and by angiocardiographic delineation of the shunt. The progress of Eisenmenger's syndrome is usually slowly downhill, death commonly occurring between the ages of 20 and 40. The main causes of death are pulmonary infarction, right heart failure and arrhythmias and, less often, infective endocarditis. Pregnancy is particularly hazardous in these patients and should be avoided or terminated early.

No surgical treatment is of value because the major defect is the irreversible change in the small pulmonary arteries. Temporary benefit may result from the conventional treatment of cardiac failure.

Displacement lesions

Transposition of the great arteries (Fig. 109)

In transposition of the great arteries, the aorta arises from the right ventricle and the pulmonary artery from the left. As a consequence, there are separate systemic and pulmonary circulations; life cannot be sustained unless there is some communication between them. Usually there is one or more of the following: a persistent foramen ovale, an atrial septal defect, a ventricular septal defect, or a persistent ductus arteriosus.

The infant is characteristically of normal size and well nourished. Cyanosis develops at birth or shortly thereafter. There is difficulty in completing feeds; increasing breathlessness, deep cyanosis, cardiac failure and death are usual within the first week or month.

On auscultation there may be a gallop rhythm and a systolic murmur.

The chest radiograph may show little abnormality at birth, but within a few days the heart becomes enlarged and the vascularity of the lung fields increased. The ECG shows little more than the right ventricular preponderance normal for this age group.

Echocardiography, especially the two-dimensional technique, is an invaluable diagnostic tool. It permits observation of the aorta, arising

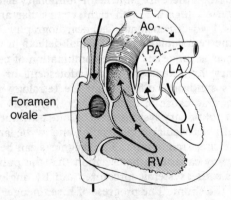

Fig. 109. Transposition of the great arteries. The aorta arises from the right ventricle and the pulmonary artery from the left. The aorta is placed anterior to the pulmonary artery, the reverse of the usual situation. Life can be sustained only if communications exist between systemic and pulmonary circulations.

from the right ventricle and lying anterior to the pulmonary artery, and also allows detection of other defects.

Transposition of the great arteries is the most common cardiac cause of cyanosis at birth and of overt heart failure in cyanotic congenital heart disease within the first few weeks of life. Accurate diagnosis at this stage is urgent; it is usually fatal to await the effects of medical treatment. Investigation should be undertaken within a matter of hours. Echocardiography is of diagnostic value in showing the abnormal connections of the great arteries. If it supports the diagnosis, it is usually then necessary to proceed to cardiac catheterization which not only enables the precise nature of the anomalies to be determined but is an essential preliminary to therapy.

In the acutely ill infant, great improvement can be achieved by producing a large defect in the atrial septum to allow mixing of the blood between systemic and pulmonary circulations (Rashkind procedure). This is done by introducing a catheter with a deflated balloon at its tip into the femoral vein and advancing it via the right atrium and foramen ovale into the left atrium. The balloon is then inflated and withdrawn abruptly so as to tear the atrial septum. This procedure is usually effective in the neonatal period and allows the child to live until the latter part of the first year of life when the venous return to the two ventricles is rerouted by the inserted of an intra-atrial baffle (Mustard's operation). This operation can be carried out with a low mortality.

Ebstein's anomaly

In this disorder, the posteriomedial part of the tricuspid valve ring is displaced towards the apex of the right ventricle. An atrial septal defect is usually present.

Dyspnoea, fatigue and arrhythmias are usual. Cyanosis may be present if there is an atrial septal defect. There are often scratchy tricuspid systolic, mid-diastolic and presystolic murmurs, arising from flow across the abnormal tricuspid valve. Tall P waves, a long PR interval and a low voltage right bundle branch block pattern are the usual ECG features. The chest radiograph shows a large right atrium and clear lung fields. Echocardiography demonstrates the abnormal position and movement.

Death usually results from arrhythmias in childhood or early adult life, but may occur later from cardiac failure or hypoxaemia.

Partial correction, with prosthetic replacement of the tricuspid valve and repair of the atrial septal defect is indicated for the disabled case but this neither restores normal function nor prevents arrhythmias.

Dextrocardia

Dextrocardia refers to all situations where the heart is in the right chest. The lung and abdominal situs or arrangement may be reversed or normal. When dextrocardia exists with complete right–left reversal of the lungs and viscera then the heart is usually normal. When the heart is in the right chest and the other organs are normally sited, or if the heart is in the left chest (laevocardia) and the other organs reversed, then the change of complex congenital cardiac lesions is high.

Right-sided aorta

In this condition, the aorta turns posteriorly and runs down on the right of the trachea and the oesophagus instead of arching upwards and to the left. It may continue to descend in this direction or may cross behind the trachea and oesophagus and attain the normal left-sided course.

As an isolated anomaly it is of no clinical significance. When associated with a congenital lesion of the heart, its detection may be of diagnostic assistance for it is found in 20 to 25% of patients with the tetralogy of Fallot. When associated with other arterial anomalies the trachea and oesophagus may be encircled and obstructive symptoms result.

The diagnosis and management of the infant with heart failure and cyanosis

The general paediatrician and the general practitioner have the responsibility of detecting heart disease in the newborn; an expert in neonatal cardiology should be contacted without delay if there is any evidence of cyanosis or heart failure. All too frequently, the clinical evidence of heart disease is overlooked until it is too late.

Central cyanosis is a serious finding in the newborn. If it persists after exposure to oxygen therapy, and there is no evident respiratory or cerebral cause, congenital heart disease should be suspected. If the cyanosis is indeed due to congenital heart disease, the prognosis without treatment is poor. Echocardiography should be undertaken immediately. The findings of this investigation may suggest that cardiac catheterization is required: this can be combined with therapy (e.g. the Rashkind procedure, see p. 235).

The commonest causes of cardiac failure, with or without cyanosis, in the newborn, are ventricular septal defect, persistent ductus arteriosus, hypoplastic left heart, coarctation of the aorta and transposition.

Heart failure in the infant is frequently overlooked because wheezing may suggest respiratory rather than heart disease. The early signs of heart failure are tachypnoea, tachycardia, gallop rhythm and enlargement of the liver. Cyanosis is often present as well. The venous pressure is a poor guide to heart failure in infants. Crepitations and rhonchi are common and should not be attributed to pulmonary disease until left ventricular failure has been excluded. Oedema, which is most likely to affect the backs of the hands and feet, is a late sign, and is common in the absence of heart failure in premature infants.

Tachycardia may be difficult to assess because the pulse rate is normally fast in infants, but it seldom exceeds 140 per minute during sleep in the healthy baby or in those with respiratory disease. If the rate is in excess of 210 per minute, there is a supraventricular tachycardia requiring urgent treatment. If the heart rate is less than 50 per minute, heart block is almost certainly present.

The digitalis group of drugs is of considerable value in the newborn. Digoxin is perhaps the best preparation; a dose of 70 μg/kg by mouth or 50 μg/kg intramuscularly is necessary for digitalization. In the acutely ill infant, two-thirds of the digitalizing dose may be given intramuscularly initially. The maintenance dose of digoxin is approximately 10 μg/kg. Infants in advanced failure also benefit from diuretic therapy such as frusemide 2 mg/kg. Oxygen should be given to all infants who are cyanosed or in cardiac failure. Measurement of the blood gases and the correction of acidosis is an essential part of the proper management of heart failure in infancy. Good nursing, temperature and humidity control, supportive frames or suspension in the propped-up position and tube feeding are essential in the early stages of treatment.

These medical measures are quite often successful in correcting cardiac failure due to a ventricular septal defect or persistent ductus arteriosus, but where the cardiac malformations are more severe, benefit is only temporary and consideration must be given to surgical procedures which can alleviate or cure the underlying abnormality.

Further reading

KEITH, J. D., ROWE, R. D. and VLAD, P. (1978) *Heart Disease in Infancy and Childhood.* London: Macmillan.
JORDAN, S. C. and SCOTT, O. (1981) *Heart Disease in Paediatrics,* 2nd ed. London: Butterworths.

13

Hypertension and Heart Disease

Hypertension is probably directly or indirectly responsible for 10 to 20% of all deaths. These deaths occur because of the deleterious effects of high blood pressure on the coronary, renal and cerebral arteries, and because of the increased work load imposed on the heart.

For reasons that will become apparent, it is impossible to define hypertension. For practical purposes, the blood pressure may be regarded as abnormally high if it persistently exceeds 140/90 mmHg in a quietly resting individual. This does not imply that individuals with raised pressure necessarily require treatment. The presence of other risk factors and evidence of adverse effects must be taken into account.

The variability of blood pressure

The level of arterial blood pressure is determined by the cardiac output and peripheral vascular resistance, two factors which vary widely from individual to individual, and within one individual at different times. The blood pressure varies to a lesser extent because the changes in cardiac output and peripheral resistance often offset each other. Persistent hypertension is nearly always due to a raised peripheral vascular resistance, the cardiac output being normal. As the peripheral resistance is determined largely by arteriolar tone, it can be concluded that hypertension is the result of arteriolar vasconstriction or organic narrowing.

Marked variations have been observed in individuals in whom the blood pressure is continuously monitored throughout the day. The mean pressure during sleep may be 30 to 40 mmHg lower than it is in the waking state. Factors which transiently increase pressure include anxiety and cold. Exercise leads to a brisk rise in systolic pressure but little change in the diastolic pressure. A transient doubling of systolic pressure may occur at the climax of coitus.

Certain identifiable factors are associated with persistently high blood pressure. Thus, at least in Western societies, both diastolic and systolic pressure increase with age. The blood pressure averages about 80/60 mmHg at birth and rises slowly throughout childhood. The resting blood pressure in the adolescent is often in the region of 120/70 mmHg, whilst in middle age 140/80 mmHg is more common. The systolic pressure often continues to rise into old age as the aorta becomes increasingly rigid. However, in many individuals and throughout some societies, e.g. in some Pacific islands, there is no rise with age. In the younger age groups, males, on average, have higher pressures than females, but this tendency is reversed after the age of 45. Obese individuals tend to have pressures higher than can be accounted for by recording errors due to increased arm circumference.

The variability of arterial pressures within one individual and between individuals makes it impossible to define normality. It has been established, however, that the higher the pressure even within the 'normal' range, whether systolic or diastolic, the more likely is the occurrence of certain disease processes such as left ventricular hypertrophy and failure ('hypertensive heart disease'), coronary artery disease, cerebrovascular disease and renal disease. The blood pressure can only be regarded as pathologically high if it has caused or is likely to lead to disordered function of the cardiovascular system, brain or kidneys.

Classification by blood pressure level

Normal adult blood pressure has been defined as a systolic blood pressure equal to or below 140 mmHg together with a diastolic (fifth Korotkoff phase) equal to or below 90 mmHg.

Hypertension in adults is defined as a systolic pressure equal to or greater than 160 mmHg and a diastolic equal to or greater than 95 mmHg.

Borderline hypertension denotes a blood pressure between normal and hypertension levels as defined above.

Hypertension may be regarded as 'mild' if the diastolic pressure is between 90 and 104 mmHg, 'moderate' if between 105 and 114 mmHg, and 'severe' if above this. Hypertension is said to be in the *malignant* or accelerated phase if there is widespread arterial fibrinoid necrosis. The diastolic pressure is very high (often above 130 mmHg), with retinal haemorrhages and exudates and frequently papilloedema.

Aetiological factors in hypertension

In some 5% of those with high blood pressure, an identifiable cause can be held responsible. When the hypertension can be attributed to one of these, it is 'secondary'; when no such factor can be unearthed it is described as 'essential' or 'primary'.

Hypertension can be secondary to a large number of conditions of which the most important are the following:
1. Renal disease including glomerulonephritis, pyelonephritis,

polycystic disease, renal tumours and renal artery stenosis.

2. Endocrine diseases including diseases of the adrenal gland such as primary aldosteronism, Cushing's syndrome and phaeochromocytoma.

3. Coarctation of the aorta.

4. Pre-eclampsia.

5. Drugs and foods including oral contraceptives, liquorice, carbenoxolone, ACTH and corticosteroids, and vasoconstrictive nose drops.

6. Acute porphyria.

7. Certain cerebral lesions such as brain tumours and bulbar poliomyelitis.

Hypertension occurring in those under the age of 40 is usually secondary, unless there is a strong family history of this condition. The relative proportion of cases with an identifiable cause decreases with age; in the elderly, secondary hypertension is uncommon.

The cause of 'essential' hypertension remains uncertain. Indeed, if it is the result of the interplay of a large number of factors, as many believe, the search for a single cause is doomed to failure. This multifactorial or 'mosaic' concept is supported by much epidemiological evidence which shows that there is an infinite gradation between the 'normal' and 'hypertensive' populations. As Pickering writes:

> What causes the rise of pressure in essential hypertension? We do not know precisely. Certainly no specific fault has been identified and I am personally doubtful if one exists. But going further back we can assign roles to inheritance, which influences pressure at any age, and environment, which influences the rate of rise with age.

The influence of heredity is unquestioned, hypertension being many times more common in the families of hypertensive patients than in those of normotensive individuals. Although some have suggested that hypertension is due to a single dominant gene, most of the evidence points to the influence of many genes.

Numerous differences have been observed between groups of individuals who are hypertensive and those who are not. The significance of these as causal factors is not established.

Dietary influences. There is an undoubted relationship between overweight and hypertension. Weight loss in the very obese substantially lowers the blood pressure; in the less overweight it has little effect. Very low salt intake appears to protect against hypertension, but there is not, as yet, sufficient evidence to incriminate excessive sodium chloride intake as a cause of high blood pressure. Alcohol has been identified as an apparent risk factor for hypertension, as has cigarette smoking, at least in regard to the malignant phase.

Haemodynamic and transient changes. A slight sinus tachycardia and a high cardiac output may be found in early hypertensives before there is a rise in peripheral resistance. These features may result from an excessive adrenergic influence. There is good evidence that baroreceptors are reset in hypertension, as bradycardia is not induced by the rise in pressure.

Some observers have reported increases in plasma catecholamine levels; others have noted abnormal responses of receptors.

Humoral changes. The possible roles of the renin-angiotensin system and of prostaglandins are being studied vigorously at present.

The causes of secondary hypertension

Renal disease

That renal disease can be the sole cause of hypertension has been clearly established both in animal experiments and in man. The components of the renin-angiotensin system are shown in Fig. 110. However, the relationship between renal disease and hypertension is

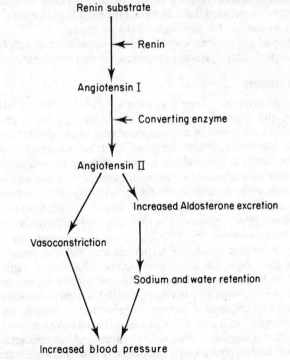

Fig. 110. The renin–angiotensin system.

complex because either may lead to the other, and it is not always easy to determine which is primary.

In *acute glomerulonephritis*, hypertension is almost invariable, but is transient and not often severe. The mechanism is not clear, but sodium and water retention may play a part. Cardiac failure occurs in about one-quarter of the cases, but the hypertension is seldom an important factor in this. The diagnosis can usually be made on the basis of the acute onset, the association with preceding streptococcal infection, and the presence of peripheral oedema and disturbed renal function.

Severe hypertension is usually a late manifestation of *chronic nephritis*, and develops only when there is evidence of advanced renal failure.

There is evidence that *chronic pyelonephritis* can cause hypertension (particularly malignant hypertension) although this has been disputed.

Hypertension occurs in more than half of those with *congenital polycystic disease of the kidneys*.

Hypertension may also be caused by *renal artery disease*, resulting from atheromatous narrowing, fibromuscular hyperplasia or aneurysm formation. Not infrequently, only one renal artery is involved. Renal artery surgery or, if the abnormality is unilateral, nephrectomy is indicated if it can be established that the renal artery disease is responsible for the high blood pressure.

Evaluation of the patient with suspected renal disease may include intravenous pyelography, isotope renography and renal arteriography.

Endocrine disease

Primary aldosteronism (Conn's syndrome). Aldosterone, which is secreted by the zona glomerulosa of the adrenal cortex, promotes sodium reabsorption and potassium excretion in the distal tubules of the kidney. Normally, aldosterone secretion is largely regulated by angiotensin, but in primary aldosteronism there is an overproduction of aldosterone as a result of an adrenal cortical tumour; angiotensin and, therefore, plasma renin levels are abnormally low. It occurs most often in young and middle-aged females. Because of the mode of action of aldosterone, the symptoms and signs are related to sodium retention, hypokalaemia and hypertension. Frequently, the patient presents with mild to moderate hypertension, but the predominant complaints are those of muscle weakness, headache, thirst and polyuria. The hypertension is seldom severe and malignant changes are rare. There is usually hypokalaemia, with a serum potassium of less than 3.0 mmol/litre, and a serum sodium that is normal or high. Characteristically, there is a metabolic alkalosis and a low serum chloride. The diagnosis should be suspected in patients with hypertension and hypokalaemia, particularly if this is associated with hypernatraemia. However, hypokalaemia is not uncommon in other hypertensive patients, particularly if they have been treated with diuretics. Furthermore, patients with malignant hypertension develop 'secondary aldosteronism' with a low serum potassium. These patients usually do not have a high serum sodium.

The diagnosis can be confirmed by showing severe potassium loss in the urine, and by demonstrating control of the hypertension by large doses of the aldosterone antagonist, spironolactone.

If the diagnosis can be made with reasonable certainty, the adrenals should be explored with a view to removing an adenoma.

Phaeochromocytoma. Phaeochromocytomas arise in chromaffin tissue in the adrenal gland or elsewhere. Most are benign, but about 5% are malignant. The tumours usually secrete noradrenaline (norepinephrine), but adrenaline (epinephrine) may predominate.

Phaeochromocytomas may produce either paroxysmal or persistent hypertension. The paroxysms are associated with the sudden onset of bilateral headache, and with perspiration, palpitation and pallor (features often regarded as neurotic). The attacks usually last from a few minutes to an hour. If the hypertension is persistent, the clinical picture is that of severe hypertension, often of the malignant variety. Because of the hypermetabolic state induced by the phaeo-chromocytoma, the patients are rarely obese.

During a paroxysm of hypertension, there is a sharp rise in blood pressure, which can be reversed by intravenous phentolamine (Rogitine) 5 mg.

The diagnosis should be suspected in any severe case of hypertension, and in patients who do not seem to be neurotic at the time of examination but who give a characteristic history. It is confirmed by the detection of total metanephrines or vanillylmandelic acid (VMA) in the urine. It is important that patients should not have been on such drugs as reserpine, guanethidine, methyldopa, broad-spectrum antibiotics and the phenothiazines prior to the test. Plasma catecholamine assays, which are becoming available, are likely to prove of superior diagnostic value.

Phaeochromocytomas should be removed surgically. This is a potentially hazardous procedure and requires close control of the blood pressure and careful anaesthesia. Beta-adrenergic blocking drugs should not be used alone; they may induce an extreme alpha-adrenergic effect. This can be avoided by the initial use of an alpha-adrenergic blocking drug.

Cushing's syndrome. This results from cortisol excess and may be due to hyperplasia of the adrenal cortex, adrenal adenoma or carcinoma, or to the excessive administration of glucocorticoids or ACTH. Adrenal hyperplasia is often the result of increased ACTH production by basophilic or chromophobe pituitary adenomas.

Hypertension, which occurs in about 80% of cases, may be severe and proceed to the malignant phase. Other features of the syndrome are muscle weakness, osteoporosis, purple cutaneous striae, obesity of the trunk, a 'buffalo' hump, a 'moon' facies and diabetes mellitus. There may also be hirsutism, amenorrhoea and weight gain.

The diagnosis should be suggested by the combination of hypertension, diabetes and truncal obesity. It can be confirmed by the dexamethasone suppression test.

Treatment depends upon the aetiology of the condition. Surgical removal of one or both adrenal glands or of the pituitary tumour may be necessary, but pituitary irradiation may be effective.

Coarctation of the aorta
See p. 226.

Pre-eclampsia
Pee-eclampsia is a condition of unknown aetiology exclusive to pregnancy, the characteristic features of which are hypertension and proteinuria. It may progress to eclampsia, in which there are convulsions.

Pre-eclampsia develops during the last three months of pregnancy and is most common in young primigravidae. The occurrence of oedema, hypertension and albuminuria at this time in such a patient should suggest the diagnosis, but this triad is also encountered in patients with essential hypertension, chronic glomerulonephritis and pyelonephritis.

The first abnormality is usually mild hypertension, with or without proteinuria, but oedema may be the presenting symptom. If the patient is promptly treated with rest and is carefully supervised improvement usually takes place. However, the condition may progress until she develops headache, nausea, vomiting and drowsiness. At a later stage, fits may occur, and there may be cerebral haemorrhage, renal failure and left- and right-sided cardiac failure.

There is a considerable risk of fetal death, which is roughly proportional to the severity of the hypertension.

The patient should be treated with rest and restriction of sodium intake. Methyldopa is probably the most successful drug and is freer of side-effects in this context than are, for example, beta-adrenergic blocking drugs and diuretics. In the patient with severe hypertension, especially if there are fits or pulmonary oedema, acute antihypertensive treatment is necessary. Termination of pregnancy is essential in cases not responding to treatment because this is the most effective measure for relieving 'toxaemia'.

The blood pressure of women with pre-eclampsia usually returns to normal after the end of the pregnancy. However, the affected patients seem more liable to develop hypertension subsequently than do those who have not had this condition.

Oral contraception

Oral contraceptive pills give rise to an increase in blood pressure in nearly all women. This is usually slight and falls on stopping the drug. It is wise to check the blood pressure at least during the first year of administration.

Acute porphyria and certain cerebral lesions such as brain tumours and bulbar poliomyelitis

Hypertension may occur as a feature of these conditions but is usually overshadowed by the other manifestations.

Pathophysiology of hypertension

The high blood pressure in essential hypertension is due to increased peripheral vascular resistance as a result of widespread constriction of the arterioles and small arteries. The cardiac output and the viscosity of the blood are normal. In the earlier stages, the hypertension is largely explicable on the basis of increased arteriolar muscle tone, but subsequently structural changes which may be secondary to the hypertension take place in the arterioles. These changes may account for the fact that hypertension tends to beget further hypertension, and the removal of the cause of hypertension does not necessarily lead to a fall in the blood pressure to normal. The increased work of the heart imposed by the high resistance results in left ventricular hypertrophy and, eventually, left ventricular failure. As it progresses, the hypertrophy may outstrip the coronary blood supply, particularly if, as is so often the case, there is associated coronary artery disease.

Hypertension accelerates the development of atherosclerosis in the coronary, cerebral, renal and other arteries, perhaps because of long-standing mechanical stress. It often leads to the formation of microaneurysms of the cerebral arteries, especially those of the basal ganglia.

The clinical features of hypertensive heart disease

The development of hypertensive heart disease is usually a slow process; no symptoms or abnormal cardiac signs may occur for many years after high blood pressure has been detected.

The earliest symptom is dyspnoea, at first on exercise and later at rest. At a more advanced stage, the features of right heart failure may develop. Angina pectoris is common.

Abnormal cardiac signs include a forcible and displaced apex beat due to left ventricular hypertrophy, an accentuated aortic component of the second sound, and a systolic murmur in the right second intercostal space. Occasionally, the early diastolic murmur of aortic regurgitation is also present. As hypertrophy progresses a fourth (or atrial) heart sound may be heard. These signs often antedate symptoms.

As failure develops, tachycardia and a third heart sound occur. At this stage, there may be pulsus alternans and the apical pansystolic murmur of functional mitral regurgitation.

Examination of the optic fundus is of great importance in the evaluation of patients with hypertension, for it is only in the retina that the state of the arterioles can be directly observed. The grading introduced by Keith, Wagener and Barker is widely used. Grades 1 and 2 include narrowing of the retinal arteries and compression of the veins at arteriovenous crossings. In grade 3 retinopathy, these features are complicated by exudates of a soft 'cotton wool' appearance and haemorrhages which are flame- or fanshaped. In grade 4 retinopathy there is papilloedema; the disc is pink with blurred edges and the optic cup is obliterated.

ECG, chest radiography and echocardiography

The ECG provides useful evidence of the severity of hypertensive heart disease. In patients with mild elevation of the blood pressure, the ECG is normal. With the development of left ventricular hypertrophy, there is an increase in the voltage of the R waves in the left chest leads and the S waves in the right chest leads. At a more advanced stage, the T waves in the left chest leads become flattened and, later, ST segment depression and T wave inversion develop. Coexistent coronary artery disease may complicate the appearances. Radiographic evidence of left ventricular hypertrophy increases with the passage of time; eventually, the features of pulmonary congestion may develop.

Echocardiography is probably the most reliable technique for evaluating the severity of ventricular hypertrophy.

Abnormalities in the blood and urine

The blood urea is often raised in patients with hypertension. In many cases, this is attributable to renal disease; in others it is secondary to the hypertension and may be corrected if the blood pressure is returned towards normal. If the blood urea exceeds 80 mg/100 ml (13 mmol/l), it is likely that renal damage is severe. The serum potassium may be reduced in essential hypertension, particularly if this is of the malignant type or if diuretics have been used. A low serum potassium in the untreated patient should lead to a search for primary aldosteronism.

Proteinuria, hyaline and granular casts may be found when there is renal disease or malignant hypertension. There is little or no protein in the urine of patients with benign essential hypertension.

Diagnosis of hypertensive heart disease: determination of cause

The diagnosis of hypertensive heart disease is usually easy as it depends on the recognition of the high blood pressure and of left ventricular hypertrophy. However, as mentioned, coronary artery disease often coexists and may be the cause of symptoms and signs in patients with hypertension. Angina pectoris and the ECG features of myocardial ischaemia or infarction suggest the presence of coronary artery disease. Hypertension is unlikely to be the sole cause of heart failure if the diastolic pressure is constantly less than 110 mmHg.

It is of great importance to determine the aetiology of the hypertension, particularly in the younger patient in whom it is often secondary, and in whom correction of the cause is more likely to be successful. The diagnosis of acute nephritis is usually relatively easy but the differentiation of essential hypertension from chronic nephritis may be impossible unless there is a history of acute nephritis, or unless renal function is found to be worse than could be accounted for by the severity of the hypertension. Chronic pyelonephritis may be diagnosed by the history, and by the presence of pus cells and micro-organisms in the urine. The kidneys of patients with polycystic disease are usually easy to feel; there is frequently a family history of the condition. Renal artery disease should be suspected in any younger patient with hypertension and in the older patient with an abrupt acceleration of pre-existing hypertension. A bruit over the renal arteries provides further evidence.

Primary aldosteronism (p. 242) is suggested by muscular weakness, headache and polyuria; suspicion should be aroused by hypokalaemia, particularly if there is also a high serum sodium, Cushing's syndrome (p. 243) is suggested by obesity, moon facies, purple striae, hirsutism and amenorrhoea, combined with glycosuria and an increased urinary excretion of 17-ketosteroids. Phaeochromocytoma (p. 243) is to be suspected when hypertension is paroxysmal, with severe headache, palpitation and perspiration during the attacks. In those cases in which the hypertension is not paroxysmal, there may be no clinical clues and the diagnosis depends upon the demonstration of abnormal quantities of catecholamines or their metabolites in the blood or urine.

Coarctation of the aorta (p. 226) should be sought for in all patients with hypertension. The diagnosis is usually not difficult if the femoral pulses are routinely palpated. In this condition, the femoral pulses are small and delayed and there is almost always a systolic murmur audible over the upper thoracic spine posteriorly. Confirmation is obtained by finding collateral vessels, by the radiographic evidence of rib notching and, if necessary, by aortography.

It may be difficult to diagnose pre-eclampsia (p. 244) with certainty if the patient is seen for the first time in the latter part of the pregnancy. Pre-eclampsia seldom develops until the last trimester, and is usually accompanied by a weight gain, proteinuria and oedema.

Hypertension occurs in acute intermittent porphyria, but is usually accompanied by abdominal pain, fits and various neurological lesions. These features may suggest hypertensive encephalopathy; in cases of doubt the urine should be tested for porphobilinogen.

The investigation of the hypertensive patient

A thorough search for a cause should be undertaken in all patients with severe hypertension (e.g. diastolic pressure greater than 110 mmHg) and in those under 40 years of age in whom the diastolic pressure exceeds 100 mmHg. Investigations are also required to determine what effects the high blood pressure has exerted on the heart and kidneys.

Investigations routinely necessary to determine the nature and severity of the hypertension include serum urea, sodium, potassium and bicarbonate and urinary contents. If all these findings are normal, and there are no clinical clues to a causal disease, it is reasonable to begin treatment. One can then reserve further investigation for those with specific indications or those in whom treatment fails.

Prognosis

Almost all patients with untreated malignant hypertension die within one year. Death is usually due to uraemia, but heart failure and cerebrovascular accidents are common.

The prognosis of benign essential hypertension is relatively good in the absence of cardiac, renal or cerebral involvement. Even in such patients, the death rate from myocardial infarction and cerebrovascular accidents is much higher than that in the normotensive population. In general, the higher the blood pressure, the greater is the risk of these complications.

Other factors related to prognosis are age, sex, cardiac status, retinopathy and renal function.

High blood pressure at any particular level is more sinister in the young patient than in the old, and in males than in females. Cardiac enlargement and the ECG abnormalities indicate a substantial risk of developing cardiac failure. Grade 3 retinal changes (haemorrhages and soft exudates) carry a prognosis only little better than grade 4 changes.

Proteinuria and urea retention are associated with advancing renal failure.

In the absence of treatment, cardiac failure and cerebrovascular accidents are the major causes of death, myocardial infarction and uraemia being less common, though not infrequent. Several studies have demonstrated the improvement in prognosis that results from antihypertensive therapy. This is most evident in those whose diastolic pressures exceed 105 mmHg, but some benefit is also achieved in individuals with diastolic pressures of 100 or even 95 mmHg. Such treatment has almost eliminated death from cardiac failure and has reduced the incidence of fatal and non-fatal strokes. Myocardial infarction has, therefore, become relatively more common as a cause of death.

The treatment of hypertension

Treatment is undoubtedly indicated when hypertension has led to deleterious effects on the heart, cerebrovascular circulation or kidneys. Therefore, if there is evidence of hypertensive heart disease, or if there are advanced retinal changes with papilloedema, haemorrhages or soft exudates, the blood pressure should be lowered. It is more difficult to determine whether antihypertensive measures are called for when the blood pressure is persistently raised in the absence of evidence of vascular or renal involvement.

Before initiating drug therapy one must ensure that no treatable cause, such as unilateral renal disease, phaeochromocytoma or coarctation is responsible for the hypertension. If surgically correctable disorders can be excluded, one should consider the most appropriate type of treatment for the individual patient. Some individuals respond well to sedative therapy alone; in others reduction in sodium intake or weight is effective. However, in virtually all patients in whom there is evidence of secondary effects from the hypertension, specific antihypertensive drugs are required. Even in the absence of these complications, there is a strong case for such therapy if the diastolic pressure remains high. In the young patient, one should consider treatment if the diastolic pressure is constantly in excess of 95 mmHg. In the middle-aged or elderly patient one might raise the level for which treatment is indicated to 100 or 105 mmHg, respectively.

There are a large number of drugs in current use for the treatment of hypertension; new ones are continually being added. It is only possible to mention those which, at present, seem to be of greatest value. Every physician should be familiar with the use of four or five of these drugs as patients vary from one another in their response to therapy and no one drug can be regarded as superior in all respects to others.

Although the aim should be to make the blood pressure 'normal', this may not be possible without producing side-effects. Furthermore, too great a fall in blood pressure may impair the circulation to the heart, brain or kidneys and precipitate a myocardial infarction, a stroke or renal failure.

Drugs used in the treatment of hypertension

Drugs acting on the sympathetic nervous system

Alpha-methyldopa (Aldomet, Dopamet).   This drug is metabolized to alpha-methylnoradrenaline, which replaces noradrenaline in adrenergically innervated tissues; as a consequence, there is a diminished response to nerve stimulation. Oral methyldopa begins to lower the blood pressure in about 4 hours and its effect lasts for up to 24 hours. Therapy is started with 250 mg three times a day and increased, if necessary, after a few days to 500 mg three times a day. If this dose is insufficient, a diuretic should be added. The total daily dose should not exceed 3 g. Transient sleepiness is almost invariable during the first 24 hours, but a more subtle drowsiness may persist. Other complications include fluid retention, loss of libido and a Coombs' positive haemolytic anaemia.

Clonidine (Catapres).   This is a potent hypotensive drug which appears to act mainly on the vasomotor areas in the brain stem. It produces bradycardia but does not affect cardiovascular reflexes and therefore does not caust postural hypotension. The starting dose is 100 μg twice daily. This may be increased to a daily total of 1 mg, but above this toxic effects become common. These resemble those of methyldopa, except for haemolytic anaemia. Clonidine should not be withdrawn suddenly; an abrupt rise in blood pressure may result.

Reserpine.   This produces a lowering of blood pressure through peripheral vasodilatation, probably depleting central and peripheral catecholamine stores. The side-effects include nasal stuffiness, bradycardia, diarrhoea, fluid retention and depression. Dose should not exceed 0.25 mg once or twice a day.

Adrenergic blocking drugs.   These, such as guanethidine, bethanidine and debrisoquine, partially replace noradrenaline in its storage sites and inhibit its uptake. They have a strong antihypertensive effect but are particularly liable to give rise to orthostatic hypotension and have largely been abandoned.

Alpha-adrenoceptor blocking agents.   These, such as phentolamine and phenoxybenzamine, are of little clinical value except in phaeochromocytoma.

Labetalol (Trandate).   This blocks both alpha- and beta-adrenoreceptors and has proved useful both in essential hypertension (particularly in hypertensive emergencies) and phaeochromocytoma.

Prazosin (Hypovase). This blocks post-synaptic alpha-adrenergic receptors. It has marked arteriolar and venous vasodilating effects and the initial dose may produce profound postural hypotension. The starting dosage is 0.5 mg thrice daily.

Beta-adrenoceptor blocking drugs. These are effective antihypertensive drugs whose mode of action remains uncertain. They are more effective when combined with a diuretic or other antihypertensive drugs but are often sufficient on their own and produce no marked orthostatic effects. To ensure compliance, it is best to utilize a preparation that needs to be given only once or twice a day. Provided these drugs are not prescribed for patients with obstructive airways disease or heart failure, serious complications are unusual. Minor side-effects, such as lethargy, nausea, nightmares and cold extremities are common.

Vasodilator drugs

Hydralazine (Apresoline). This is a potent arteriolar dilator and increases cardiac output and heart rate. It is best combined with a beta-adrenoceptor blocking agent. Initially 25 mg three times a day should be given; the dose may then be increased if necessary to a total daily dose of 200 mg. It has well-known side-effects of tachycardia, headache and systemic lupus erythematosus-like reaction; these can largely be avoided by combining with other drugs so that only a small dosage is required.

Diazoxide (Eudemine). This is very effective in acute antihypertensive treatment (150 mg intravenously) but may cause diabetes in prolonged use.

Minoxidil (Loniten, Minipress). This is a potent vasodilator and antihypertensive. It produces a reflex tachycardia and fluid retention and should be combined with a beta-blocker and diuretic. It may cause hypertrichosis.

Nitroprusside. This is a very effective antihypertensive drug when given intravenously but should be reserved for hypertensive emergencies.

Diuretics

The mode of action of diuretics remains uncertain, but appears to have two components. Initially, there is a reduced plasma volume and cardiac output, but these are transient changes. With more prolonged treatment, the total peripheral resistance diminishes and this may be the result of changes in the sodium content of vessel walls.

Thiazide drugs.   These have been used predominantly in this context and are effective, but have the disadvantage of producing hypokalaemia and occasionally hypoglycaemia and hyperuricaemia. Another side effect is impotence.

The potassium-conserving diuretics such as spirolonactone, amiloride and triamturene have only mild antihypertensive effects but can be used together with thiazide diuretics to preserve potassium equilibrium. The loop diuretics, such as frusemide, ethacryonic acid and bumetanide, may produce a considerable reduction in blood pressure when given intravenously, but they are not suitable for long-term treatment in hypertension because their effects are relatively short-lived.

Drugs interfering with the renin angiotensin system

The drug most in use in this context is captopril (Capoten) — this is a very effective antihypertensive drug used either on its own or in association with other antihypertensive drugs. A variety of side-effects have been reported including disorders of taste, rashes and leucopenia.

Calcium-blocking drugs

Nifedipine (Adalat).   This is an effective antihypertensive drug, particularly when combined with other antihypertensive therapy, such as beta-adrenoreceptor blocking drugs. Verapamil also has some antihypertensive effect.

Choice of therapy for the individual patient

There is no doubt of the need for therapy when the complications of hypertension, such as cardiac failure or advanced retinal changes are encountered. However, to an increasing extent it has become clear that asymptomatic patients with hypertension benefit from antihypertensive treatment insofar as it protects them from stroke, cardiac failure and renal failure and, less certainly, from angina pectoris and myocardial infarction.

Randomized control studies of treatment in a number of countries have demonstrated clearly that if the diastolic pressure constantly exceeds 105 mmHg, antihypertensive treatment reduces the incidence of complications. Recent studies have suggested that there is a clear-cut benefit from antihypertensive treatment if the diastolic pressure is 100 mmHg or more; there is less certain evidence of those with a diastolic pressure exceeding 95 mmHg. In particular, the role of antihypertensive treatment in the elderly has not yet been defined. Currently, it seems reasonable to treat middle-aged patients whose diastolic pressure exceeds 100 mmHg with antihypertensive drugs, but to use such drugs only for patients with diastolic pressures exceeding 95 mmHg if they are young or there are features suggesting that hypertension may be causing secondary effects on the heart, kidney or retina.

A 'stepped' approach to therapy is now to be recommended. By this it is meant that one should start treatment with a single drug which has relatively minor side-effects. It is now customary to start either with a diuretic or a beta-blocker, the latter being favoured if there is angina. The next step is to try the one of these two drugs which has not been given initially and if this fails to combine the two. If such measures fail, methyldopa, hydralazine or prazosin might be added. If the combination of such therapy still fails to control the blood pressure, careful review of the whole case needs to be undertaken ensuring that a secondary form of hypertension has not been overlooked and that the patient is complying with treatment. If such is not the case, then the more potent drugs such as captopril, minoxidil or the adrenergic blocking drugs might be considered.

The patient embarking on antihypertensive treatment must be advised that drug therapy will probably be required for the rest of his life. Regular checking of the blood pressure is essential.

Occasionally, urgent antihypertensive therapy must be undertaken for acute left ventricular failure or hypertensive fits. The most effective drugs are intravenous sodium nitroprusside, (50 mg in 500 ml 5% glucose), labetalol (25 mg) and diazoxide (150 mg). All require the most cautious administration and careful monitoring.

References

ABC of hypertension. (1981) London: BMJ Publications.
HART, J. T. (1980) *Hypertension*. London: Churchill Livingstone.

14

Diseases of the Aorta

The aortic wall is composed of an endothelial lining or intima, a media containing smooth muscle and elastic tissue, and a fibrous adventitia. The media is largely responsible for the elasticity of the aortic wall, and the adventitia for its strength and resistance to rupture.

Dissecting aneurysm

A dissecting aneurysm (Fig. 111) results from the entry of blood into the media, either as a consequence of the rupture of vasa vasorum or from a tear of the aortic intima. It is probable that dissection only affects an abnormal media, the commonest abnormality being medial necrosis with mucoid and cystic softening and degeneration of the elastic fibres. Dissecting aneurysm is an important complication of the Marfan syndrome and of pregnancy, but the majority of cases occur in middle-aged or elderly men with systemic hypertension. The dissection usually starts either in the ascending aorta a short distance above the aortic valve, or just beyond the origin of the left subclavian artery. The blood dissects a channel between the intima and the adventitia and usually advances distally. In so doing, it may occlude branches of the aortic arch and the descending aorta, including the renal and iliac arteries. If the dissection spreads proximally, the aortic valve may be involved, producing aortic regurgitation and, occasionally, occlusion of a coronary artery. The aneurysm usually ruptures externally into the pericardium, pleural cavity, mediastinum or retroperitoneal tissues, but sometimes it perforates the intima and the dissection 're-enters' the aortic lumen. Occasionally, the dissection becomes chronic without perforation.

Dissecting aneurysms usually present with the sudden onset of a 'tearing' pain of extreme severity. The site of the pain depends upon the location of the dissection and moves as the dissection progresses. The pain may start in the anterior or posterior chest or in the abdomen, but nearly always affects the upper back at some stage. Intervals of freedom from pain may occur; with recurrences, the pain may involve the neck, arms, chest, trunk or legs. Occasionally, the pain is slight; breathlessness or syncope may then be the presenting symptom.

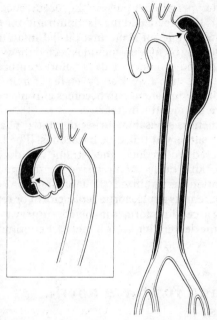

Fig. 111. Dissecting aneurysm of the aorta. This usually starts either a short distance above the aortic valve (left) or just below the origin of the left subclavian artery (right).

On examination, the patient appears pale and sweaty and has a tachycardia; although he may have the appearance of shock, the blood pressure is usually within normal limits, having fallen from hypertensive levels. Other signs depend on which branches of the aorta are occluded. Thus, one or more of the arteries to the limbs may become impalpable. Other complications include aortic regurgitation, tamponade, hemiplegia, mental disturbances, haematuria, bloody diarrhoea and haemothorax.

The ECG is of little diagnostic value, but pre-existing hypertension may have caused left ventricular hypertrophy. The appearances of myocardial ischaemia or myocardial infarction may be present if there has been encroachment on a coronary artery. The chest radiograph shows an increase in the width of the mediastinum. The diagnosis can be further confirmed by injecting radio-opaque material into the aorta which is irregular and narrowed, and may have occluded branches.

The diagnosis may not be difficult when there is a severe but shifting pain associated with the occlusion of vessels. Differentiation from myocardial infarction may be almost impossible clinically. Dissection is suggested by the following: the distribution and progression of the pain, the relatively high blood pressure, the development of differences in the peripheral pulses, the occurrence of an aortic diastolic murmur, the broadened mediastinum and the absence of the ECG and enzyme changes of acute myocardial infarction.

Although death may be sudden and unexpected the symptoms often progress over a period of hours or days before rupture occurs. Few patients survive more than a week and even fewer more than 3 weeks. Occasionally, a dissecting aneurysm becomes chronic and the patient may then survive for months or years.

Medical treatment is advisable during the initial phase: the fragile aortic wall makes surgery at this time hazardous. The blood pressure should be lowered to reduce the strain on the aorta; beta-adrenoceptor blocking drugs are preferred for this purpose.

When the situation has stabilized (perhaps after 2 or 3 days), surgery should be considered. As a rule, aortic replacement or repair should be undertaken if the ascending aorta is involved; surgery is only required for dissection of the descending aorta if there are continuing symptoms or major vessels are obstructed.

Saccular and fusiform aortic aneurysms

These are localized distensions of the wall of the aorta, being fusiform if the whole circumference of the vessel is involved and saccular if only part of it is affected.

Atherosclerotic aneurysms, which are usually situated in the descending aorta, result from atrophy of the media and adventitia with fibrous replacement. Syphilis, formerly the major cause of aortic aneurysm, has become uncommon. Syphilitic aneurysms usually affect the ascending aorta and the aortic arch, as a result of inflammatory changes in the aortic wall and subsequent fibrosis and calcification (see p. 273). Aortic aneurysms are also seen in association with the Marfan syndrome and coarctation of the aorta. They can also result from trauma, particularly car accidents, in which the aortic wall is partially or completely transected. A distinctive type of aneurysm is that of the sinus of Valsalva, which will be considered separately.

The clinical features resulting from an aneurysm of the thoracic aorta depend upon its size and site. When the aneurysm is in the ascending aorta, there is often associated aortic regurgitation which leads to cardiac failure. As the aneurysm enlarges and encroaches upon neighbouring structures, there may be pain as a result of erosion of ribs and sternum. A pulsating mass may be seen in the front of the chest and obstruction of the superior vena cava may occur. When the aneurysm is situated in the aortic arch, wheezing, cough and hoarseness may arise from compression of the trachea, bronchus or recurrent laryngeal nerves. Aneurysms of the descending aorta are most likely to produce symptoms as a result of encroachment on the vertebrae, ribs or spinal nerves. Often, however, an aneurysm of the thoracic aorta is first diagnosed in an asymptomatic patient by the radiographic demonstration of a localized dilatation of the aorta. The diagnosis can be confirmed by the injection of radio-opaque medium into the aorta.

Asymptomatic patients with relatively small aneurysms may survive for many years. However, the prognosis is generally poor and the patient with symptoms is unlikely to survive more than 1 or 2 years.

Most patients with aneurysms of the aorta have severe associated disorders such as hypertension, ischaemic heart disease or cerebro-vascular disease, and death more often results from one of these than from the aneurysm. Perhaps only one-third of the patients die from aortic rupture; before surgery is undertaken, the cardiovascular and cerebral circulations must be carefully evaluated. Surgery should be considered for those aneurysms which are large or producing symptoms. Saccular aneurysms, which usually have a narrow neck, can be treated by transection of the neck with repair of the underlying aorta. If much of the aortic wall is involved, resection must be undertaken with replacement by a graft.

Aneurysm of the sinus of Valsalva

This is most commonly caused by a congenital localized absence of the aortic media, but can result from syphilitic aortitis or infective endocarditis. The aneurysm forms a thin-walled sac which in most instances protrudes into the right ventricle or right atrium (Fig. 112). No symptoms or signs are produced until the aneurysm ruptures. When it does so a fistula is formed between the aorta and the relevant

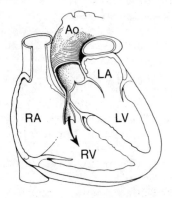

Fig. 112. Aneurysm of sinus of Valsalva rupturing into right ventricle.

chamber. Congenital aneurysms of the sinus of Valsalva are often associated with other congenital lesions, particularly a ventricular septal defect.

Sudden death sometimes occurs; more often rupture causes the abrupt onset of chest pain and breathlessness. These symptoms subside over a period of days or weeks. Cardiac failure develops subsequently, but is very variable in its rate of progression.

On examination the patient may have a collapsing pulse due to the aortic diastolic leak, and there is usually a continuous systolic and diastolic murmur, resembling that of a persistent ductus arteriosus, but loudest over the sternum at the level of the third or fourth interspace.

The ECG may be normal initially, but the signs of right ventricular hypertrophy or right bundle branch block may develop later. The chest radiograph shows cardiac enlargement with pulmonary plethora. The definitive diagnosis is made by showing the leak by aortography, and by the demonstration of a left-to-right shunt on cardiac catheterization.

The ruptured sinus of Valsalva should be treated by repair of the aortic wall.

Further reading

DALEN, J. E., PAPE, L. A., COHN, L. H., LESTER, J. K. (Jr.) and COLLINS, J. J. J. (1980) Dissection of the aorta. *Progr. Cardiovasc. Dis.* **23**, 237.
LIDDICOAT, J. E., BEKASSY, S. M., RUBIO, P. A., NOON, G. P. and DEBAKEY, M. E. (1975) Ascending aortic aneurysms. *Circulation*, **52** (Suppl. I), 202.

15

Disorders of the Lungs and Pulmonary Circulation

Pulmonary embolism, thrombosis and infarction

Pulmonary thrombo-embolism can cause or aggravate heart disease, and is a common and serious complication of cardiac disorders.

Pulmonary embolism results from the obstruction of the pulmonary arterial vessels by thrombus or by material, such as fat or air, originating in some other site. *Pulmonary thrombosis* implies the formation of clot in situ. *Pulmonary infarction* is the necrosis of a wedge of lung tissue resulting from pulmonary arterial occlusion.

Pulmonary embolism is usually a consequence of thrombophlebitis or phlebothrombosis in the leg veins but may also follow thrombosis of the pelvic veins, or clot formation in the right atrium in patients with right-sided cardiac failure, particularly if there is atrial fibrillation. Deep vein thrombosis is often asymptomatic, but the leg may be warm, tender, slightly dusky and swollen by oedema. Thrombosis is most likely to occur when there has been stasis in the veins, especially in association with childbirth, abdominal surgery, acute myocardial infarction and right-sided cardiac failure. There is a slightly increased risk in women taking oral contraceptives. Pulmonary thrombosis is uncommon except as a complication of pre-existing disease of the pulmonary arteries.

Pulmonary embolism can be prevented by measures which prevent the development or progression of venous thrombosis. Simple measures to encourage venous flow such as the use of leg exercises and elastic stockings in those confined to bed are important and effective ways of doing so. Once thrombosis has been diagnosed treatment should be initiated with heparin, unless there are contraindications. A bolus of 5000 units may be given, followed by a continuous infusion of the drug. The dosage should be controlled by the activated partial thromboplastin time (APTT). Oral warfarin should be started at the same time as described on p. 156. Heparin may be stopped after 3 days. Warfarin should be continued for 3 months for calf thrombosis and six months for iliofemoral thrombosis.

There are three syndromes of pulmonary thrombo-embolism which

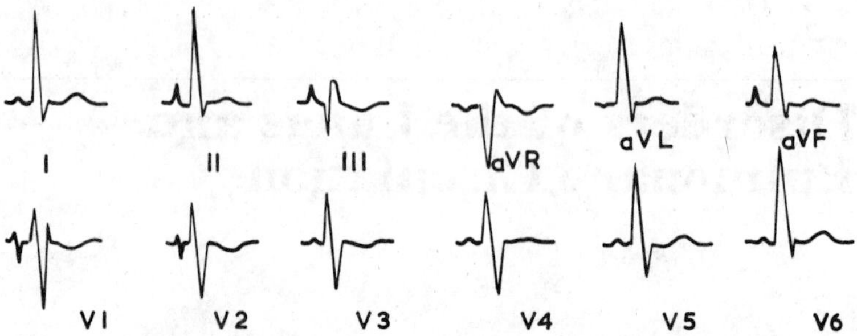

Fig. 113.   ECG appearances in pulmonary embolism. Note tall, peaked P waves, partial right bundle branch block (rSr in V1), S in lead I, Q and negative T in III, and inverted T waves in V1 to V3.

may occur at different times in the same patient. They are massive pulmonary embolism, pulmonary infarction and thrombo-embolic pulmonary hypertension.

Massive pulmonary embolism

A large embolus may block the main pulmonary artery or one of its major branches, or multiple emboli may occlude many smaller branches. If two-thirds of the pulmonary arterial bed is occluded, acute right-sided cardiac failure occurs with a low cardiac output and a rise in venous pressure. Sometimes the onset of massive thrombosis is more insidious, with symptoms and signs increasing progressively over two weeks or more.

When massive embolism occurs, the patient may drop dead suddenly. In other cases there may be syncope, chest pain and dyspnoea. The syncope is probably attributable to a sudden fall in blood pressure, the chest pain to inadequate coronary blood flow, and the dyspnoea to impaired pulmonary ventilation and reflex factors. On examination, the patient is pale, cyanosed and breathless, with cold extremities. There is tachypnoea and sinus tachycardia. The jugular venous pressure is often raised and there may be right ventricular third and fourth heart sounds. Occasionally, there are pulmonary systolic or diastolic murmurs.

The ECG often shows the effects of acute dilatation of the right ventricle and atrium. One or more of a number of features may be observed (Fig. 113): a narrow Q wave and inverted T wave in lead III, accompanied by an S wave in lead I as a result of a change in the position of the heart produced by dilatation of the right ventricle and atrium; P pulmonale, or an atrial arrhythmia; partial or complete right bundle branch block; T wave inversion from V1 to V4 ('right ventricular strain').

The chest radiograph is seldom helpful, although it may show enlarged proximal pulmonary arteries and small peripheral ones. Pulmonary angiography reveals the presence of pulmonary arterial obstruction. Areas of ischaemic lung may be demonstrated by radio-isotope scanning after the intravenous injection of albumin labelled with ^{131}I or ^{51}Cr.

Massive pulmonary embolism should be suspected in any patient who suddenly develops the features of shock, syncope, acute dyspnoea or chest pain, particularly if the subject has evidence of a venous thrombosis or has been confined to bed during the preceding days. The differential diagnosis from acute myocardial infarction may be extremely difficult. The ECG is of considerable value, but the patterns associated with massive pulmonary embolism are often misinterpreted as being those of a combination of inferior and anteroseptal infarction. The appearance of Q waves and negative T waves in lead III (but not in lead II) in association with inverted T waves from V1 to V4 strongly suggest pulmonary embolism. The definitive diagnosis can be made by angiocardiography, but this is potentially hazardous; radio-isotope scanning is safer though less specific.

The prognosis of massive pulmonary embolism is poor; some 10% die almost immediately of a ventricular arrhythmia or circulatory failure, a further 20% die within the next few hours or days. In those who survive, complete recovery is usual, but there is a risk of further pulmonary embolism.

The patient should be treated with oxygen and digoxin. Anticoagulation should be started with intravenous heparin and continued with an oral preparation such as warfarin for 3 to 6 months. Fibrinolytic therapy with drugs such as streptokinase or urokinase accelerates recovery from massive pulmonary embolism and is indicated for the critically ill patient. The expense of these drugs has prevented their widespread use. If an appropriately skilled surgeon and cardiopulmonary bypass techniques are immediately available, the embolus can sometimes be successfully removed. The diagnosis should be confirmed by angiocardiography or, at least, by radio-scanning before this dramatic procedure is undertaken.

Pulmonary infarction

Pulmonary infarction follows the occlusion of smaller pulmonary arteries (and, rarely, veins). A necrotic area develops which is usually haemorrhagic because of the exudation of blood from still patent bronchial arteries. The infarction may reach the surface of the lung and produce pleurisy with an effusion which is usually blood-stained. Typically, there is a pleuritic pain accompanied by low pyrexia and, in about 50% of cases, the expectoration of bright red blood. Pulmonary infarction may, however, be silent, or cause only a low-grade pyrexia.

Often there are no abnormal physical signs, but tachycardia, tachypnoea, the signs of pulmonary consolidation and a pleural rub may occur. Right-sided failure may develop or be aggravated in those with pre-existing heart disease. The ECG is often normal but may show changes similar to those of massive pulmonary embolism. The chest radiograph often reveals a small and sometimes wedge-shaped opacity. It may also show an effusion or elevation of the diaphragm on the affected side. A radio-isotope scan is abnormal, usually revealing several scattered areas of reduced perfusion.

It is frequently difficult to differentiate pulmonary infarction from pneumonia if there has not been previous evidence of deep venous thrombosis. Pulmonary infarction is commoner than pneumonia in hospitalized patients; it differs in that the sputum is seldom infected but is often frankly bloody, and the fever does not respond to antibiotics.

Pulmonary infarction should be treated by heparin and oral anticoagulants, the main purpose of which is to prevent further embolization.

Recurrent pulmonary emboli and thrombo-embolic pulmonary hypertension

Recurrent pulmonary embolization, which is usually associated with chronic or recurrent venous thrombosis, may appear as massive emboli, as pulmonary infarction or be silent. Eventually, the vascular obstruction may become so widespread as to cause a substantial increase in the resistance of the pulmonary arteries and lead to pulmonary arterial hypertension. Once this has become established, the prognosis is poor and most patients die within a period of 5 years. The process may sometimes be reversed or prevented from progression by permanent anticoagulant therapy. If anticoagulant therapy fails, inferior vena caval ligation or plication sometimes prevents further embolism, but is not always effective and may lead to severe oedema of the legs.

Pulmonary hypertension

The pulmonary arterial pressure is determined by the pressure in the pulmonary capillaries, the pulmonary blood flow and the resistance of the pulmonary arteries (especially the arterioles).

The small pulmonary arteries of the fetus have a thick muscular media and the pulmonary vascular resistance of the non-aerated lung is high. This muscular layer regresses over the first 2 to 3 months of life. As a consequence the pulmonary vascular resistance and arterial pressure start to fall shortly after birth and within a few weeks have declined to normal adult levels.

The pulmonary arteries in the adult are relatively thin-walled, the smaller vessels having considerably less muscle in their walls than corresponding systemic arterioles. The resistance to flow is much lower and the pressure in the pulmonary artery (about 20/10 mmHg) is approximately one-seventh that in the aorta. It is believed that many of the capillaries in the lung are closed at rest, particularly those of the upper parts of the lungs. When the cardiac output increases, as on exercise, the vascular resistance falls as capillaries open and small arteries dilate. As a consequence, blood flow through the lungs can increase threefold before any rise in pressure occurs.

Pulmonary arterial hypertension (greater than 30/15 mmHg) may result from:

1. An increase in pulmonary capillary pressure
2. An increase in pulmonary blood flow
3. An increase in pulmonary vascular resistance

1. Passive pulmonary hypertension due to a raised pulmonary capillary pressure occurs in all conditions in which the left atrial pressure rises, such as mitral stenosis and left ventricular failure. The pulmonary artery pressure rises in proportion to the pulmonary capillary pressure and the pulmonary hypertension is not severe.

2. Pulmonary hypertension due to increased flow develops in disorders in which there are left-to-right shunts. These include septal defects and persistent ductus arteriosus. In atrial septal defect, a large pulmonary blood flow of 10 to 15 litres per minute may be unassociated with pulmonary hypertension because there is a compensatory vasodilatation with a fall in vascular resistance. In many cases of ventricular septal defect and persistent ductus arteriosus, there is no vasodilatation, and the resistance remains normal. The pulmonary arterial pressure may therefore rise even with comparatively small shunts. With large shunts, pulmonary arterial pressure may reach systemic levels.

3. Pulmonary vascular resistance may be increased by several mechanisms:

   a. Pulmonary vasoconstriction. This may be a reaction to an elevated pulmonary capillary pressure and to hypoxia. It is particularly common in mitral stenosis, much less so in mitral regurgitation, and seldom develops unless the mean pulmonary capillary pressure is constantly in excess of 20 mmHg.

   Hypoxia is a potent pulmonary vasoconstrictor and is a factor in the pulmonary hypertension that occurs in respiratory disease.

   b. Disease of the small pulmonary arteries. In infants with large ventricular septal defects, there may be delay in the regression of the muscular media of the small pulmonary arteries (see above). As a consequence, the pulmonary vascular resistance may stay high, thereby limiting the left-to-right shunt. Hyaline and fibrotic changes may take place and thickening of the arteries may progress and lead to severe pulmonary hypertension (Eisenmenger's syndrome).

Arterial muscular hyperplasia and fibrosis may take place in older patients in response to long-standing pulmonary hypertension.

c. Obliteration of the pulmonary arteries by thrombosis and embolism (see p. 260), of the arterioles in schistosomiasis, and of the pulmonary capillaries by emphysema.

Combinations of 1, 2 and 3 are common. In mitral stenosis, for example, the initial phase of passive pulmonary hypertension is often complicated by vasoconstriction and by the obliterative changes of pulmonary embolism. In many cases of ventricular septal defect, both high blood flow and pulmonary vascular disease contribute to pulmonary hypertension. In emphysema, obliteration of the vascular bed and hypoxia are contributory factors.

Independent of causation, certain clinical features are characteristic of severe pulmonary hypertension. The symptoms include dyspnoea, fatigue, syncope, anginal pain and haemoptysis. Hoarseness may occur as a result of stretching of the left recurrent laryngeal nerve. Eventually, the symptoms of right-sided cardiac failure develop.

The arterial pulse is normal or small; the venous pulse is often abnormal due to a prominent 'a' wave. There is a forceful right ventricular thrust along the left sternal edge and there may be a shock in the second left interspace due to pulmonary valve closure. There is a loud pulmonary second sound, which may be followed by the early diastolic murmur of pulmonary regurgitation, and there may also be a fourth heart sound at the lower left sternal edge. Both right atrial and right ventricular hypertrophy may be seen on the ECG, and the radiograph shows prominent main pulmonary arteries with normal or unusually clear peripheral lung fields.

The prognosis of pulmonary arterial hypertension depends upon its aetiology and on its severity. Passive pulmonary hypertension responds well if the underlying disorder can be corrected. Pulmonary hypertension due to high pulmonary arterial flow can usually be reversed by the correction of the underlying congenital abnormality. Increased pulmonary arterial resistance due to vasoconstriction can often be diminished by relieving hypoxia or by the successful treatment of mitral valve disease. When pulmonary hypertension is due to severe pulmonary vascular disease, as in the Eisenmenger syndrome, the prognosis is poor and life is usually sustained for only a few years. In these cases, cardiac failure is progressive in spite of treatment.

Primary ('unexplained') pulmonary hypertension

• Pulmonary hypertension is said to be primary when the aetiology cannot be determined. It is possible that small pulmonary emboli are responsible for some cases. The condition, which is rare, is most apt to affect young women. The diagnosis is made by exclusion in patients found to have the clinical features of pulmonary hypertension. The prognosis is poor; death is likely to occur within 5 years. Some improvement may be achieved by the use of vasodilators such as hydralazine, diazoxide and nifedipine.

Pulmonary heart disease

The understanding of pulmonary heart disease (cor pulmonale) has been made difficult by problems of nomenclature. Here it is defined as heart disease secondary to disorders of ventilation and respiratory function. Right-sided heart failure due to pulmonary arterial disease or secondary to left-sided heart failure is not included in this definition, and is considered under Pulmonary Hypertension (p. 262).

The prevalence of pulmonary heart disease varies greatly between one geographical area and another. There is abundant evidence that heavy cigarette smoking and air pollution are major factors in the production of chronic bronchitis; cor pulmonale is commonest in communities exposed to these influences. It is predominantly a disease of middle-aged and elderly men, and is uncommon in young men or in women of any age.

Pathogenesis of heart failure in lung disease

Lung disease causes heart disease mainly because of its effects on the pulmonary vessels. Due to a number of different mechanisms, there is an increase in pulmonary vascular resistance, leading to pulmonary hypertension, right ventricular hypertrophy and right heart failure. These mechanisms include:

1. Pulmonary arteriolar constriction due to low alveolar oxygen tension in areas of underventilated lung.

2. Anatomical reduction of the pulmonary vascular bed from rupture of alveolar walls and from fibrotic or thrombotic obliteration of capillaries.

3. Compression of pulmonary capillaries by high intra-alveolar pressures when there is air trapping.

Pulmonary hypertension is seldom severe in pulmonary disease except when there is superadded respiratory infection.

Abnormalities in the blood gases nearly always precede the appearance of heart failure due to lung disease. Hypoxaemia is almost invariable. Even if the arterial oxygen tension is normal at rest, it is reduced on exercise. The hypoxaemia results either from disturbances in the ventilation–perfusion relationship or from interference with the diffusion of oxygen through the alveolar wall.

The carbon dioxide tension is raised when the heart failure is secondary to chronic obstructive airways disease and alveolar hypoventilation. If there is a rapid rise in carbon dioxide tension, the pH is low, but in the chronic stage of the disease the renal retention of bicarbonate maintains a normal or near normal acid–base balance.

These blood gas abnormalities are responsible for many of the characteristics of pulmonary heart disease:

1. Polycythaemia and increased blood volume due to hypoxaemia.
2. Peripheral vasodilatation, due to high carbon dioxide tension, producing a large pulse and warm extremities.
3. Cerebral vasodilatation, due to high carbon dioxide tension, which leads to a raised cerebrospinal fluid pressure, with tremor, confusion and papilloedema. The more advanced symptoms of carbon dioxide retention occur mainly, if not exclusively, in patients receiving oxygen in high concentration. Such treatment is dangerous if there is carbon dioxide retention because it abolishes the hypoxaemia which is a major stimulus to respiration.
4. Impaired myocardial function due to hypoxaemia.

Diseases causing pulmonary heart disease

Diseases primarily affecting air passages of the lung and the alveoli

1. Chronic bronchitis with generalized airways obstruction with or without emphysema. In chronic bronchitis there is hyperplasia of the mucus-secreting glands of the tracheobronchial tree, with chronic infection and bronchial obstruction. In emphysema, the air spaces distal to the terminal bronchioles are abnormally enlarged, and the alveolar walls are, to a greater or lesser extent, destroyed.
2. Bronchial asthma.
3. Emphysema without bronchitis or asthma.

In all these three conditions, airways obstruction is an important factor. This is transient in asthma and usually disappears between attacks; pulmonary heart disease is uncommon. In chronic bronchitis and emphysema there is uneven matching between ventilation and perfusion. Some alveoli are well perfused with blood but poorly ventilated, whilst others are well ventilated but inadequately perfused.

Pulmonary hypertension results from a combination of hypoxia, destruction of pulmonary capillaries and the effects of high alveolar pressure on the pulmonary vessels. Often, pulmonary hypertension is experienced only during episodes of infection which aggravate bronchial obstruction.

4. Pulmonary fibrosis due to tuberculosis, pneumoconiosis, bronchiectasis, other pulmonary infections, radiation and mucoviscidosis.

Pulmonary hypertension due to these causes is relatively uncommon, unless there is associated emphysema.

5. Pulmonary granulomata and infiltrations due to sarcoidosis, fibrosing alveolitis, berylliosis, eosinophilic granuloma, histiocytosis, malignant infiltration, scleroderma, systemic lupus erythematosus, dermatomyositis and alveolar microlithiasis.

In these conditions there is a diffusion defect in the lung due to thickening of the alveolar membrane. Because oxygen diffuses much less quickly than carbon dioxide, this disturbance leads to hypoxaemia but not carbon dioxide retention. The hypoxaemia causes hyperventilation and eventually leads to pulmonary hypertension and cardiac failure. The early diagnosis may be difficult as the chest radiography may show no abnormality.

6. Pulmonary resection.

7. Congenital cystic disease of the lungs.

Diseases primarily affecting the movements of the thoracic cage and respiratory muscles

1. Kyphoscoliosis and other thoracic deformities
2. Thoracoplasty
3. Pleural fibrosis
4. Chronic neuromuscular weakness, e.g. poliomyelitis
5. Obesity with alveolar hypoventilation
6. Idiopathic alveolar hypoventilation

In these conditions, there is inadequate pulmonary ventilation, due either to a deformity of the thoracic cage, or to interference with the function of the respiratory muscles. Alveolar hypoventilation leads to hypoxaemia and carbon dioxide retention.

Clinical features of pulmonary heart disease

The patient is usually a cigarette-smoking middle-aged man with a long history of morning cough and sputum. There may have been recurrent attacks of winter bronchitis. These symptoms are slowly progressive until breathlessness becomes disabling. Overt cyanosis and peripheral oedema are usually late features but are sometimes the first clear manifestation of pulmonary disease. Recent worsening of cough and the production of purulent sputum is common.

The subject is usually breathless and wheezing even at rest. Cyanosis varies from the scarcely detectable to the gross. When carbon dioxide retention is present, there may be clouding of consciousness or confusion, accompanied by tremor of the hands. The hands are usually warm and the pulse large due to peripheral vasodilatation.

The jugular venous pressure may be raised due either to cardiac failure or increased blood volume, or because venous return is hindered by high intrapleural pressure. Cardiac failure produces oedema and hepatic enlargement. The chest moves poorly and may be barrel-shaped and hyper-resonant. Expiratory rhonchi are usual and there may be crepitations. The breath sounds are often difficult to hear.

Emphysema may make the apex beat impalpable and prevent right ventricular hypertrophy from being detected at the left sternal edge, although it may be palpable in the epigastrium. The first and second heart sounds are soft; when cardiac failure ensues there may be a right ventricular third heart sound and a systolic murmur over the lower sternum due to tricuspid regurgitation.

Electrocardiogram and chest radiograph.   The ECG is often normal, but may show P pulmonale, right axis deviation, right ventricular hypertrophy, right bundle branch block, or an rS pattern across the chest. In emphysema the QRS complexes are often small.

The radiological appearances depend upon the nature of the lung disease. When there is emphysema with an increased total lung volume, one may see a low diaphragm and a narrow heart. Enlargement of the main pulmonary artery and its major branches occurs when there is pulmonary hypertension. The radiograph is, however, often normal.

Pulmonary function tests. Spirometry.   In chronic bronchitis and emphysema, and in bronchial asthma during the paroxysms, the forced vital capacity (FVC) is reduced, but to a smaller extent than forced expiratory volume in one second (FEV_1). Normally, the FEV_1/FVC is 75% or more; in obstructive airways disease it is considerably less. In restrictive lung disease due to pulmonary fibrosis there is no obstruction and FEV_1/FVC is often greater than 75%.

Blood gas estimations.   In virtually all cases of pulmonary heart disease there is hypoxaemia. Carbon dioxide retention is usual in obstructive airways disease and in those disorders in which the movements of the thoracic cage and respiratory muscles are impaired.

Carbon dioxide tension is normal or even reduced when there is a diffusion defect.

Diagnosis

Two types of diagnostic problem arise:

1. Is there cardiovascular involvement complicating known pulmonary disease?

2. Is right heart failure due to pulmonary disease or to some other factor?

Cardiac involvement in pulmonary disease is suggested by clinical, ECG or radiological evidence of pulmonary hypertension or right ventricular enlargement, by the presence of a right ventricular third heart sound and by signs of right-sided cardiac failure.

The pulmonary origin of cardiac failure is often overlooked, particularly when it coexists with known ischaemic, rheumatic or hypertensive heart disease. This is particularly the case with hypertension; mild hypertension is often blamed for heart failure which is secondary to chronic bronchitis and emphysema. The history of chronic cough with sputum and wheezing should suggest the diagnosis, as should poor chest movement and the presence of rhonchi. The diagnosis is usually best made by studies of ventilation and blood gases; carbon dioxide retention makes it almost certain that there is a pulmonary component in heart failure.

Prognosis

The prognosis is poor once cardiac failure has complicated pulmonary heart disease. Treatment may overcome individual attacks, but the subject is liable to further episodes with recurrent infection, and is unlikely to survive more than two or three such attacks over a period of a few years.

Treatment

When a patient is seen in cardiac failure due to pulmonary heart disease, the major objects of treatment should be to combat respiratory infection, correct hypoxaemia and carbon dioxide retention and relieve airways obstruction.

Infection is most commonly due to haemophilus influenzae and pneumococcus. The antibiotics of choice are either ampicillin or oxytetracycline in a dose of 250 mg 6-hourly for 10 days.

Oxygen therapy is essential, but oxygen in too high a concentration may lead to carbon dioxide retention and coma. The oxygen should therefore be administered using one of the special types of mask which deliver 25 to 29% oxygen. If oxygenation remains inadequate in spite of this type of oxygen therapy, it may be best to employ intermittent positive pressure ventilation, if necessary with tracheostomy. Bronchodilators such as salbutamol or orciprenaline by inhalation or intravenous aminophylline are helpful. Corticosteroids may be necessary in severe attacks of asthma. Digitalis and diuretics should be used, if necessary, but are relatively ineffective until infection has been controlled and hypoxaemia corrected.

Once the patient has recovered from the attack of cardiac failure, efforts must be made to ensure that he does not recommence smoking, that he avoids dusty atmospheres, that obesity is corrected and that respiratory infections are promptly treated.

Further reading

Current problems in pulmonary embolism (1974–5) *Prog cardiovasc. Dis.*, **17**, 161–391.

Editorial (1981) Primary pulmonary hypertension. *Br. med. J.* **282**, 170.

FERRER, M. I. (1974) Present day status of cor pulmonale. *Amer. Heart. J.*, **89**, 657.

FLENLEY, D. (1981) *Respiratory Disease*. London: Baillière Tindall.

HARRIS, P. and HEATH, D. (1977) *The Human Pulmonary Circulation*. 2nd ed. Edinburgh: Churchill Livingstone.

HIRSCH, J. (1981) Prevention of deep venous thrombosis. *Br. J. Hosp. med.*, **143**.

WEST, J. B. (1977) *Pulmonary Pathophysiology*. Baltimore: Williams and Wilkins.

16

Systemic Disorders and the Heart

Infections and the heart

Infections can affect the circulation in a variety of ways:
1. Direct invasion of endocardium, myocardium and pericardium
2. Toxic myocarditis
3. Acute circulatory failure due to toxic effects on the vasomotor centre or peripheral vessels, or to dehydration

Pericarditis and infective endocarditis are considered in Chapter 9 and will not be considered in detail here.

Diphtheria

Diphtheria causes an acute myocarditis in approximately 20% of subjects. The myocarditis is due to an exotoxin of the diphtheria bacillus rather than to local infection with the organism. Acute circulatory failure may occur in the first few days but the major cardiovascular effects are more common at the end of the first and during the second week. Tachycardia may be present in the absence of myocardial involvement and may be replaced by a bradycardia due to heart block. Gallop rhythm is common and there may be cardiac enlargement. The myocarditis may lead to cardiogenic shock, sometimes accompanied by cardiac failure.

ECG abnormalities often precede the clinical signs of myocarditis, the commonest change being flattening or inversion of the T waves. All grades of heart block may occur.

The presence of acute myocarditis is suggested by gallop rhythm, cardiomegaly, ECG abnormalities, heart block or cardiogenic shock.

Nearly all infants with acute diphtheritic myocarditis die; the mortality in adults is less than 25%. In those who recover from the acute attack, there is little evidence of residual cardiac damage.

Diphtheria should be prevented by immunization; if it occurs the patient requires treatment with antitoxin and penicillin. Electrical pacing may be required for heart block; conduction disorders are seldom, if ever, permanent.

Tuberculosis

Tuberculosis may cause pericarditis, with or without subsequent constriction (p. 168). It may also be responsible for heart disease secondary to pulmonary fibrosis. Tuberculous myocarditis is very rare.

Virus infections

Viruses cause both pericarditis and myocarditis. Coxsackie viruses of group B are probably the commonest organisms affecting the heart. The clinical picture is usually one of fever, malaise and muscular pains, accompanied by evidence of pericarditis and, if there is myocarditis, tachycardia, gallop rhythm, cardiomegaly and cardiac failure. The ECG usually shows non-specific abnormalities, but there may be ST and T wave changes suggesting pericarditis or myocardial infarction. The diagnosis can be made by isolating the organism from the stool or by demonstrating a rise or fall in serum antibodies. The patient nearly always recovers completely, but there may be residual myocardial damage and recurrences are not unusual. A myocarditis may also be associated with infectious mononucleosis, acute anterior poliomyelitis and other virus infections.

Trypanosomiasis (Chagas' disease)

Myocarditis due to infection by *Trypanosoma cruzi* is common in South America. It is transmitted by infected bugs. There are two major forms, acute and chronic. Acute Chagas' disease, which occurs predominantly in childhood, may be asymptomatic but can produce tachycardia, cardiomegaly and cardiac failure. Much more important is the chronic form which produces cardiac failure of insidious onset. It particularly affects men between the ages of 20 and 40. The left ventricle is enlarged, and there may be dyspnoea, chest pain and palpitation. Eventually, evidence of right-sided heart failure develops. Arrhythmias are almost invariable and complete heart block is common. The ECG usually shows right bundle branch block. Death is often sudden due to ventricular fibrillation or asystole. Chagas' myocarditis should be suspected when patients who have lived in the tropical or subtropical areas of America develop arrhythmias, cardiac failure and right bundle branch block.

Toxoplasmosis

Toxoplasma gondii can give rise to a myocarditis which may complicate either the disseminated form of the disease, in which there is hepatitis, pneumonia and meningo-encephalitis, or the less acute form which resembles infectious mononucleosis with lymphadenopathy the most obvious abnormality. The myocarditis usually gives rise to tachycardia and may cause heart failure, pericarditis and arrhythmias. Complete recovery is unusual.

Syphilis

Cardiovascular syphilis used to be an important cause of death, but is now uncommon. It seldom affects the myocardium, although gummata can occur. The organism localizes in the aorta soon after the primary infection, but a latent period of 10 to 25 years elapses before clinical evidence of aortitis develops.

The initial lesion involves the vasa vasorum of the aorta which become obliterated. The muscle and elastic tissues of the media necrose and are replaced by scar tissue which becomes calcified. Atherosclerotic changes are frequently superimposed. The lesions are usually most severe immediately above the sinuses of Valsalva, and predominantly affect the ascending aorta. The inner aspect of the aorta appears wrinkled, with radial or parallel grooves. The process may involve the mouths of the coronary arteries producing stenosis and, occasionally, occlusion of the coronary ostia. Damage to the aortic valve ring produces dilatation with aortic regurgitation. Aortic stenosis does not occur. Aneurysms of either saccular or fusiform type may be formed.

The symptoms and signs of syphilitic disease depend mainly on whether there is coronary artery involvement, aortic valve disease or aneurysm formation. Coronary artery stenosis leads to angina pectoris and, rarely, myocardial infarction. Syphilitic aortic regurgitation may cause the clinical features of left-sided cardiac failure. Because syphilitic aortic aneurysms affect predominantly the ascending aorta and arch, the major symptoms are those of chest pain due to erosion of bone, cough and dyspnoea due to pressure on the trachea and bronchi, and hoarseness from paralysis of the left recurrent laryngeal nerve. The aneurysm may be visible in the second or third right intercostal spaces, and a systolic thrill may be palpable in this area. Occasionally, a tracheal tug pulls down the thyroid cartilage with each heart beat. There is often a loud systolic murmur over the aneurysm and the second heart sound may be accentuated.

The ECG appearances depend on the nature of the complications and are not specific. A chest radiograph shows a dilatated aorta, often with linear calcification. Aneurysms may be observed, but can be difficult to differentiate from uncoiling of the aorta, which is common in the elderly. Angiography is helpful in delineating the shape of the aorta.

Syphilitic aortitis should be suspected if the aorta is conspicuously dilated or aneurysmal, or if there is aortic regurgitation unassociated with stenosis.

The prognosis is quite good in asymptomatic syphilitic aortitis, survival for 10 or 20 years being probable. The patient is unlikely to live more than 2 or 3 years if there is angina due to coronary stenosis or left ventricular failure due to aortic regurgitation.

Syphilitic cardiovascular disease does not develop if early syphilis is adequately treated. It is uncertain whether treatment of established cardiovascular syphilis is effective in preventing progression. It is customary to give 6 to 12 million units of penicillin over a period of 10 days in an attempt to control the infection. Surgery may be necessary for relief of coronary ostial stenosis, for the correction of aortic regurgitation, or for the repair of an aneurysm.

Endocrine and metabolic diseases

Hyperthyroidism

The hypermetabolic state characteristic of thyroid overactivity is associated with increased oxygen consumption and heat production. The augmentation in cardiac output which occurs in response to these demands, and to the direct effect of thyroid hormone on the heart, is achieved mainly by tachycardia and increased myocardial contractility rather than by an enlarged stroke volume.

The heart has to support the burden of a greatly enhanced cardiac output when its own metabolic requirements are increased. The normal heart may, in these circumstances, be unable to supply an adequate circulation; a diseased heart is likely to fail. Clear manifestations of cardiac abnormality, such as cardiomegaly or heart failure usually imply that the hyperthyroidism has aggravated underlying heart disease. This is most commonly ischaemic but it may be hypertensive or rheumatic. Occasionally, hyperthyroidism is the sole cause of heart failure.

Most of the cardiovascular features of hyperthyroidism can be accounted for by the hypermetabolic state, but it is difficult to attribute the common complication of atrial fibrillation to this cause. This arrhythmia may be due to a direct toxic effect of the thyroid hormone on the myocardium.

Cardiac symptoms are common in hyperthyroid patients, even in the absence of cardiac disease. Palpitation is particularly frequent, and is usually attributable to the combination of sinus tachycardia and a vigorous cardiac action. Atrial flutter or fibrillation may be responsible for regular or irregular palpitation.

Breathlessness is also common, and can be due to hyperventilation, anxiety or left ventricular failure. Hyperthyroidism may aggravate angina pectoris in those with coronary artery disease. Sinus tachycardia is almost invariable if there is not atrial fibrillation or flutter, and persists during sleep. The pulse is of large volume and may have a collapsing character. The systolic blood pressure is frequently high, whilst the diastolic is normal or low.

The apical impulse is vigorous, but is usually not displaced. The heart sounds are loud, and there is often a pulmonary midsystolic murmur, due to high flow.

Cardiac enlargement and the signs of left- or right-sided heart failure may develop if the thyroid disease is of long standing or if there is coexistent cardiac disease.

The classical features of hyperthyroidism such as weight loss, moist warm extremities, tremor, lid retraction, exophthalmos and goitre are usually present, but these signs may be slight or absent in the older patient. There are no distinctive features on the ECG or chest radiograph.

Hyperthyroidism can be recognized easily if the characteristic features are present, but the diagnosis can be difficult if the obvious abnormalities are confined to the cardiovascular system. Hyperthyroidism should be suspected whenever sinus tachycardia, atrial flutter, atrial fibrillation or cardiac failure are unexplained.

The diagnosis of hyperthyroidism is established by finding abnormally high blood levels of thyroxine, protein-bound iodine or an enhanced uptake of radio-iodine (^{131}I).

Hyperthyroidism may be treated by antithyroid drugs (such as carbimazole and propylthiouracil), radio-iodine or partial thyroidectomy. Radio-iodine is the most suitable therapy for most patients with thyrotoxic heart disease, but surgery may be indicated if there is a danger of tracheal compression.

When the rapid control of the tachycardia of hyperthyroidism is necessary, propranolol should be given.

The atrial fibrillation of thyrotoxicosis responds poorly to digitalis until the disease process is controlled. When it is, dc shock is usually effective in restoring sinus rhythm.

Heart disease in hyperthyroidism usually responds well to therapy unless it has been untreated for several years or there is serious independent cardiac disease.

Hypothyroidism

Hypothyroidism affects the cardiovascular system in several ways:

1. The reduced level of body metabolism is associated with a low cardiac output, a diminished peripheral blood flow, a reduction in venous return, and sinus bradycardia.

2. The deficiency of thyroid hormone seems to be responsible for

interstitial oedema and mucoid infiltration of the myocardium, and for a pericardial effusion.

3. The hypercholesterolaemia characteristically present may be responsible for premature coronary atherosclerosis and ischaemic heart disease; the evidence for this is inconclusive.

4. 'Myxoedema coma' is associated with hypotension and bradycardia.

The patient with hypothyroidism seldom has cardiac symptoms, except for angina pectoris due to coexistent coronary disease. The symptoms and signs of cardiac failure rarely, if ever, occur in the absence of some additional form of heart disease.

The pulse rate is usually between 50 and 60 per minute. The sluggish apex beat is difficult to feel and the heart sounds are soft.

The ECG is abnormal in showing low voltage of all components of the PQRST complexes; the T waves are flattened or inverted. The chest radiograph reveals a large cardiac shadow, often accompanied by a pericardial effusion; on fluoroscopy, cardiac movement is seen to be diminished.

Hypothyroidism is usually suspected because of the general sluggishness, the cold and thickened skin, the husky voice, the coarse but scanty hair and the slow pulse, but minor forms of the disorder may easily escape detection. The most sensitive test is the serum level of thyroid-stimulating hormone.

Treatment with thyroid substances is effective but may provoke angina pectoris. For this reason, in those suspected of having coronary disease, small doses (e.g. thyroxine 0.05 mg) should be used initially and the dose should be increased very cautiously, if necessary, but not beyond 0.15 mg. The addition of a beta-adrenoceptor blocking drug may protect the patient from angina but often fails, in which case coronary artery bypass surgery may be required.

Carcinoid syndrome

Malignant carcinoid tumours with metastases in the liver may be associated with pulmonary stenosis, and with tricuspid stenosis or regurgitation, the valve cusps being fixed by fibrosis. The cardiac lesions are probably due to the actions of kinins or of 5-hydroxytryptamine (5HT, serotonin) secreted by the tumour. These substances are also responsible for the flushing attacks, telangiectasia, diarrhoea and bronchospasm characteristic of this syndrome.

The cardiac findings in the carcinoid syndrome are those of the particular valve lesion and of right-sided heart failure. The diagnosis is established either by identification of the tumour at laparotomy or by the detection in the urine of large quantities of 5-hydroxy-indole acetic acid (5-HIAA), a breakdown product of 5-HT.

Haemochromatosis

In this disorder there is excessive iron storage associated with cirrhosis of the liver, diabetes and pigmentation of the skin, and a substantial proportion of patients die from a cardiomyopathy, which is often of the constrictive type. The clinical picture may resemble constrictive pericarditis; the features are predominantly those of right-sided cardiac failure. Treatment of the failure may be temporarily effective, but the prognosis is poor.

Gout

There is a statistical association between hyperuricaemia and coronary artery disease, but there is no definite evidence of an increased incidence of coronary disease in those with clinical gout. Gout may be provoked by diuretics; it may occur in severe cyanotic congenital heart disease in association with secondary polycythaemia. Gout occasionally causes an acute pericarditis.

Glycogen storage disease

In this familial disorder, excessive glycogen is deposited in skeletal and cardiac muscle. Breathlessness, feeding difficulties and muscular weakness usually develop about the third month of life and the progression of cardiac failure is relentless. The ECG and the chest radiograph demonstrate biventricular enlargement. Death occurs before the age of 3 years — usually within the first year of life.

Pseudoxanthoma elasticum

This is a familial disease affecting connective tissue and is associated with the development of calcification and proliferation of the media of the coronary and peripheral arteries which may give rise to ischaemic heart disease and vascular insufficiency. The skin, particularly in certain areas such as the elbow creases and back of the neck, takes on a crêpe-like appearance with much redundant tissue. Characteristic dark 'angioid' streaks occur in the fundi; there is a liability to hypertension, gastrointestinal haemorrhage and blindness.

Obesity

This is associated with heart disease in a number of ways. In the first place, obese patients often appear to be hypertensive. This is to some extent, but not exclusively, due to falsely high blood pressure recordings in those with fat arms.

A specific 'Pickwickian' syndrome of hypoventilation with carbon dioxide retention, hypoxia, somnolence, polycythaemia and right-sided heart failure is sometimes caused by obesity. The obesity is directly responsible for the hypoventilation because it restricts respiratory movement; improvement can be achieved by weight loss.

Obesity is important in patients with cardiac disease of any type because the demands on the heart are increased. Weight reduction is an essential component in the prevention and treatment of angina pectoris and cardiac failure.

Beri-beri

This disease is due to thiamine deficiency, which is usually the result of a diet with a high proportion of polished rice in eastern countries but is associated with alcoholism in North America and Europe. The deficiency leads to a lack of co-carboxylase which is necessary for the oxidation of pyruvic acid to acetyl coenzyme A. The citric acid cycle is inhibited and the accumulation of lactate and pyruvate may lead to peripheral vasodilatation and impaired cardiac function. The characteristic haemodynamic features are those of a low peripheral vascular resistance and a high cardiac output. Cardiac failure eventually occurs and in the later stages the cardiac output may fall.

The clinical features of beri-beri heart disease include palpitation, fatigue, breathlessness and peripheral oedema. In some cases there may be acute circulatory failure with hypotension and syncope. There is usually sinus tachycardia with a large pulse and right-sided cardiac failure. The heart is enlarged and there may be a gallop rhythm and systolic murmurs.

The neurological features are those of an ascending peripheral neuritis, commonly accompanied by mental confusion. Paraesthesiae occur in the hands and feet and there is weakness of the legs. The calf muscles are tender and areas of anaesthesia occur.

Neither the ECG, which usually shows non-specific T wave changes, nor the chest radiograph, which reveals cardiomegaly, are helpful in diagnosis. This is usually achieved by obtaining a history of nutritional deficiency or of alcoholism, and by finding evidence of both peripheral neuritis and cardiac failure.

Most cases respond quickly to thiamine chloride, 50 mg intramuscularly per day. Subsequently, thiamine should be given orally in dose of 10 mg three times a day.

Alcoholic cardiomyopathy

There is increasing evidence that a large intake of alcohol, even in the absence of nutritional deficiency, can lead to cardiomyopathy. The patients are often middle-aged relatively wealthy men who are excessively fond of both food and alcohol. The initial symptom is either breathlessness or palpitation, due to ectopic beats or atrial fibrillation. The ECG may show low, dimpled T waves. In the early stages, abstinence may reverse the picture, but otherwise there is progression with increasing cardiac failure to death.

Treatment consists of complete abstinence from alcohol and the use of conventional measures for controlling atrial fibrillation and cardiac failure.

Miscellaneous disorders

Rheumatoid arthritis and the connective tissue disorders

Rheumatoid arthritis. This is accompanied by valve disease rather more often than would be expected by chance, although by no means as frequently as is rheumatic fever. Acute pericarditis and pericardial effusion are quite common; pericardial constriction is rare.

Ankylosing spondylitis (rheumatoid spondylitis). This is associated with aortic regurgitation due to focal destruction of the elastica and media of the aorta.

Systemic lupus erythematosus. This often affects the heart, although cardiac symptoms and signs seldom dominate the clinical picture. Acute or chronic pericarditis, with or without effusion, is usually the most obvious evidence of cardiac involvement. Myocarditis sometimes develops, and may be due to disease of the small coronary vessels. Endocarditis also occurs, with large warty excrescences which may involve any of the four heart valves. These lesions seldom give rise to clinical heart disease, but may act as a focus for infective endocarditis.

Polyarteritis. This may result in myocardial infarction, or in cardiac failure without evidence of infarction. The heart failure may be, in part, the result of hypertension which is common in this disorder. Pericardial effusions occasionally occur.

Scleroderma. This may lead to cardiac failure either by producing a cardiomyopathy, usually of the constrictive type, or as a result of pulmonary heart disease secondary to diffuse pulmonary fibrosis.

The Marfan syndrome

This familial disorder of connection tissue may result in many skeletal, cardiovascular and other abnormalities. These include great height,

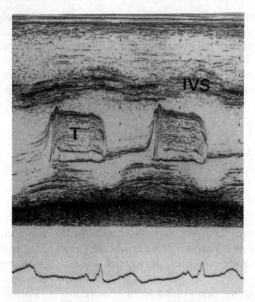

Fig. 114.   Parasternal M-Mode echocardiogram of a left atrial myxoma.
Multiple echoes are seen behind the anterior mitral valve leaflet
in diastole as the tumour prolapses downwards towards the left
ventricle. IVS = interventricular septum. T = tumour.

long limbs with spidery fingers (arachnodactyly), a high arched palate
and dislocation of the lens.

A weakness of the aortic media is common and leads to dilatation,
aneurysm formation and dissection. Aortic regurgitation may follow
dilatation of the valve ring. Mitral valve disease may result in cusp
prolapse and regurgitation.

These abnormalities can be evident in childhood but may not
develop until the fifth decade.

There is no specific treatment. Surgery may be required for the
valve disorders and aortic disease.

Cardiac tumours

Cardiac tumours are rare. The commonest is the *myxoma* which occurs
most frequently in the left atrium, but occasionally in the other
chambers. It varies from 1 to 8 cm in diameter, and is usually attached
by a pedicle to the atrial septum. Because its position may vary with
posture, transient or complete obstruction of the mitral valve may
result. The tumour may prolapse into the left ventricle and cause
mitral regurgitation. The haemodynamic effects of left atrial myxoma
usually resemble those of mitral stenosis. The tumour may also be

responsible for embolic phenomena, and can produce constitutional effects such as fever, weight loss, anaemia, finger clubbing, raised sedimentation rate and abnormal serum proteins. The obstruction of the mitral valve may lead to dyspnoea and, rarely, syncope or vertigo related to posture. Variable mitral systolic and diastolic murmurs may be heard, and there may be a loud first sound and opening snap. The diagnosis should be suspected in patients with signs of mitral stenosis, who have a history of syncope, or variable murmurs, or unexplained fever with a high ESR. The diagnosis can be most readily established by echocardiography which demonstrates a mass within the left atrium (Fig. 114). The tumour should be removed under cardiopulmonary bypass.

Trauma

Traumatic lesions of the heart may be due to penetrating chest injuries as, for example, from gunshot wounds or stabbing, or from non-penetrating injuries produced by blows to the chest such as steering wheel accidents.

Penetrating injuries may cause lacerations of any of the heart chambers or great vessels, and death may ensue from haemorrhage or cardiac tamponade. If the victim does not die within a few hours late complications may occur due to infective pericarditis, valve damage or intracardiac shunts. The diagnosis is usually not difficult and can be deduced from the site of the injury, the evidence of blood loss or cardiac tamponade, or ECG abnormalities. The chest radiograph may be valuable in locating foreign bodies in or around the heart. Pericardial aspiration may relieve tamponade, but for the other serious complications, immediate surgery is usually necessary.

Non-penetrating injuries may occur with or without rib fractures. Complications include haemopericardium with cardiac tamponade, contusion of the myocardium with subsequent rupture and myocardial infarction due to coronary artery damage. Valves or chordae tendineae may be ruptured; aortic transection is relatively common, particularly in road and air accidents. Cardiac involvement should be suspected from persistent chest pain, or the development of arrhythmias, of loud murmurs or of ECG abnormalities. The patient may require surgical treatment for cardiac tamponade, valvular regurgitation or aortic rupture.

Anaemia and the heart

Anaemia imposes increased demands upon the heart and, at the same time, impairs its function. It aggravates the symptoms of the patient with heart disease and has important circulatory effects even in the individual with a normal heart.

The haemodynamic effects of anaemia probably result mainly from a decrease in blood viscosity and from tissue hypoxia, which is responsible for peripheral vasodilatation. As a consequence, the peripheral arterial resistance is diminished, the diastolic pressure falls and the pulse pressure widens. Ventricular afterload is decreased. The stroke volume and cardiac output are increased when the haemoglobin level falls below 7 g/100 ml blood, and both respond to exercise to a greater degree than normal. The hypoxia produces coronary vasodilatation when this is possible, but in the patient with coronary artery disease the ability to dilate is restricted. If anaemia is both severe and prolonged, a fatty degeneration of myocardium takes place.

For the reasons described, anaemia may precipitate or aggravate cardiac failure in the patient with pre-existing heart disease, and it may induce or exacerbate angina in those with coronary artery disease.

It is rare for either heart failure or angina to develop in anaemic patients with normal hearts, but signs and symptoms may occur in such patients which mimic those of heart disease. Dyspnoea, tachycardia and peripheral oedema are common in patients with chronic and severe anaemia.

Anaemia produces the warm skin and bounding arterial pulse of the high output state. A venous hum in the neck is common. Cardiac enlargement may be seen in the advanced case. The murmur most commonly found in anaemia is systolic and situated in the second or third left intercostal space close to the sternum. It is probably due to turbulence resulting from increased flow and reduced blood viscosity. There is often a loud third heart sound and, in very severe cases, there may be a short mitral mid-diastolic murmur, due to increased flow.

The ECG is usually normal, but non-specific ST and T wave changes may occur and the ST depression of myocardial ischaemia may develop.

The clinical features of anaemia are usually readily corrected either by appropriate drug therapy, or by blood transfusion. Rapid transfusion is dangerous, particularly if there is heart failure; in this situation, it is advisable to use packed cells. If whole blood only is available, a diuretic such as frusemide 40 mg should also be given.

Pregnancy and the heart

Pregnancy imposes a substantial load on the heart and circulation. There is a progressive increase in cardiac output and blood volume from the second month onwards, until, about the 30th week, they are some 30 to 50% above normal levels at which they remain during the rest of pregnancy. During the last 8 weeks, the inferior vena cava may be obstructed by the uterus when the subject is supine; as a consequence, the cardiac output may fall when this position is assumed. Other factors affecting the cardiovascular system are an increased metabolic rate, a corresponding rise in oxygen consumption, the arteriovenous shunt in the uterus and an elevation in the venous pressure due to the increased blood volume.

These circulatory changes produce characteristic physical signs in the normal pregnant woman. The hands are warm and the pulse is large. A tachycardia is present and the venous pressure slightly raised. The apex beat is vigorous and may be displaced outwards, partly as a consequence of cardiomegaly and partly by the high diaphragm. The high flow almost always produces a soft pulmonary midsystolic murmur and a third heart sound. These are often mistaken for cardiac disease. The chest radiograph shows an increase in cardiac diameter.

The circulatory burden of pregnancy frequently reveals pre-existing heart disease for the first time. Symptoms may start at about week 12 and tend to progress until they may become severe from week 24 onwards. A period of particular danger occurs after delivery, when the sudden reabsorption of blood from the uterus into the circulation may precipitate pulmonary oedema.

Heart disease in pregnancy is frequently rheumatic; mitral stenosis is the most serious lesion encountered. Patients with tight mitral stenosis may become breathless in early pregnancy and progress to pulmonary oedema or right-sided cardiac failure. Even those with less severe lesions may develop symptoms during the last months or shortly after delivery. Patients with mild mitral stenosis, mitral regurgitation and aortic regurgitation usually tolerate pregnancy well, but may become increasingly breathless.

The management of rheumatic heart disease in the pregnant woman depends upon a number of factors including her age, parity and religious beliefs, the stage of the pregnancy, the nature of the lesion, and the response to treatment. In the patient with severe mitral stenosis, pregnancy should be avoided or deferred until mitral valvotomy has been performed. If such a patient becomes pregnant, a decision should be made before week 16 as to whether valvotomy should be undertaken or the pregnancy terminated. As pregnancy progresses beyond this time, both termination and valvotomy become more hazardous. If the patient is seen for the first time at a later stage of pregnancy, she should be managed medically, for with adequate bed-rest, digitalis and diuretics, the maternal mortality is low. Furthermore, in the last half of pregnancy, there is a danger of misdiagnosis because the circulatory changes may so alter the physical signs that patients with predominant mitral regurgitation may appear to have tight mitral stenosis, and vice versa. Patients with rheumatic valve lesions other than mitral stenosis should be managed medically or have the pregnancy terminated.

Patients who were born with congenital heart disease are being seen with increasing frequency in pregnancy, but the cardiac abnormality is usually mild or has been corrected by surgery prior to conception. Pregnancy is tolerated well if there is an uncomplicated septal defect or persistent ductus arteriosus. Severe pulmonary hypertension of whatever aetiology is extremely hazardous, with a 25 to 50% risk of maternal death during the pregnancy or in the puerperium; termination in early pregnancy is to be strongly recommended.

Toxaemia of pregnancy is discussed in Chapter 14.

Cardiomyopathy ('peripartal') of unknown aetiology sometimes develops during later pregnancy or the puerperium. Although about one-third of patients recover permanently, there is a risk of progression and of recurrence during subsequent pregnancies.

Termination of pregnancy

With good medical preparation and skilled anaesthesia there is little risk in terminating a pregnancy in the presence of cardiac disease. This procedure is indicated in women with advanced heart disease and severe symptoms in early pregnancy, if they are not suitable candidates for mitral valvotomy. Termination should also be considered for those with less severe disease who would find the care of an additional child burdensome.

Sterilization

This should be considered in patients with heart disease who have completed their families or in whom further pregnancies would be harmful. It should not be undertaken lightly. The religious beliefs of the patient must be respected, the risk of psychological disturbance considered, and the possibility of surgical correction of the cardiac lesion borne in mind.

Contraception

Patients with cardiac disease may wish or need to practise contraception. Advice should be proffered to those for whom pregnancy is temporarily inadvisable.

Oral methods of contraception have the major advantage of reliability. They may, however, cause venous thrombosis and embolism, exacerbate hypertension, produce weight gain and, possibly, promote the development of pulmonary hypertension. The risk of developing any of these complications is small; oral contraceptives are well tolerated by most patients with cardiac disease.

Further reading

ABER, C. P. and THOMPSON, G. S. (1964) The heart in hypothyroidism. *Amer. Heart J.*, **68**, 428.

ALDERMAN, E. L. and COLTART, D. J. (1982) Alcohol and the heart. *Brit. med. Bull.*, **38**, 77.

BRIGDEN, W. and ROBINSON, J. (1964) Alcoholic heart disease. *Brit. Heart J.*, **2**, 1283.

BURCH, G. E. and GILES, T. D. (1972) The role of viruses in the production of heart disease. *Amer. J. Cardiol.*, **29**, 231.

CHEITLIN, M. D. (1982) Key References. Cardiovascular trauma. *Circulation*, **65**, 1429; **66**, 244.

DAVIDSON, P., BAGGENSTOSS, A. H., SLOCUMB, C. H. and DOUGHERTY, G. W. (1963) Cardiac and aortic lesions in rheumatoid spondylitis. *Proc. Staff Meet. Mayo Clin.*, **36**, 427.

FLEMING, H. A. (1974) Sarcoid heart disease. *Brit. Heart J.*, **36**, 54.

GRAHAME-SMITH, D. G. (1968) The carcinoid syndrome. *Amer. J. Cardiol.*, **21**, 376.

HARVEY, H. P. B., McLEOD, J. C. and TWITTER, J. R. (1966) Myocarditis associated with toxoplasmosis. *Aust. Ann. Med.*, **15**, 169.

HETMANCIK, M. R., WRIGHT, J. C., QUINT, R. and JENNINGS, F. L. (1964) The cardiovascular manifestations of systemic lupus erythematosus. *Amer. Heart J.*, **68**, 119.

KIRK, J. and COSH, J. (1969) The pericarditis of rheumatoid arthritis. *Quart. J. Med.*, **38**, 397.

LEVIN, A. B. and GOLUM, A. (1953) Heart in haemochromatosis. *Amer. Heart J.*, **45**, 277.

METCALFE, J. and UELAND, K. (1974) Maternal cardiovascular adjustment in pregnancy. *Progr. cardiovasc. Dis.*, **16**, 363.

ROSENBAUM, M. D. (1964) Chagasic myocardiopathy. *Progr. cardiovasc. Dis.*, **7**, 199.

SANDLER, G. and WILSON, G. M. (1959) Nature and prognosis of heart disease in thyrotoxicosis. *Quart. J. Med.*, **28**, 347.

SMITH, W. G. (1970). Coxsackie B myopericarditis in adults. *Amer. Heart J.*, **80**, 34.

Symposium on Cardiac Tumors. (1968) *Amer. J. Cardiol.*, **21**, 307.

SZEKELY, P. and SNAITH, L. (1974) *Heart Disease in Pregnancy*. Edinburgh: Churchill Livingstone.

VARAT, M. A., ADOLPH, R. J. and FOWLER, N. O. (1972) Cardiovascular effects of anaemia. *Amer. Heart J.*, **83**, 415.

WAGNER, R. I. (1965) Beri-beri heart disease. *Amer. Heart J.*, **69**, 200.

WEBSTER, B., RICH, C., DENSE, P. M., MOORE, J. E., NICOL, C. S. and PADGET, P. (1953) Studies in cardiovascular syphilis. Natural history of syphilitic aortic insufficiency. *Amer. Heart J.*, **46**, 117.

WEINTRAUB, A. M. and ZVAIFLER, N. J. (1963) Occurrence of valvular and myocardial disease in patients with chronic joint deformity. *Amer. J. Med.*, **35**, 145.

17

Psychological Aspects of Heart Disease

The relationship between psychological factors and heart disease is complex. Many anxious individuals believe, erroneously, that they have heart disease; anxiety and depression often complicate and aggravate organic heart disease.

Anxiety state and the heart

Individuals with an anxiety state often have complaints suggestive of heart disease. A large number of labels have been applied to the complex of symptoms of such patients, including 'effort syndrome', 'cardiac neurosis' and 'neurocirculatory asthenia'. It is particularly common in the armed services during war-time, and has therefore been called 'soldier's heart', but it also occurs frequently in civilians.

Breathlessness, palpitation and fatigue are almost invariable, and are usually accompanied by feelings of faintness and dizziness. Chest pain is less common, but is often the reason for referral to a physician.

The breathlessness may be related to exertion, but also occurs at rest. Frequent complaints are that 'I can't take a deep breath' or 'I can't get enough air'. The palpitation is usually the awareness of a sinus tachycardia, but can be due to ectopic beats which cause the patient to think that his heart is about to stop.

The chest pain of anxiety state is usually situated in the left sub-mammary region but may be elsewhere in the left chest and may radiate to the left arm. It is sometimes provoked by effort, but tends to come on after exercise rather than during it; it can develop at rest and at night time. It often takes the form of a persistent ache lasting for hours or days; sharp momentary stabs of pain are also frequent. The patient will often say that the pain is 'in his heart'. The muscles in the area may be tender, and in some cases the pain can be abolished by infiltration with local anaesthetics.

Whilst recounting his history, the patient gives an impression of distress, and is tense or rather withdrawn in manner. Sighing respiration is common and there may be hyperventilation. Sinus tachycardia is usual, and palpation reveals a hyperdynamic heart. The hands are often sweaty but cool; there may be a coarse tremor.

The ECG confirms sinus tachycardia and may show non-specific flattening or slight inversion of T waves.

The diagnosis can usually be made from the characteristic symptoms and from observing the patient. The poor relationship of the breathlessness and pain to exertion, and the site, character and duration of the chest discomfort differentiate the syndrome from angina pectoris. The palpitation can be distinguished from that of paroxysmal tachycardia by the lack of sudden onset and by the relationship to emotion.

The prognosis with regard to the relief of symptoms is poor if it is a chronic condition or if there is a serious personality derangement. If the complaints have occurred in response to an obvious emotional stress, the outlook is relatively good. When anxiety about the heart has been induced by the thoughtless or ill-informed comments of physicians, it is particularly difficult to eradicate.

Psychiatric treatment is necessary for the more severe cases, but strong reassurance by the physician may be effective in those patients in whom cardiac symptoms predominate, particularly when an unfounded fear of organic heart disease has provoked them. The patient should be instructed to embark upon a programme of gradually increasing physical activity. Sometimes, it may be necessary to give tranquillizers such as diazepam (Valium) 2 to 5 mg three times a day. Propranolol in a dose of 10 or 20 mg four times a day is helpful if the palpitation of sinus tachycardia is distressing.

Psychological disturbances in patients with heart disease

Many individuals equate heart disease with total disability and death. Patients with cardiac disorders may regard themselves and be considered by others as 'invalids', even though their lesion may be of little importance or be correctable.

Fear of sudden death is common in those who experience angina and palpitation. Anxiety and depression are important causes of symptoms and disability in patients who have sustained a myocardial infarction. Headache in hypertensive patients is usually due to tension and only rarely to the high blood pressure.

Excessive anxiety can be prevented by thoughtful management of the patient and his relatives. Frankness should be combined with optimism. One must be careful in one's choice of words; if such terms as angina, murmur or heart failure are to be used, they must be explained in such a way that they do not cause alarm.

Advanced heart disease can cause confusion and delirium as a result of hypoxia or hypotension or, when associated with pulmonary disease, carbon dioxide retention. Similar symptoms may arise from lignocaine overdosage, or following cardiac surgery. Depression may result from a number of cardiac drugs including methyldopa. Fatigue is common in patients on beta-blocking drugs. These psychological disturbances, which are secondary to medical disorders, should be treated by correcting the underlying cause.

18

Surgery and the Heart

Anaesthesia and general surgery in patients with heart disease

Anaesthesia is potentially hazardous in the patient with heart disease because it may cause hypoxaemia, hypercapnia, hypotension and cardiac arrhythmias; these complications can be almost completely avoided by skilful management. The choice of anaesthetic technique is dependent on the type and severity of the cardiac lesion and the nature of the operation being undertaken.

The period of induction is particularly dangerous, as hypotension may result from the intravenous barbiturates commonly used, and endotracheal intubation may stimulate vagal reflexes with resultant bradycardia, heart block or asystole. The dose of barbiturates should be small; muscle relaxants facilitate quick intubation. Halothane may be employed for maintenance of anaesthesia but should be avoided if a fall in blood pressure is undesirable. Cyclopropane has the advantage of not being hypotensive, but may provoke ventricular arrhythmias if underventilation and carbon dioxide retention are allowed to occur. It should not be used if diathermy is required.

Patients with heart disease often tolerate major operations without serious complication but the necessity for surgery must always be balanced against the cardiac risks. The greatest problems usually arise in those with ischaemic heart disease because hypotension may provoke serious arrhythmias or result in myocardial infarction. These risks diminish as time passes after a coronary occlusion, being high during the first 3 months, and reaching a relatively low level by the end of a year. Only surgery which cannot safely be deferred should be undertaken in those who have had a myocardial infarction within the preceding 6 months. On the other hand, when a patient has survived a year or more after a myocardial infarction without major disability, it is reasonable to consider cholecystectomy, prostatectomy and other major, but relatively elective, procedures.

Hypertensive patients usually tolerate surgery well, provided no sharp fall in blood pressure is permitted. There is an enhanced risk of hypotension in those on rauwolfia compounds and adrenergic blocking agents, but if the anaesthetist is aware of this possibility, it is usually not necessary to discontinue the treatment prior to surgery.

Major surgery should, if possible, be avoided in those with severe heart valve disease; it is better to defer this until the valve lesion has been corrected. However, if prosthetic valve surgery is contemplated, it may be preferable to carry out general surgery first in order to avoid operating on a patient receiving anticoagulants.

Particular care is required in the presence of pulmonary heart disease. Affected patients tolerate surgery poorly, and are susceptible to respiratory infection, pulmonary collapse and bronchitis postoperatively. It is important that these individuals stop smoking some weeks prior to surgery and are free of pulmonary infection.

Cardiac failure and arrhythmias should always be brought under control as far as possible prior to surgery. Complete heart block should be managed by temporary or permanent insertion of an endocardial pacemaking electrode.

Surgery for heart disease

Indications and contraindications

Most types of congenital and rheumatic heart disease are amenable to surgical treatment (for discussion of individual lesions see Chapters 11 and 12). Surgery also has a major part to play in the management of ischaemic heart disease, infective endocarditis, constrictive pericarditis and in diseases of the aorta. In deciding whether surgery is necessary in an individual case, one must weigh up the prognosis of the patient without surgery and the risks of morbidity and mortality imposed by surgery. For example, most patients with atrial septal defects or persistent ductus arteriosus are asymptomatic, but have a life expectancy reduced to about 30 years. Surgery in childhood is justified in these cases because the mortality is very low. At the other end of the scale, severe aortic stenosis carries a very poor prognosis and surgery should be undertaken in spite of a mortality which commonly exceeds 5 %. Contraindications to surgery include poor left ventricular function, extreme pulmonary hypertension and advanced disease of other organs such as the brain, liver and lungs.

Types of cardiac surgery

Cardiac surgery may be 'closed' or 'open'. In closed-heart surgery, the circulation continues through the patient's heart throughout the operation, and the interior of the heart is not inspected. The operations are relatively simple and safe but are limited in scope to such procedures as mitral and pulmonary valvotomy, pericardiectomy for

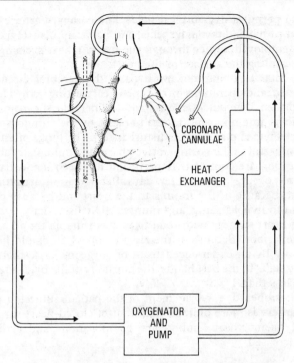

Fig. 115. Cardiopulmonary bypass.. Venous blood drains from cannulae in the venae cavae into an oxygenerator, and is then returned to the femoral artery or aorta by a pump. The temperature of the perfusing blood can be controlled with a heat pump. The coronary arteries can be selectively perfused.

constrictive pericarditis, division of persistent ductus arteriosus, resection of coarctation and shunt operations for tetralogy of Fallot. In experienced hands, the mortality of these operations is low, but postoperative complications are common. These include systemic embolism (after mitral valvotomy), arrhythmias, pulmonary collapse and infection, pulmonary embolism and the postcardiotomy syndrome (see p. 197).

In total cardiopulmonary bypass, the heart and lungs are completely excluded from the circulation. Venous blood is drained by gravity into an oxygenator through cannulae inserted into the inferior and superior venae cavae. A pump is used to recirculate the blood through a cannula positioned in the aorta (Fig. 115). When operations are undertaken on the mitral valve, the aortic valve prevents regurgitation into the left ventricle of the blood pumped into the aorta by the artificial heart—lung apparatus. When operations are being carried out on the aortic valve, the aorta must be clamped below the origin of the innominate artery to permit a dry surgical field. The coronary arteries may be supplied with blood through special coronary cannulae. Hypothermia is often employed, either through the use of a heat exchanger or by directly cooling the surface of the heart.

With total cardiopulmonary bypass, the cerebral circulation is maintained, and operations on the open heart lasting up to 5 hours can be performed. The potential risks are considerable; the major hazards are cerebral air embolism, trauma to blood by the pump-oxygenator, and electrolyte and acid–base disturbances. The lungs often become abnormally stiff in the postoperative phase, and pulmonary atelectasis and infection are common. If perfusion has been inadequate, renal failure may occur. In the first few days after operation, arrhythmias are frequent, because of the trauma to the heart and because perfusion may lead to hypokalaemia and unmask digitalis toxicity.

Open-heart surgery with total bypass is suitable for all surgically treatable lesions. Because of the risks involved, it should be undertaken only by an experienced team of surgeons, anaesthetists, and ancillary staff. In the best hands, the mortality of the bypass technique itself is less than 1 %.

The postoperative management of the patient subjected to open-heart surgery is more difficult than that of closed-heart surgery, the risks of haemorrhage, pulmonary complications and arrhythmias being increased.

The replacement of heart valves
(see also Chapter 11)

Heart valves may be replaced by prostheses, homografts or heterografts. In appropriately selected cases, valve replacement leads to the amelioration or abolition of symptoms and striking haemodynamic improvement.

There is a large variety of prosthetic valves available, of which the Starr–Edwards ball valve has been the most widely used (Fig. 116). With all artificial valves, there is a risk of thrombosis and of infection in relation to the prosthesis, and of haemolysis. Long-term anticoagulant therapy is necessary to prevent embolism; the addition of agents which prevent platelet aggregation, such as dipyridamole and sulphinpyrazone may further decrease this risk. By contrast, if homograft or heterograft valves are used, haemolysis is rare and anticoagulants are unnecessary unless there is some other indication, such as atrial fibrillation.

Prosthetic valves produce characteristic clicks, a mitral prosthesis causing a 'first sound' and 'opening snap', and an aortic prosthesis an 'ejection click' and 'aortic second sound'. Slight aortic regurgitation is not uncommon whether prosthetic or graft material is used. Re-

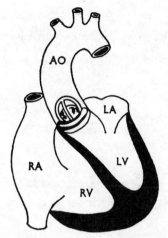

Fig. 116.   Starr–Edwards caged ball prosthesis in the aortic valve position.

operation is necessary if there is more severe regurgitation, particularly if there is a prosthesis because considerable haemolysis is often provoked.

Intra-aortic balloon pumping (counterpulsation)

Mechanical support may be given to the circulation by a balloon introduced via a femoral artery into the descending thoracic aorta which is inflated in diastole and deflated in systole by an external pump. This reduces afterload and increases coronary and peripheral diastolic blood flow. It greatly improves the patient with poor cardiac performance, particularly immediately after bypass surgery. It is of value in cardiogenic shock, as after myocardial infarction, only if it allows the patient to survive until some surgically corrective procedure can be undertaken.

Cardiac transplantation

There is now quite an extensive experience of transplantation of the heart from a recently deceased donor to a recipient with advanced heart disease. Several individuals have survived more than 5 years after the operation. The applicability of this procedure is limited by the paucity of suitable donors and by the problems associated with the use of immunosuppressive drugs. It is probable that cardiac transplantation will be used only for patients with intractable cardiac failure due to ischaemic heart disease and cardiomyopathy.

Further reading

BONCHEK, L. J. (1981) Current status of cardiac valve replacement. *Amer. Heart J.*, 101, 96.

SABISTON, D. C. and SPENCER, F. C. (1976) *Gibbon's Surgery of the Chest*, 3rd ed. Philadelphia: Saunders.

Index